PSYCHOSIS: PHENOMENOLOGICAL AND PSYCHOANALYTICAL APPROACHES

FIGURES OF THE UNCONSCIOUS 3

Psychosis:
Phenomenological and
psychoanalytical approaches

Edited by

Jozef Corveleyn
Paul Moyaert

Leuven University Press
2003

Published with the Support of
"K.U.Leuven Commissie voor Publicaties"

ISBN 90 5867 279 4

D / 2003 / 1869 / 5

Cover: Lejon Tits

Illustration cover: "Madame Gern" (inventory nr. 3964) by Oskar Herzberg (case nr. 355),
Sammlung Prinzhorn der Psychiatrischen Universitätsklinik Heidelberg, photographer M. Zentsch.

TABLE OF CONTENTS

PREFACE

Jozef Corveleyn & Paul Moyaert

These days a book on psychosis composed entirely of psychoanalytic contributions is a rarity indeed. It can create surprise that, in what some have called 'the decade of the brain', scholars in psychoanalysis, psychiatry and psychology still continue to develop a project for understanding and explaining psychosis from a phenomenological and psychodynamic perspective. And yet such a project not only continues to exist in spite of the dominance of the neuro-biological model but elaborates itself self-consciously in contradistinction to and even as a corrective to this model. The contributors to this reader share the following concern: "The present-day biologisation and neurologisation of psychiatry has dangerously de-emphasized the concern with the individual suffering soul, with the psyche in psychiatry. But if this means a gain in the scientific status of psychiatry, it is at the same time a loss for patients and practitioners alike." (Lothane, 2002, p. 78)

Most of the contributions made to this volume build globally on the ideas of De Waelhens, known for his studies in phenomenology on Heidegger and Merleau-Ponty as well as for his phenomenological and psychoanalytic research into psychosis. The limits of phenomenology as formulated by De Waelhens in the last chapters of his *La philosophie et les expériences naturelles* (1961) incited him to broaden the scope of his perspective; to unravel the basic existential structures of *Dasein* it is necessary, according to De Waelhens, to study human existence in its vulnerability and this vulnerability breaks through in phenomena such as schizophrenia and paranoia. The broadening of his perspective obliged him to combine phenomenology with psychoanalysis and this resulted in his major work *Schizophrenia: A philosophical reflection on Lacan's structuralistic interpretation* (1978). This work has recently been partially re-edited in our series *Figures of the unconscious* and is there preceded by a large essay by Ver Eecke on the tension between biological psychiatry and psychoanalysis in explaining and understanding psychosis. De Waelhens stated, "Whatever success the studies on the anatomical-physiological or biochemical foundations of psychosis in general and schizophrenia in particular may have in realizing the hopes of Kraepelin and many others for the achievement of their ideal of a term for term correspondence between the organic and the psychic,... this would not change a thing as far as we are concerned. Our effort aims at laying the foundation for a *comprehension* of the structure of psychosis and, if possible for an understanding of the different forms of psychosis." (De Waelhens and Ver Eecke, 2001, p. 125, De Waelhens' underlining).

Antoon Vergote, friend and *compagnon de route* of De Waelhens, nonetheless criticizes him for his one-sided emphasis on negative symptoms in schizophrenia.

De Waelhens, according to Vergote, conceives psychosis mainly in terms of a failure. This is to say that he conceives it as a lack in the symbolic order due to the absence of 'the Name of the Father', as a deficiency in the process of symbolisation which causes confusion both in the image of the body and in the perception of sexual identity. This mainly negative view hinders him from seeing that psychosis is an active process in which the subject protects himself against some traumatic experiences, a process in which he tries to restructure his inner chaos with the remains of his fractured imaginary and symbolic order. Further, argues Vergote, with his solely negative view De Waelhens can hardly understand why psychosis is not an unchangeable state. Without the assumption that psychosis is a reaction against a threat coming from within the body, one can hardly understand, he argues, why psychotherapy makes sense.

In their contribution to this volume, Stefaan Soenen and Jozef Corveleyn focus on the crucial role of negative experiences of the libidinous body, both in the pathogenesis of schizophrenia and in the affective experience the psychotic person has of his/her own body. These experiences, the authors show, are not mere epiphenomena of a defective brain process. Clinical observation demonstrates that they also play an important role in rebuilding a world to live in, a world which is continually at risk of falling apart. The authors note that psychoanalysts like Gisela Pankow and Piera Aulagnier have also emphasised the necessity of focusing on the experience of the body not only in their theoretical endeavours but in their actual psychoanalytic practice as well.

In his contribution, Paul Moyaert argues that Freud's interest in schizophrenia was not primarily based on clinical and psychotherapeutic experience but arose from meta-psychological interests. In his remarks on schizophrenia, Freud noticed the peculiar understanding of those linguistic expressions that contain a reference to the body: metaphorical word-representations are taken literally and reduced to bodily thing-representations. To this reduction corresponds the hypochondriac symptoms almost never missing in a psychotic upsurge. According to Moyaert, the negative experience of the body is grounded in the subjective experience of drives as a source of pain and destruction. Auto-mutilation can be seen as a destructive protection against the threatening power of drives that attack the body from within.

Jan Godderis focuses on the clinical phenomenon of the elderly paranoiac. The author argues that this type of paranoia has not really benefited from the great advances made in the fields of neurobiological or neuropsychological research. He claims that the mirror stage as analysed and interpreted by Lacan and De Waelhens is a much more fruitful means to understand the inner organisation of the worldview of an elderly person suffering from paranoic delusion.

Rudolf Bernet focuses on the scopic drive, the body and the gaze in Lacan, Freud and Merleau-Ponty. For both Lacan and Merleau-Ponty the scopic drive is basically an erratic movement depending on an impersonal gaze that gives birth to a divided subject. The scopic drive is incompatible with vision understood as an intentional consciousness belonging to an ego-logical subject. The question then arises of how to understand the difference between an impersonal gaze such as that arising from a painting (Holbein) or from a thing (Cézanne) and a psychotic experience. According to Bernet, Merleau-Ponty makes it possible to better understand what Lacan calls a desymbolisation of the gaze in the traumatic experience of a psychotic hallucination.

The last two essays handle aspects of the famous Schreber case. Freud's first profound study of psychosis was based on the autobiographical writings of Daniel Paul Schreber. Freud gave him the diagnosis of paranoia and 'dementia paranoides'. After Freud, a great number of psychiatric and psychoanalytic scholars as well as a host of historians, sociologists and literary critics have studied this fascinating person. Devreese demonstrates the fruitfulness of an hermeneutical approach that contextualises madness in its historical context and shows the manner in which it is built up within different types of discourse. For his part, Lothane discusses the traditional diagnosis of Schreber. Referring to the conditions of his psychiatric imprisonment, to the disturbances in his behaviour and to the crucial events in his life, Lothane argues that depression would be a more appropriate diagnosis.

REFERENCES

De Waelhens, A. (1961). *La philosophie et les expériences naturelles.* (Phaeno-menologica 9). The Hague: Martinus Nijhoff,

De Waelhens, A. (1978). *Schizophrenia : A philosophical reflection on the structuralist interpretation of J. Lacan.* [Introduction, Explanatory Footnotes and a Bibliography by W. Ver Eecke] (W. Ver Eecke, Trans.). Pittsburgh: Duquesne University Press.

De Waelhens, A. and Ver Eecke, W. (2001). *Phenomenology and Lacan on schizophrenia, after the decade of the brain.* Leuven: Leuven University Press, Figures of the unconscious 2.

Lothane, Z. (2002). The Perrennial Sullivan (1892-1949). Review of M. Conci, *Sullivan Rivisitato la sua rilevanza per la psichiatria la psicoterapia e la psicoanalisi.* Massari Editore, 2000. *International Forum of Psychoanalysis, 11,* 78-80.

PHENOMENOLOGY AND PSYCHOANALYSIS: REFLECTIONS IN REFERENCE TO THE BOOK OF ALPHONSE DE WAELHENS, *SCHIZOPHRENIA*

Antoine Vergote

My reflections on psychosis first of all engages the intention that animated Alphonse De Waelhens when, after about thirty years of work in philosophy, he crossed over into another domain which he nevertheless intended to explore as a philosopher. This means that I will essentially think along with De Waelhens on psychosis and raise questions whenever I find it difficult to think like him.

In his book *Schizophrenia* (De Waelhens, 1978), there is a claim which I would immediately like to accentuate, a claim which must have been an important one for the author since it is found in his foreword and in his conclusion. Thus framing his whole work, this claim is meant to make its perspective explicit. The author affirms that he will show that a philosophical anthropology cannot be constituted without the help of psychiatry and psychoanalysis. One wonders whether the readers of this brief introductory and concluding statement take notice of it and, if they do, how they understand it. For it does not seem to be self-evident.

The final chapter, which is the properly philosophical part of the book, is significantly entitled "Existential Elucidation of the Unconscious and of Psychosis". Actually, this chapter does more to allow psychiatry and psychoanalysis to benefit from phenomenological analyses than to renew phenomenology through the contributions made by psychiatry and psychoanalysis. In view of our topic, which is that of "phenomenology and psychoanalysis," this paradox calls for examination. I will not pretend to completely elucidate this paradox, but I think I can clarify it a bit by recalling the conception of philosophy that De Waelhens expounded in his most personal philosophical work, on philosophy and natural experience: *La philosophie et les expériences naturelles* (De Waelhens, 1961). "Philosophy," he wrote "is reflection upon non-philosophical experience. For indeed, philosophy is both akin to, yet alien, to non-philosophical experience; for while it manages to make the latter aware of itself as non-philosophical, it thereby sometimes allows natural experience to set itself up as an explicit rival of philosophy. Correlatively, non-philosophical experience is close enough to philosophy for it to find a hearing in philosophy, to disquiet it, and thereby to transform it as philosophy" (De Waelhens, 1961, 2-3). And further on, De Waelhens proposes, "thus, the task of philosophy is to comprehend, by contact with human experience and with its history, the rationality that man progressively and interminably institutes in his very existence, in his sensitivity, in his relations with others, in his reflection on himself, on things and their transformation, in

11

the process of his community life, in political activity, in contemplation or aesthetic creation, and finally in religious faith" (De Waelhens, 1961, 39). Or again, "The world, as constitutive of the non-philosophical experience which philosophy must elaborate, achieves its meaning in language, which is not explicitly philosophical yet from which philosophical language is inseparable, because man is inseparable from it, since man *is* language" (De Waelhens, 1961, 117). It is this very conception of philosophy that De Waelhens has implemented in his study on psychosis. What is of interest in psychoanalytic experience and theory is to comprehend the rationality that humanity progressively and incessantly institutes from the prehistory of its existence. This means in particular comprehending how the human person, taken up in language, through those events which are existentially first, becomes what he is in principle: subject of the speech act. The author's project can be understood in this way as the project of showing that a philosophical anthropology cannot be constituted without the help of psychiatry and psychoanalysis. Indeed, psychoanalysis deals with non-philosophical experience, experience at once the most heterogeneous to philosophy, and which is moreover not even natural because, in the process of rememoration, it reawakens a history which precedes all natural experience. Yet, at the same time, this experience has the greatest affinity with philosophy since it concerns the very advent of language suited to articulate existence. For De Waelhens as a philosopher, what was fascinating about psychoanalysis was to discover how the human person becomes human insofar as the very questions which the philosopher raises are at work in him long before any self-conscious thought: questions of one's birth and of one's contingency, of one's death and of one's finitude, of one's relationship to others, of desire and of the law. If there is a contribution of psychoanalysis to philosophical anthropology within this perspective, it consists essentially in furnishing the non-philosophical experience which allows philosophy to reach its accomplishment as philosophy by shedding light on the rationality which man progressively achieves, prior to any thematic thought. Psychoanalytic experiences likewise serve to prop up the phenomenological critique of an idealist or naturalist philosophy which are unable to account for the experiences psychoanalysis observes.

PSYCHOSIS

Within this perspective, Alphonse De Waelhens has viewed psychosis as the failure to reach the rationality which the human person is called to achieve. By considering the most radical human lack, he wanted to comphrehend most radically the constitution of human being. The contrasting alternative between the analysis of the early constitution of human being and that of its non-constitution in psychosis comprises the framework of his book. The emphasis placed on psychotic non-constitution can seem disconcerting; but it can be understood from the author's view of the shore opposite to the constitution of human being, the shore of its catastrophic drift. His exploration of this drift has allowed him to pose for himself, with heightened awareness, the question already opened for him by his study of Heidegger: who am I being there, *Da-sein*. The psychotic, the most heterogeneous other to the one who questions his own being, remains no less a witness to the humanity of man, for madness is proper to man. If this is so, the human person cannot be understood unless there is an elucidation of "... the potentiality for madness lying at the very heart of the structures that are constitutive of the human condition" (De Waelhens, 1978, X). Correlatively, the perilous proximity of madness to the constitutive structuring of the human condition vividly elucidates that condition.

It might seem surprising that De Waelhens has, to a certain extent, abandoned properly philosophical research in order to apply himself with such fervor to the study of psychosis, to the point of undertaking a systematic study of the great psychiatric works, of spending a month in the psychiatric clinic of the University of Utrecht in the Netherlands, of devoting innumerable hours of conversations with psychotics at the psychiatric clinic of the University of Leuven at Lovenjoel in Belgium. All things considered, these efforts were simply continuing his longstanding interest in how the human person comes to be in and through an historical path. While it was the existential analysis of *Dasein* that De Waelhens favored within the philosophy of Heidegger, the *Phenomenology of Spirit* within the philosophy of Hegel, and the phenomenology of constitution within the philosophy of Husserl, it was psychoanalysis that opened up for him an insight into the early constitution and history of human being.

The options which ground the thought of De Waelhens are animated by the same concern that is recognizable in his effort to dialectically reconcile the two tendencies inherent to philosophy which pull it asunder and which are its salutary peril. These tendencies are, on the one hand, to elaborate a system of ideas that claims to render an exhaustive account of human experience, and, on the other hand, to dissolve rationality into the savage being of brute experience. It is curious that, without elaborating the common ground between these two extremes from which his thought sought to be freed, De Waelhens studies two forms of psychosis, schizophrenia and paranoia, and that he presents them as the two forms which typify those two extremes. Through his constitutive phenomenology, De Waelhens has conjured up this double danger in philosophy, of destroying itself either by changing into something other than philosophy, or by constructing a vault of concepts over an abyss. The constitutive thought he practiced was receptive to the latency of reason emerging in the wake of human gesture, but was above all dedicated to enlarging reason in active thought. Far from being a thinker who is an eternal beginner, *'ein ewiger Anfänger'*, De Waelhens has worked like an architect, measuring the weight and counterweight of stones and constructing an edifice from them.

Thus, in order to comprehend psychosis, the author gave it a place within a constitutive construction. For this reason, his book *Schizophrenia* is in a certain sense a fundamentally phenomenological work. The question is whether the psychotic can be relagated to the place fixed for him by the author within his architectural blueprint for human abodes.

In seeking to understand psychosis according to the model of constitutive construction, De Waelhens has opposed the causal explanation which he attributes to the mechanistic conception of pre-analytic psychiatry. At the same time, he has likewise rejected the purely phenomenological comprehension presented by the existential analysis of L. Binswanger. Phenomenological psychiatry describes changes in one's relations to the real world, that is to say, the impossibility of consenting to things as they are, and it tries to understand psychosis by the interlinking chains of the subjective reactions to this impossibility. But, as De Waelhens has rightly affirmed, the changes which the existential analysis describes are not the enigmatic point of departure of the illness; they are the illness itself. There is consequently a need to understand "why does the coherence of the world cease to prevail in this particular subject" (De Waelhens, 1978, 44). An existential analysis can isolate the deficiencies but, incapable of understanding them, it calls upon a mechanistic causalisty. Psychiatry and non-analytic phenomenology thereby easily come to ally themselves with a mechanistic explanation. Refusing the alternatives of either an existential description or a mechanistic explanation, De Waelhens has sought to understand psychosis through the vicissitudes of the constitutive unconscious. It can be asked whether this third way so radically excludes the causalistic explanation he had refused. Indeed, as the author has pointed out, microbes, by attacking cerebral tissue, cannot be held accountable for a delirium of megolomania or of one of pettiness (De Waelhens, 1978, 31). Yet it is doubtful whether De Waelhens would still have maintained so sharp an opposition between understanding and causal explanation since, after the publication of his book, he has declared that he had on many occasions been impressed by the favorable effects certain neuroleptics have upon delirium.

This opposition between understanding and explaining has likewise had its consequences for his interpretative rereading of Freudian theory. Just like Merleau-Ponty, De Waelhens has sought to free psychoanalysis from "a biologically oriented naturalism that he (Freud) never completely overcame" (De Waelhens, 1978, 182). Actually, the fundamental Freudian concept of pulsion (*Trieb*), as a double-faceted reality, at once organic and psychic, force and signification, poses insuperable limits upon understanding. The psychical is found to be in part causally determined by its inherence within the biological. Psychic meaning is in part subjected to the force of pulsional energy, to a pulsional economy which can be observed or inferred afterwards by its effect but which, by its very nature, eludes the sort of comprehension associated with meaning. This is indeed why psychoanalysis is an analysis which more or less restores the significant history afterwards by reassembling the past without ever being able to reconstitute the lived present by logical chains of meaning. Jacques Lacan has likewise sought to free psychoanalytic theory from its economic concepts; yet he just as forcefully refused the idea of comprehending psychosis. For him, psychosis is definitely not a question of meaning. It represents an invasion by signifiers which set about speaking in the void of non-subject. De Waelhens himself has taken up this idea of Lacan, which shows that the expression 'to comprehend psychosis' is not a simple one.

SCHIZOPHRENIA

A first stage in understanding the project of De Waelhens consists in identifying what he calls the psychotic structure, which gathers together the symptoms of psychosis into a coherent figure. One might think that unprejudicial observation would be sufficient for this project, yet this is not the case. Chapter one, which retraces the essential psychiatric notions which have advanced the knowledge of schizophrenia, shows how operative concepts borrowed from psychology and philosophy has already governed and inflected the perception of the manifestations of psychosis. This is not surprising. Both philosophy of science and phenomenology teach us that perception and listening go to meet phenomena with regulatory ideas which bring a significance stand out in the facts observed. Thus, the academic psychology of faculties led Kraepelin to draw up a list of their particular alterations. Similarly, his existential analysis prompted Binswanger to evoke the bizarre and capricious (*eigenartig*) way of relating to things which causes the loss of an assured basis for a veritable project. Convinced by the history of psychiatry as he reasoned it out and by his own philosophical conception that observation of facts and theoretical concepts envelop each other reciprocally, De Waelhens accordingly began to offer an account of psychosis by developing his own explanatory conception. Psychoanalytic theory provided the grid through which to read the facts. It was only afterwards that he presented the diagnostic table upon which he derived the internal coherence of symptoms.

Together, in their co-originality, five traits pertain to schizophrenia. First, the schizophrenic experiences her body as fragmented, which reveals the absence of a subjective identity that ought to have unified the lived body by assuming it. Secondly, a specific disturbance is characteristic of schizophrenic language: the words are signifiers according to their literal sense. Thus the yellow (*geel* in Dutch) wall of her cell proves to a patient that she is crazy. It is necessary to realize that *geel* (yellow) is also the name of a town (Geel) where many insane people came to live together (Roosens, 1979). De Waelhens designated this phenomenon as the confusion of the signifier and the signified which manifests that the split between the two has not been made. Thirdly, the father tends to be confused with the mother, a confusion which opens the way for the delirious idea of being one's own incestuous father. Fourthly, sexual identity has not been assumed, which leads the psychoanalysist to suspect that the subject has not entered into the Oedipal structuration. Finally, birth and death are confused; in other words, the psychotic does not situate herself within a historicity marked by the law of generations, which also must be related to the non-accomplishment of the Oedipal triangulation. This remarkable table of revelatory signs makes a veritable phenomenon of schizophrenia since it draws attention to presence insofar as it is manifest in its essential dimensions: the lived body, being of language, being for others in difference, and temporalization. What is striking is that, with the exception of the fragmented body, all these traits are characterized by confusion. A split has not been made, differentiation has not been achieved, and an opening has not been produced within which there would be room for presence. This table of revelatory symptoms makes us think of the negativity at work in Hegel's system, Husserl's notion of intentionality, and Heideggers's philosophy of existence and difference. Only one who has been instructed by the philosophy of an efficacious structuration through disjunction could identify psychosis by the negation of constructive negativity.

The philosophical conviction that there is meaning only in a distantiation and that one only finds oneself by going outside oneself governs De Waelhens' understanding of psychosis which, for the author, is essentially a non-becoming. Becoming is accomplished through negativity. Yet the symptoms of psychosis attest precisely to the absence of negativity. One wonders how the author could account for a fundamental characteristic of psychosis which Freud very aptly called the generalized pleasure of a denying rejection (the *'allgemeine Verneinungslust'*) (1925 h, 239).

CONSTITUTION

Let us now consider how the concept of constitutive unconscious sheds light on psychosis. I shall take the liberty of summerizing the ideas of De Waelhens in a highly succinct fashion. I will first develop his comprehension of schizophrenia and then will present his interpretation of paranoia.

The first moment of the constitution, that of the accession to language, is decisive. Not being a matter of simple apprenticeship, this accession requires the renunciation of the immediacy in which the infant bathes. This step represents an anguishing loss. Thus a psychological labor must be accomplished: that of the primary repression of gratifying representations of the dual union with the mother. If the pre-subject "consents to live as a being who lacks," then "such a way of living is marked by negativity since the various partial objects will then be for him so many possible signifiers of his desire to be recognized by the Other's desire" (De Waelhens, 1978, 59). The accession to language and to desire thus is realized by the acceptance of distance and the renunciation of immediacy. The schizophrenic, not having accomplished this primary repression, will be incapable of learning a language as a universe of signs which mediate the real recognized as such.

It could be asked what motivates the pre-subject to accept this loss. What sustains the work of the negative, whose crucial necessity the author went on to demonstrate at each stage? Clearly, the author preferred to concentrate on describing the drama of successive renunciations, and took less care than does Françoise Dolto, for example, to pinpoint the experiences or tendencies which also prepare for and promote transgressive ruptures from within. His eagerness to understand psychotic deficiencies made him remark forcefully the moments of transmutations which are not realized in the schizophrenic, moments which are in fact always renunciations since renunciations are necessary conditions for an access to a new mode of being.

While this is the fundamental thesis of De Waelhens, it is not the thesis of

Lacan. Lacan places the foreclosure (the rejection within the exterior, within the "real") of the order of language (signifiers) at the origin of psychosis. This foreclosure is for him correlative to a non-accomplishment of a first consenting affirmation. To be sure, De Waelhens did address the Lacanian idea of foreclosure as the non-accession to language, but in doing so he wants to give it an explanation that would combine the philosophy of language with a psychology or psychoanalysis of attachment. He begins his exposition by pointing out that "The accession to speech can be explained in Hegelian terms as the passage which guides immediacy to mediation" (De Waelhens, 1978, 49). Immediacy, in the constitutive becoming of being, is the mother, the first object of attachment. The pre-subject experiences himself in a fusional union with her. Child and mother form a oneness. "The immediate which must be renounced, is the state of consciousness as it sets in as a savage and dangerous rush to, and within the other, who actually is still the same as the pre-subject itself" (De Waelhens, 1979, 55. Translation changed, AV). When De Waelhens calls renunciation the primary repression, he thereby gives his concept a meaning which Freud did not.

Manifestations can probably be observed in schizophrenia of this avid, fusional attachment to a maternal figure or symbol, but the author does not cite any. An analysis of such manifestations, however, would not be enough to prove his thesis anyway. From my acquaintance with schizophrenic discourse, they are not dominant there; I think they are more prevalent in certain grave neuroses. The thesis of De Waelhens is manifestly an interpretative construction propped up by his philosophy and a developmental psychology. This interpretative construction is meant to account for the revelatory signs of schizophrenia in the way he describes it, as marked by confusion.

The relationship of the schizophrenic to his/her own mirror image, further in the development, repeats and confirms the early failure. Even if the author does not thoroughly develop the structuring relations of the maternal bond, he does analyze in depth the formation of subjectivity at work in the 'mirror-stage' as Lacan articulated it (Lacan, 1977, 1-7): the assumption of oneself as corporeal ego unified by the apperception of one's own image, doubled and reflected in one's likeness. The schizophrenic, deprived of an autonomous signifier, by his/her reintegration within his/her closure with his/her mother, does not grasp in his/her specular image the reference to an 'other'. Therefore, she will not assume herself as a lived totality, just as she will be incapable of constructing a world as a totality organized by a subjective center of projects (De Waelhens, 1978). Thus, the schizophrenic will be unable to enter within the vicissitudes which normally structure the subject definitively: the Oedipal complex. The author vividly enlightens the importance of the structuring Oedipal complex in contrast with the 'absence' of the Oedipal triangle in psychosis. However, the expression 'absence of the Oedipal triangle' lends itself to misunderstandings. His whole development indicates to us that this 'absence' must be understood as a presence which is not recognized. I think I am being faithful to the author's intention in saying that the father who has been excluded (by the mother, but with his unconscious connivance) is installed as negatively present in the subject. This is what gives the schizophrenic her status, not of being a child who is a retarded pre-subject, but of being an alienated non-subject. "The maternal elements which contribute to the formation of the Oedipal relations do not lead to a correct position of the Oedipus complex ...". We understand this to mean that the Oedipal is not posed and worked through as such since "the pseudo-subject remains, in his being, identified with the phallus of the mother and could therefore not be another for her" (De Waelhens, 1978, 88-89). In continuity with Lacan, De Waelhens then exposes the structuring efficaciousness of the paternal figure. It definitely makes present the law and the bestowal of a name which identifies the child. The famous Oedipal prohibition confirms the process of primary repression and breaks the mother-child coalescence at the level of desire, which now is already sexually signified. Splitting up the narcissistic mother-child couple by his very position, the father castrates the child in the sense that he tears him/her away from his/her desire to be the phallus of the mother. 'Castration', which bears upon the 'imaginary' of the child, has the result that the child will be capable of entering into the exchange of desire precisely by the assumption of his/her own sexually differentiated body. Likewise the paternal figure which bestows his name situates the child within inter-subjective relationships identified in time (generations) and within socially differentiated relations (family and exogamy).

Psychoanalytic theory, according to De Waelhens, thus follows an understanding of a fact of psychosis which non-analytic psychiatry never has managed to grasp within its differentiated structure. "Blocked in his first position as the imaginary maternal phallus ...," (De Waelhens, 1978, 128) not having acceded to the other that is that which the father signifies as such by the sign of his name, the schizophrenic is not capable of symbolizing the real by his/her language. His/her language does not de-realize the immediate and so does not signify the world. His/her language immediately transfers onto the real (which is only so for us, being imaginary for him/her) phantasms which emanate from the most archaic realms of the unconscious (being devoured by the mother, castration by the father imagined to be real, omnipotent grandeur). In this manner, delirium is an endeavor to escape from the unavoidable voices that speak in him/her but from which there is no distance in default of a true language which would allow him/her to repress his/her phantasms. This ejection of phantasms into the outside also represents the substitution of a pseudo-real and fills the radical void yawning at the extreme limit of an autistic retreat from the world.

Put to the test by a thorough case study, analytic theory proves its value by its power to shed light on it, unlike the philosophies which inspired classical psychiatry. Delirium can now be understood as resulting from several processes: an effort to restore a dimension of reality that has been disinvested, a compromise with unconscious representations, the utilization towards this end of material that has been perceived. Furthermore, in light of this dynamic conception, the absence of delirium in a schizophrenia takes on the meaning of being the most radical regression toward an absolutely insular autism.

PARANOIA

This autism is the terrible and fatal destiny of schizophrenia. Paranoia is a somewhat more fortunate psychosis, for the paranoiac has in fact accomplished the primary repression and has thereby acceded to language. He nevertheless remains fixed to the mirror stage. As I have already pointed out, De Waelhens, following Lacan, understood by 'mirror stage' that precocious moment when the small child forms a certain awareness of himself as corporeal unity by seeing himself in a mirror as someone who looks like him/her and who is perceived as a double figuring himself. By remaining fixed at this constitutive moment, the paranoiac reduces every relationship with others to a reproduction of this specular couple. This is the fundamental thesis of De Waelhens. It seems to furnish him with an understanding of two symptoms characteristic of paranoia. First of all, it helps him understand the passionate interests of a homosexual nature for one's likeness, an interest which, according to Freud, returns through defensive inversions in delirium, whether of persecution, erotomania, or of jealousy. Secondly, and most importantly, the fixation at the mirror stage seems to provide the key to comprehending that strange phenomenon which is the delirious conviction of possessing absolute evidence. The paranoiac, indeed, knows with an unshakeable certitude what he/she affirms in his/her delirious interpretations. For De Waelhens, this knowing is a seeing. Of the paranoiac, one can say that 'it' (*das Es*, the id) only discourses; 'it' possesses absolute truth because 'it' sees a world without transcendence, a world reduced to the imaginary. For, says the author, "... the imaginary is, by its very nature, always a 'thing', always *something* finished" (De Waelhens, 1978, 151).

The author does not quote Sartre, but it seems it is indeed the Sartrean phenomenology of the imaginary which he has taken up there. Recall Sartres fine analysis of the imagined Pantheon: as imagined, it offers itself as a whole, in an absolute transparency, without letting itself be grasped by an exploration of it. In his later book on the duke of Saint-Simon (De Waelhens, 1981), De Waelhens applies himself, with a secret jubilation, to a description of the piercing, unveiling, infallible look of the duke. The duke knows with an absolute certainty because he sees.

I ask myself if the phrase cannot be turned around: does not the paranoiac see with a regard that penetrates things and men because he knows? Is it not rather the way his/her language is relieved from its inherence in perception which fills his/her concern for an absolute knowing? So we think of Schreber who stays often half-naked looking at himself in the mirror and who 'sees' his breast becoming that of a woman. He does not look to explore the unknown, but to verify that which he knows. Paranoiac delirium seems to me rather to represent the absorption of the world in pure language. I would apply to the paranoiac the famous statement of Lacan: it speaks in him/her. It is undoubtedly no accident that this thesis on the unconscious was formulated by one who began his work with a thesis on paranoia (Lacan, 1932), a thesis which seems to have given Lacan the model for his theory of the unconscious, which is where I cannot follow him without some qualifications.

19

Freud saw a likeness between philosophy and paranoia, but he did not assimilate the one to the other. Yet both have in common the reconstruction of the world starting from concepts. For Freud, the paranoiac is he/she who is entirely dominated by the quasi-corporeity of signifiers. His/her verbal system has integrally incorporated the real. He/she thereby shuts out all contingency and exorcizes any disquietude. Let us admit that he thus attains a completeness of knowing of which philosophy as a rigorous science dreams. In this sense, paranoia is inscribed in humanity as one of its fundamental possibilities. However, the idea of reconstructing the world with concepts remains, for the philosopher, a dream which he knows is, according to the untranslatable word of Husserl, *ausgetraümt*, dissipated because it is demystified as the dream of a utopian knowledge.

By inverting the thesis of De Waelhens, I am evidently overthrowing his theory of a developmental constitution which would explain paranoiac psychosis by a fixation to a stage. In doing so, I am likewise radicalizing the psychotic nature of paranoia. Readers of his book on the duke of Saint-Simon will have had occasion to remark that there the author hesitated on this point. De Waelhens in fact interpreted this celebrated memorialist entirely in reference to his theory of paranoia. He even explained the strange passion that set the duke to writing his memoires night and day over a period of years by his passion to be the absolute witness and quasi-divine judge of good and evil. Nonetheless, De Waelhens did not dare to declare him to be paranoiac without further ado because the duke showed no evidence of being a psychotic. Is not this an implicit avowal that the fixation to the mirror stage does not determine the psychotic structure?

PHENOMENOLOGY AND PSYCHOANALYSIS

Phenomenology and psychoanalysis: what does psychoanalysis contribute to phenomenology? First, psychoanalysis draws the limits of phenomenology. De Waelhens warns us that an existential elucidation of psychosis must recognize the discontinuity between psychoanalysis and phenomenology since the 'unconscious constitution' escapes all direct phenomenology. Positively, psychoanalytic experience presents irreducible observations for which certain philosophies are unable to account: the rationalist tradition, dualism, a philosophy which gives primacy to rational consciousness. This is what the author shows in the second part of his work.

From all appearances, phenomenology is the philosophy most in accord with analytic observations; it is for this reason that De Waelhens concludes his book with a summary of his interpretations, elucidating them by the phenomenology of the body, of perception, of temporalization, of signifying language, and of presence. How indeed could one listen intelligently to what is said in analysis about the most personal and existential experiences of the body, others, self-representation, desire, and finitude, without hearing in it the resonances of all that phenomenology has developed? The extraordinary genius of Freud is admirable in that he was able to describe in an *existential language* the themes phenomenology has strived to elucidate. If the psychoanalyst had the immense culture and genius of Freud, he could dispense himself from a philosophical formation. But, in repeating the schemas of Freudian theory, his heirs risk reducing them to a mechanics of a few formal schemas. A phenomenological elucidation like De Waelhens practices opens up the theoretical concepts of psychoanalysis and restores their life to them, their power of guiding and enlightening clinical listening.

Inversely, what does psychoanalysis contribute to philosophical anthropology? In what respect is psychoanalysis indispensable for a philosophical anthropology as De Waelhens affirms?

It indeed seems that for him psychoanalysis represents above all the discovery of the archaic massif of psychic formation which remains imperceptible to the phenomenologist. For De Waelhens the analytic experience reveals above all the structuring effect of the existential assent to absence and distance. The renunciation of an undifferentiated fullness marks the three great moments evoked in the constitution of human being: in the dual relationship with the mother, in the dual relationship of the mirror stage, and in their retrieval in the Oedipal triangulation. The exploration of the prehistoric archeology of human existence justifies for philosophy what its analysis of perception and temporality had already taught it. This exploration makes it understand once and for all why its secret passion to recuperate all signification within an absolute knowing is an illusory nostalgia. To comprehend psychosis is, in the final analysis, to comprehend why there is meaning only in the retreat before the fullness of meaning. By positing an exterior limit to philosophical comprehension, psychoanalysis establishes the internal limit of comprehension that philosophy deploys as the establishment of rationality.

CRITICAL QUESTIONS AND PROPOSITIONS

We must still ask whether psychosis is entirely comprehensible as the early reflux and retreat before language which prompts us to consent to separation and distance. This question opens an interrogation of two fields between which De Waelhens' book on psychosis moves: the field of psychiatry and psychoanalysis, and the field of phenomenology. On the one hand, has not constitutive phenomenology the tendency to hide data which are essential to psychoanalysis yet which arise precisely due to our corporal being? On the other hand, does not psychoanalysis yield some essential meanings which philosophical rationality tends to misunderstand?

In the first place, can psychosis really be entirely understood as resulting from the absence of rupture with an originary coalescence? Are psychotics psychotic from the very beginning, to the point that one could say that "whatever their language may be, these patients only speak dead languages," (De Waelhens, 1978, 207) that they have never inhabited their language or their body except beneath a covering of learned but not interiorized language, that they have always been psychotics and will be definitively always? We ought to give credit to De Waelhens who, instructed by his further observations, did not try to elude any revision of what he had written in this regard. Beyond the practical consequences for a theory of psychosis, what is important for our topic is to see what psychiatric and psychoanalytic observations have to teach the philosopher. What these observations seem to me to shake is precisely this very principle of a sufficient comprehension according to the model of genetic constitution. The explanatory power of this model seems to me to be much more limited than a phenomenologist thinks who reconstructs afterwards the logic of human prehistory and history. A constitutive analysis of meaning naturally tends to think according to the model of definitive stratifications and reworkings. Like the philosophy of Hegel, it has the advantage of disclosing, e.g., through wanderings and illusions, a history becoming spirit. De Waelhens accordingly describes extremely well the becoming of a person through the imaginary doubling of the mirror stage or the Oedipal conflict. But, just like the bird of Minerva, the phenomenologist of genetic constitution flies over the daytime of accomplished history and thinks that history has been definitively achieved in that one passage. The evening peace of comprehensive reason effaces the traces of upheavals which continue to take place underground. Let us illustrate this with an observation. The experience of a fragmented body is one of the signs revealing schizophrenia. In contrast to the psychiatrist who is attentive to disturbances of the psychological faculties, the phenomenologist makes an analysis of the lived body, perceiving all the importance of the observation to lie there. But the phenomenologist comes to a comprehension of the fragmented body as the non-formation of the unity of the lived body. Two principles of perception orientate his explanation. First of all, perception grasps a *Gestalt* in the dispersion of sensible data. The perception of one's image in the mirror thus yields the *Gestalt* of the body which allows one to assume it as a unity. In his *Phenomenology of Perception*, Merleau-Ponty even proposed to interpret all pathology, and thus the unconscious, as the residue of what has not been integrated within the living *Gestalt*. Phenomenology goes on to develop a second principle which can be invoked to comprehend the fragmented body: the principle of transcendence toward the world which must animate the body by its intentional arc. Consequently, it can be inferred that the maintenance of an immersion in the confusional unity with the mother congeals the movement of transcendence and leaves the body unanimated, squirming in its early chaotic dislocation.

Whatever light phenomenology might thus shed upon the psychotic phenomenon of the fragmented body, it does not permit a comprehension of what, in my opinion, is so impressive in much observation of psychosis: that the anguishing experience is not of a fragmented body but of a body being fragmented by the force of aggressions, imaginary ones to be sure, which are devouring from within, which corrupt it, which turn pleasure into suffering, which tear it apart. Or, further, there is the horrifying experience of the decaying body, of the bad body, the experience that can be evoked by the expression attributed to Luther: that you are but shit that has dropped from the devil's ass. A negativity is manifest there which can no longer be understood as the absence of the positive work of negativity. Only by taking the human pulsional conflict into account can one to some slight extent elucidate such death-dealing negativity. This means that the advent of presence is under submission to what Freud called the economy of pulsions, pulsions of life and 'death'. Alongside the language of meaning, it is also necessary to adhere to a language of conflictual forces. This is not the place to develop these considerations, but it is necessary to mark the limits of a phenomenological comprehension, and to insist at the same time upon the limits of a psychoanalytic explanation.

Moreover, the constitution of presence is dependent upon the neurophysiological body, which the specialists admit still retains an immense reserve of secrets. Further, psychoanalytic observation likewise teaches us that access to language, transcendence toward the world, and openness to presence are not simply accomplished within some remote prehistory, but that this archaic history remains the underpinning of the present, that it remains as inscribed, with its failures, its progressions and regressions, in the psychic memory ever active beneath the present history. In this sense the psychotic has always been psychotic, but he also has never been before late adolescence really a psychotic. An autistic child is not schizophrenic and I doubt very much that an adolescent could be. It is necessary that a new crisis of existence takes place upon entry into adult life, to activate, by significant analogies, the buried memory of old fixations, the solidified results of early conflicts which, like embedded cells of meaning, regressively aspirate the present drama. If this is so, psychosis and particularly schizophrenia are no longer to be seen as a destiny inexorably determined by the very first vicissitudes of existence. By depriving the phenomenologist and even the psychoanalyst of an assured understanding, psychoanalysis to some extent restores to the psychotic a hope of recovering presence.

THE UNCONSCIOUS OPEN TO OBSERVATION?

I would like to conclude by reflecting for a moment more on a claim repeated in De Waelhens's book. Following the observations of Freud, but in taking up a formulation which I think came from Lacan, De Waelhens has written that psychosis spreads the unconscious wide open. I am not contesting his technical explanation according to which the psychotic, due to his lack of a primary repression, is incapable of repressing what he calls phantasms, phantasms concerning birth, castration, the paternal figure. That in a certain sense the unconscious errupts into the open in psychosis not only poses the question of non-repression, but, even beyond this, the question of repression in a person who is not psychotic. Freud was struck by the similarities with myths which he heard in deliria. He also insisted upon the likenesses between dreams and symptoms on the one hand, and folkloric narratives, sayings, fairytales, and expressions of popular language on the other. A prescientific, even preconscious perception of the psyche expresses itself in natural language, and this gives access to hidden representations which, to some extent, constitute the meaning of pathological phenomena. It was even a literary work, a drama of Sophocles, which furnished the essential grid for deciphering the unconscious, and it is well known that Jung's psychology took the same observation as its point of departure. On the basis of this resemblance between myths and delirium, Jung constructed his dubious theory of archetypes inscribed within the collective unconscious. In a completely different way but nonetheless reminiscent of the Jungian attempt, Lacan tried to account for this strange phenomenon by elaborating his conception of the symbolic order, the 'treasury of signifiers' which governs the unconscious and shows how, in phantasms and deliria as much as in myths and rites, 'it' speaks. The difference between the psychotic and anyone else is that, for the psychothic, 'it' returns from outside, in the 'real'; whereas for the non-psychotic, 'it' speaks from within, across significations which metaphorize the signifiers.

This opens up an immense question which there is no question of closing up again through some psychoanalytic rationalizations. In explaining myths as the projection of unconscious content, Freud only displaced the question towards the problem of the constitution of the unconscious, thus clearing the way for the Jungian theory. And his pseudo-ethnological essay in *Totem and Taboo* is but a grandiose failure, redeemed by the greatness of its enterprise (Vergote, 1996, 243-263).

What is most important about the repeated connection Freud saw between the structures of the unconscious and myths and literature is his recognition that pathology itself is still a modality of human existence such as is expressed in cultural works and such as culture constitutes it precisely as human. This was Freud's first revolutionary discovery, and it was starting from this comprehension of pathology that he then posed the question of comprehending or explaining why this humanized existence is only realized in some mode of its partial or more radical failure. A person who is ill is so in and through that which is most fundamentally human in him/her. Therefore, it is necessary to comprehend how pathology is inscribed as a possibility of that which is most essentially human. It was at this juncture between meaning and distorted meaning that Freud introduced the link between meaning and the energetic.

Meaning must be produced, yet this only happens by a psychic action. But the idea of action implies the idea of forces and conflicts. Hegel already insisted upon this in his philosophy of life. Meaning, which is semantic, is produced by the encounter between language and the psyche, which is life. Thus, at the basis of the production of meaning, pulsion is discovered with its two facets. This production begins from the entrance into human relationships which is always articulated and signified by language. From this came Freud's effort, not only to decipher meaning, but also to comprehend it as production. This perspective, which joins the deciphering of meaning with the description of its production, likewise allowed him to situate the production of that meaning which is preserved and displaced in order to be put in the service of life and to defend against pain and anxiety.

Language, which is related to meaning, surely has only metaphors at its disposal with which to describe the conflictual production of meaning. Do not all sciences resort to such metaphors to construct their theoretical concepts? Besides, is not the linguistic term metaphor itself a metaphor? Insofar as it is, it recalls that metaphorization as the production of meaning requires an action and thus a psychic force. The speech acts which the philosophers of language analyze already imply a movement of production. To reproach Freud for having borrowed his models from physics and biology is not only to reduce psychoanalysis to a hermeneutic of meaning cut off from its clinical aspect but is even to fail to recognize the force producing new meaning to which metaphors attest.

Let us consider a bit further the similarity between deliria or hallucinations and myths, since it provides us with a guide for a certain understanding of psychosis. At any rate, it shows how the psychotic finds himself beneath the sway of the great signifying realities that the language of humanity brings to him even more forcefully than to those who have suppressed the question of existence. It is precisely within these fundamental references that psychotics, due to a collapse, no longer situate themselves. The essential words have lost their power to anchor them within an existence that has been assumed. The phenomenology of presence, of the body, and of temporality provides a powerful analysis of this point which helps to explain the destructuration of the capacity to situate themselves relationally. An existential hermeneutic, however, is not capable of explaining how the collapse is produced; it can only describe an absence which it is then inclined to place at the origin as a pure non-arrival. Personally, as I have already indicated, I think that a premature drama in the life of the libidinal body, by its force of retroactive attraction, makes a cleavage between existence as it is experienced and the allocutive and evocative power of language to signify, in such a way that the latter loses its subjective significance. That is what I think I can read, for example, in that catastrophe which took place at a certain moment in the existence of President Schreber, a catastrophe which he called soul murder. It had to do with the experience of an event which was death-dealing.

As I did mention, De Waelhens thinks that psychotic delusions eject the unconscious phantasms in the exterior, or quoting Lacan: in the real. Do psychotic delusions actually reveal universal unconscious phantasms? Can they be compared with myths which would be witnesses of archaic times of humanity? Freud thought so. He isolated some similar traits in myths, deliria, dreams and phantasms and he saw in them the hereditarily transmitted representations of the early stage of human development. But the similarity Freud enhances should not make us fail to recognize most essential differences, which accurate linguistic analysis should examine thoroughly. Myths are very specific, well structured tales in the objective order of language, without a speaking subject mentioned. They are like the talk of humanity and the construct of a common world of meaning. Delirium, on the contrary, is awkward idiosyncratic talk, mostly logically chaotic, often using semantics, grammar and cultural ideas in an odd way. Dreams exist only as told sequences of images; in this way they are a combination of primary and secondary processes. Their private content gives way to common talk and communication.

In the conception of psychoanalysis, delirium, just like all psychopathologic symptoms, has a positive meaning and cannot be characterized as in purely negative terms. Psychotics use their memories of language, of the human world of family and society, of religion and literature in order to reconstruct with them a lost common world. They do not create a new meaningful ensemble, but they endeavor to recreate a common world. As such their intention is functional: they try to repair. Therefore they construct a private pretence of a world. In this way, Schreber did use his exceptionally rich memories of cultural facts and ideas.

It thus would oppose the idea that in psychosis the unconscious is open to observation. We cannot compare psychosis with neurosis. In neuroses and in dreams the unconscious is to some extent unveiling itself to the trained observer. In psychosis it is lacking, because it has been destroyed by destructive impulses. Consequently, language, which is in the memory, is no more rooted in the unconscious which mediates the perception of the real world. Hence the psychotic, in so far she is psychotic, no longer uses semantics, grammatical competence, cultural data with a personally conscious intention to refer to a common human and natural world. The functional intention is to recreate a world. Psychosis is not, as neurosis, a permanent repression of representations, plus a partial lifting of it; psychosis is a struggle to save some world from its destruction through a psychological death.

THE VICISSITUDES OF CORPOREALITY IN SCHIZOPHRENIA: A PSYCHOANALYTIC APPROACH

Stefaan Soenen & Jozef Corveleyn

Disturbances of the body image are allocated a primary, even a central role in Alphonse De Waelhens' reflections on the fundamental structures of schizophrenia. In the classical literature of clinical psychiatry, these phenomena have frequently been described at length (see Soenen & Corveleyn, 1998), but they have never occupied such an important place as in the work of De Waelhens. His book, *La Psychose*, presents the fragmentation of the body image as one of the five existential and psychodynamic criteria for being able to speak of a schizophrenic personality structure (De Waelhens, 1972). De Waelhens draws here on Lacan's early texts on the mirror stage and on the ideas of Gisela Pankow and Pierra Aulagnier regarding the body image in schizophrenia. Each in their own original manner, these psychoanalytic authors have made a detailed analysis of the way in which the schizophrenic subject relates to his or her body. This article aims primarily to draw more attention to the work of Pankow and Aulagnier. The particular features of corporeality in schizophrenia have received very little attention in the contemporary, mainly neurobiological and cognitive-psychological literature on schizophrenia. The authors just mentioned have nonetheless shown that, on this point at least, there are important points of connection for diagnostic and therapeutic approaches to psychosis. We will examine successively the theories of Pankow and Aulagnier, and conclude with a section about the work of Andreoli, a psychiatrist inspired by the thought of Bion. Andreoli's theses will turn out to converge in a striking way with the ideas put forward by the first two authors, to whom we now turn.

GISELA PANKOW AND THE DISSOCIATION OF THE BODY IMAGE

Certain situations are found to be so intolerable and life-threatening that there is no other possibility than to escape from one's own body. During prolonged and severe torture, prisoners of war have been able to transform their experience to such a degree that they no longer had the feeling they inhabited their own bodies. They situated themselves elsewhere, for instance in an apple tree which could be seen from the place where they were undergoing their traumatic torment. A similar, though even more radical escape can be seen in schizophrenic subjects, according to Pankow (Pankow, 1969). In contrast to the prisoner of war, however, the schizophrenic person no longer succeeds in returning to his body on his own initiative. The body remains behind, uninhabited and abandoned, like a form without content, an empty shell.

The schizophrenic subject's radical turn away from the libidinal body inevitably leads to a loss of identity, since along with loss of the lived body, there is also a loss of bodily experienced memory, a loss of the libidinal history in which the ego sinks its roots. The subject becomes entrapped and enclosed in a timeless, inhuman space. Pankow describes how the self-experience of one of her schizophrenic patients is mixed up with the mineral world, thus becoming, in a sense, petrified. Similarly, Gregor Samsa, from Kafka's 'The Metamorphosis', seeks an escape in another way of being, according to Pankow. While he gradually loses contact with his family, Gregor undergoes a strange transformation into vermin, into a 'Gregor insect'. Already far removed from the human world, Gregor makes various attempts to establish communication with his surroundings from within the 'skin' of an insect. In a similar way, Françoise Dolto describes the body image of psychotic (and autistic) subjects as being in the grip of animal or plant images, or of representations of inanimate things (Dolto, 1984).

Faced with this archaic level of psychic functioning, the therapist is faced with the difficult task of bringing about an encounter with the patient. Pankow's originality is precisely the way in which, in her practice, she gains access to the lifeworld of her schizophrenic patients. While the construction of a systematic theory is not her strongest suit, she nonetheless elaborates her own view of the concept of 'fragmentation' which is commonly used in psychoanalytic thought concerning schizophrenia (Laure, 1971).

Pankow (1969) defines the body image on the basis of two symbolic functions inherent in the symbolic structures that are contained and controlled by one's earliest bodily experiences (Pankow, 1960). The first function of the body image makes it possible to recognize a dynamic link between the various parts of the body and the whole. This function is only concerned with the spatial aspect of form: it is a matter of the structuring of the body as a spatial totality in which the parts dynamically refer to one another. She calls this aspect the 'corps ressenti', the felt body. The second function of the body image concerns the body as the bearer of primarily interpersonal meanings. This function organizes the body image in the subject's meaningful interaction with the world on the basis of the culture's symbolic laws transmitted from one generation to the next. This she calls the 'corps reconnu', the recognized body. With this second function, Pankow has in mind the psyche's intentional directedness to what is other (the object). This directedness is linked with the temporal dimension and, hence, with the construction of one's own libidinal history.

In L'homme et sa psychose (Pankow, 1969), Pankow shows that in schizophrenic psychosis, which she also calls 'Kernpsychose', the symbolic structures of the body image are radically destroyed, whereas in 'Randpsychose' (various forms of psychosis in which hallucinations and delusions are prominent (see Corveleyn, 1984)) and in neurosis, they are only partially affected (only the relational functions). Particularly disturbances of the first function of the body image are typical of schizophrenia. Pankow refers to this as 'dissociation'. The term dissociation is defined as a destruction of the body image in which the parts lose their link with the whole and subsequently reappear in the external world (in the guise of voices or visual hallucinations). These fragments of the body are no longer recognized by the subject as its own. For this reason, the distinction and the link between the inner world and the outer world loses its clarity. Body parts can sometimes still be experienced in a limited way, but they no longer refer to the whole body: they form a totality unto themselves.

In order to breathe some more life into this theoretical discussion, we will provide a number of examples drawn from the richly elaborated, yet unfortunately none too numerous and often repeated case studies dealt with by Pankow.

The difficulty that psychotics experience with the formal dimension of their own bodies is tellingly expressed in a pronouncement made by a schizophrenic philosophy professor: "Any acceptance of a form is a threat to my existence. The moment that I accept a determinate form, I am lost" (Pankow, 1969, 27). For this man, the acceptance of a form signifies the end of his unlimited ability to be anything and anywhere (Pankow, 1977). The fascination and preoccupation shown by schizophrenics with their own mirror image, phenomena that mostly occur in the early stages of a schizophrenic illness, refer to this same problem (Abély, 1930; Pankow, 1960). According to Pankow, recognizing oneself in the mirror loses its obvious character because this process requires a connection to be made between the world within — the felt body — and the world outside — the body as it is seen by the other (Pankow, 1969). For schizophrenics, this connection is difficult, often impossible.

Véronique, one of Pankow's patients, describes the lack of cohesion in her bodily experience in the following way: "My body had broken up, but the pieces that were separated from my body were no longer related with one another" (Pankow, 1969, 147). This detachment of the body parts from the whole can also be seen clearly in the content of Véronique's dreams (for example, her leg is eaten by a shark or stored in the refrigerator).

The dissociation of the body image is certainly not always so apparent in the story told by the schizophrenic subject. In order to gain access to the patient's spatial world, Pankow asks him or her to make a drawing or a clay model. These products are then considered as representations of the lived body, and they form the main point of reference for her technique.

Valérine, a forty-year-old woman suffering from negativistic schizophrenia, could not succeed in making a spatial representation out of clay during the first stage of her therapy with Pankow. The woman had lost all contact with her own body. Only after re-discovering her own bodily sensations with the help of relaxation exercises was she able to make use of forms (Pankow, 1956). Using drawings and especially clay models ('modelages') made by Valérine, Pankow investigates the way in which she inhabits her body.

In the first months of the analysis, the woman modelled a white block of clay with two large protrusions, one being 'the way of sin' and the other being 'the way of the holy'. It is a static sculpture in which various contrasting parts are simply juxtaposed to one another without maintaining any dynamic link between them. The parts of the body image no longer refer to each other; they stand on their own and only refer to themselves. Valérine finds it impossible to connect this ambivalent representation with elements of her own history. The content — the body in its libidinal relation with the world — is divided from the form that is presented in the clay models. Pankow speaks of a 'hiatus' between form and content. The content has been radically destroyed. This process of destruction must be strictly distinguished from the (neurotic) mechanism of repression where the threatening representation remains present in the psyche in an unconscious state. This does not occur in psychosis. In Valérine's case, the destruction of the content becomes clear in the representation of a house on fire. With Valérine, human desire is demolished and evicted. What remains is a static, empty form.

During the course of the therapy, the models that Valérine made became more dynamic. Using the model of the 'flower person', an assimilation of a person's body with a flower, Pankow finally succeeds in setting up a relation between form and content. The woman arrives at the point where she is able to recognize a content that can fill the body. The theme of the bowels that are found on the underside of the flower-person, which are presented as dynamic material ('material in a state of expectation'), brings Valérine to the question of her own sexuality and the sexualized body. Pankow wonders whether the inability to inhabit her own body as a sexualized female body is not at the basis of the body image's split between form and content.

Pankow gives the name 'phantasms' to these dynamic images that provide an access to desire, for instance Valérine's flower-person. She defines the phantasm as the culmination of a dynamic which makes the appearance of human desire possible while also providing access to the symbolic order (Pankow, 1956, 39).

In the course of her therapy, Valérine comes to recognize bodily sensations during masturbation, and in particular two different forms of bodily desire. On the one hand, there is something that she experiences as a purely physiological desire (localized in the genitals); on the other hand, there is a feeling that she perceives over the entire body, which she calls a desire to caress. This dynamic had previously been represented in the form of bowels underneath the flower-person, and later in the therapeutic relation as a gap between the legs and the person of the analyst. As a result of the event of transference between therapist and patient, these two libidinal movements are recognized as having a sexual content, and are united with each other. Valérine once again experiences her own body as a unity. Her body has truly become a relational (libidinal) body. In this way, she re-enters her own libidinal history.

In this case described by Pankow, which we have only partially reproduced here, we can see how the inability to assume sexual drives into one's own body, to psychically represent them and to deal with them in terms of unconscious psychic conflicts leads to the destruction of their meaning or content, and ultimately to the conflict being inscribed in the spatial structure of the body itself. In schizophrenia, it is not the repressed content that speaks (as in hysteria) but rather a timeless space.

The second case study that we would like to examine shows how parts of one's own body appear in the external world in the form of a hallucination (Pankow, 1956). Suzanne is an 18-year-old hebephrenic woman. A psychotic reversion at the beginning of the treatment allows Pankow to gain some insight into the structure and dynamics of the illness. It turns out that during the Easter vacation Suzanne experienced sexual sensations when she saw Alain, the boy with whom she is in love. From that moment on, she believed that every man wants to touch her. She had the feeling that a boy was following her all the time. In therapy, it becomes clear that bodily sensations are a rare occurrence with this woman. According to Pankow, it is precisely the lacunae in the body image that make the appearance and recognition of such sensations impossible. Suzanne's hallucinatory world is a 'response from without to a desire within' (Pankow, 1956, 15). Suzanne 'sees' Alain on the train and 'hears' him in the market (among other anonymous voices). In these places, she also detects soldiers who might possibly assault her. Pankow notices that the voices are sometimes even 'felt' deep within her body. This phenomena has been described by various psychiatrists, including Kraepelin (1913). Voices perceived within the body are a transition between bodily sensations and hallucinated desires. Pankow considers Suzanne's hallucinations to be pieces of the body image that have lost their link with the whole and reappear in the outside world. From there, they cover up the lacunae in affective life (Pankow, 1956). Pankow claims that it would not be correct in this case to speak of a projective mechanism; it is more a case of rejection: a dissociation and expulsion of a part of one's own body. Pankow (1978) uses the term 'rejection' (*rejet*) to translate the German word '*Verwerfung*'.

The dissociation of Suzanne's body image is apparent in the following pronouncement: "On the left I am communist; on the right, Catholic" (Pankow, 1956, 17). On one side, her body wants to obey passionate impulses ('communist'), but on the other side, her body is not permitted to do so ('Catholic'). Such a splitting of the body into a left and right side occurs frequently in schizophrenics (Herner, 1965; Seidel, 1989). Striking distortions in psycho-motor behaviour — some authors call these body scheme disturbances — can occur as a result.

According to Pankow, the first objective of psychotherapy with schizophrenics must be to allow the patient to attain a body that is limited and experienced as a unity. Only after this, can one begin to work with the world of object relations (Pankow, 1968, 1982). The transition from the dialectic of space to the dialectic of desire is strikingly formulated by Pankow as the transition from the world of 'being' to the world of 'having' (Pankow, 1978).

Already from the time of her earliest writings, Pankow explicitly refrained from proposing hypotheses about the psychogenesis of disturbances in the process of symbolization. This changes in her later work however, partially as a result of her meeting Gregory Bateson who, as is well known, regards schizophrenia as the result of a 'double bind' between parent and child (Pankow, 1977). More and more, Pankow places the emphasis on the context in which the body image is normally structured: the Oedipal triangle. In interviews with patients and their family members, she notices that there exists a correlation between destruction of the family structure and destruction of the body image. According to Pankow, the parents of the schizophrenic person, particularly the mother, live in such a strong relation of dependence with their parents that their own child cannot be recognized as the product of their relation. In such a context, the child has insufficient space to develop its own desire, and it functions only to fill the void in the mother's body image, as a part of her body.

When we relate this to Pankow's earlier work, we can assert that the pathological symbiotic link with the mother opposes any form of symbolization at the level of bodily experience (Pankow also refers to it as a process of exclusion). In the first place, what is hindered is the subject's recognition that a particular body part is not identical with, hence distinct from, another body part. This seriously threatens the establishment of the distinction between inside and outside. A further result is that the subject can find no access to the place of the father (Pankow, 1976). This makes the genitalization of the body image impossible. This genitalization implies the recognition that the body of the other is totally different from one's own body. The integration of sexual difference is, for Pankow, a precondition for the emergence of a desire for the other as other (Pankow, 1956). Genitalization, as the possibility of recognizing a non-I in a unisexual body, is the ultimate goal of therapy with the schizophrenic person. The results of treatment are most of the time quite limited: the patient's phantasmatic life remains poor. It is not very often that one gets beyond what Pankow calls, following Piaget, 'operative thinking' (Pankow, 1981).

By way of concluding this section, it is important to emphasize one more thing. The fact that Pankow makes a connection between a pathological family structure and schizophrenic disturbance does not necessarily mean that this connection can tell us anything about the cause of the disturbance (etiology). The most one can say is that the parents' relation of dependence, mentioned by Pankow, is a risk factor, but only in combination with other factors (genetic, neurobiological, etc.) that likely have much greater etiological weight. What Pankow does first of all is to analyze the psychodynamic mechanisms that have made, and continue to make, schizophrenia what it is, namely a very particular manner of being in the world.

SOME REFLECTIONS ON PANKOW'S WORK

Pankow's thought exhibits a unique style and a unique conceptual apparatus (e.g. 'form' and 'content' to clarify the difference between neurosis and psychosis). This is why it is not always so easy to make a connection between her statements and other kinds of psychoanalytic thought. Sometimes she appropriates terms from the prevailing discourse, but without much theoretical argumentation they assume a different meaning (e.g. the term 'rejection') (Corveleyn, 1984). Likewise, the connection with Freud's theory of drives is unclear in Pankow's work (Seidel, 1989).

Attempts have been made to integrate Pankow's thought into a framework inspired by Lacan (De Waelhens, 1972) as well as into a Kleinian context (Seidel, 1989). In the former case, more attention is given than in Pankow to the internal relationship between language and the body, while in the latter case more thought is given to the destructive dynamic lying at the basis of dissociation (dominance of the death drive). In our opinion, Pankow pays insufficient attention to the active mechanisms (specifically the formation of delusions) that the psychotic's psyche makes use of as a defence against internal destruction.

One author who focuses more on the destructive aspects of the problematic and on active defence mechanisms is Pierra Aulagnier. Drawing inspiration from Lacan, she places the emphasis on the disturbed relationship between the body and language.

PIERRA AULAGNIER AND THE ACTIVITY OF THE ORIGIN

Aulagnier is much more of a theoretician than Pankow. She was trained in the Lacanian school, and this will continue to influence her, no matter how innovative her own work may be. One essential difference with Lacan's thought is the greater place given in her theory to corporeality and affectivity. Aulagnier wants to avoid two theoretical extremes: on the one hand a biologizing approach to psychological development and, on the other hand, a theory of signifiers that would overlook the role of the body (Castoriadis-Aulagnier, 1975).

In her book, *La violence de l'interprétation* (Castoriadis-Aulagnier, 1975), on which our discussion will be based, Aulagnier sees the body as a totality of sensory functions. These functions accompany a continuous stream of information which the living organism receives when it encounters its psycho-physical environment. The information can be processed or metabolized by the psyche in three different ways: via the originary process, via the primary process and via the secondary process, each of which represents information in its own characteristic manner.

It was the therapeutic encounter with psychotics that led Aulagnier to introduce a third process — the originary process — into psychoanalytic thought, alongside the already accepted primary and secondary processes. She found the existing psychoanalytic models insufficient to account adequately for psychotic experience. The concept of the originary process will allow her to give a metapsychological explanation for the psychotic subject's experiences of fragmentation, disintegration and destruction of the body (Fine, 1992).

The originary process characterizes the earliest psychic functioning, but also remains constantly active in later life. While it is present only in the background, it is nonetheless structurally significant (as a representative ground: '*fond représentatif*'). The process has as its objective to maintain the body's fragile energetic balance by way of self-regulating mechanisms. The first ordeals that the child's body undergoes, such as hunger or cold, are experienced as an overwhelming and threatening interruption of the status quo of inner experience. The originary process transforms these sensations, which have their origin in the body and thereby reach the psyche, and makes them into representations (cf. Freud's theory of drives; Freud, 1915 c). Aulagnier calls these representations 'pictograms'.

The pictogram results from an encounter between a sensory organ (e.g. the mouth) and an external object that can stimulate this organ (e.g. the breast). The sensorial model of this relation is taken up by the originary process and transformed into a representation that treats this duality as an inseparable unity of the object and the corresponding sensory zone (e.g. the pictogram mouth-breast). What is particular to the pictographic representation is that the object represented is not recognized as a representation of an external source that caused the sensations. The sensations are only brought into relation with, and ascribed to, the activity of the psyche itself (as 'self-engenderment'). The object is treated then as an inseparable part of one's own body, one which can be re-actualized (e.g. in the form of a hallucination) whenever the organism undergoes a bodily ordeal.

According to Aulagnier, one important condition must be fulfilled in order to arrive at a satisfying psychic activity: the presence of a minimal amount of pleasure in the encounter with the object. When such pleasure is not present, the organ (and the object) is disinvested. So the moment when displeasure appears is a crucial one. This occurs when the state of fixation that the psyche had found in the pictogram is placed at risk, and the psyche is required to form a new representation. Within the originary process, the perception of displeasure is allocated to a part of one's own body over which it has no control. This leads to a radical feeling of hate and to the desire to expel or destroy the source of displeasure. Aulagnier refers here to Freud's ideas about the purified pleasure ego ('purifiziertes Lust-Ich', Freud, 1915 c). This process of self-mutilation is the work of the death drive, which tries immediately to destroy any tension in the psyche (cf. Freud, 1920 g). Whatever is pleasurable is incorporated (life drive); whatever provokes displeasure is expelled (death drive).

A body that gains sufficient pleasurable experiences can be libidinally invested (cf. primary narcissism). Here, it is not a question of merely physiological pleasure, since it is dependent on the libinal link between mother and child. A satisfying link with the mother transforms sensory zones into auto-erotic zones. The pleasure that is experienced in a single, determinate auto-erotic zone will also spread to other zones, so that a sort of general feeling of bodily well-being is attained. The experience of the breast, for instance, is multi-sensory: it is simultaneously seen, felt, heard and smelt, etc. One could say, then, that a sound can be seen and that a smell can be felt. In this, Aulagnier anticipates what Stern (1985) will refer to as amodal perception. The spread of pleasure over various partial zones is a precursor of the experience of one's own body's unity (the narcissistic libido: 'le libido narcissique') and of the affect that will later be referred to as 'enjoyment' ('jouissance'). However, if the affect of displeasure predominates in the child's experience, then the total experience can come under serious threat. In such a case, there is a real danger that the death drive will have free rein and fasten itself to the body, whereby the experience of the body becomes completely fragmented. In particular, the organ that is the source of displeasure is destroyed and expelled. This process can ultimately lead to a complete destruction of the libidinal body. According to Aulagnier, this is what occurs in schizophrenia. In order to fully understand the function of the originary process in schizophrenia, the workings of the primary and secondary processes must be taken into account, as well as the environmental factors that are necessary for the proper functioning of these processes.

Aulagnier also believes, just as Pankow did, that it is difficult for the mother of the psychotic child to see it as the creation of new life, of a desiring and autonomous subject in the making. As a result of an inadequate activity of repression, the relationship with her child is experienced as the repetition of a primitive relationship with her own mother. So as to prevent archaic incestuous representations from breaking through into the mother's consciousness, the child, in order to provide support for the repression, must conform to the model that the mother has in mind. Anything not conforming to this model is either denied or interpreted according to this model. The body of the child is not anticipated as the bearer of its own desires. Aulagnier calls the desire of these mothers (a non-desire of desire: 'un non-désir du désir'). Characteristic features of their behaviour are an (over-)investment of the child's separate bodily functions (e.g. in the form of feeding programmes), without any anticipation on the part of the mother that the body is a totality in the making. The body is seen as 'un corps en morceau' (a body in pieces). The mother's inability to libidinalize the body of the child results in the child not experiencing its own body as pleasurable. This ends up by making the death drive even stronger.

The transition from the originary to the primary process takes place, according to Aulagnier, when the child comes to recognize, in the dialectic of the mother's presence and absence, a body that is separate from its own body. Within the fantasmatic thing-presentation ('l'image de chose') the various erogenous zones are now put in relation to one another and with the other's body, specifically with the body of the mother. Aulagnier also calls this the body image. What is characteristic of the primary process is that sensations inside the body are ascribed to the all-powerful desire of the other. Once it has evidence of the mother's desire for something other than itself, the child builds up a representation, within the fantasy of the primal scene, of its own body in relation to the parental couple. The primal scene can either be interpreted as an act of love lying at the origin of its own existence, or as an act of rejection. For Aulagnier, the attitude that the mother effectively adopts with respect to the child determines to what extent the child can attain a body image that is unified and integrated by the life drive. For the schizophrenic subject, imprisoned in an archaic image of the mother, the primal scene will assume a persecutory form. The child will not see itself as the product of an active desire on the part of the parents. The child's unnameable and extremely threatening experiences, often intensified by somatic illnesses, become in this way unusually overwhelming. The child interprets this as a rejection of its existence. The auto-erotic function falls into the destructive grip of the other's desire for displeasure ('désir d'un déplaisir'). This means that the subject will deny itself every possible form of pleasurable experience (cf. primary masochism).

It is particularly the transition from the primary to the secondary process that goes amiss in schizophrenia, according to Aulagnier. The secondary process makes it possible that the relation between mother and child is no longer mediated by the omnipotence of her desire, but by independent signifiers provided by the symbolic order (word presentations: *'les images de mot'*). What previously existed as an affect (pleasure-displeasure) is transformed through a process of metaphorization into a bodily experience that can be communicated (it is inter-subjective). Aulagnier calls this 'feeling'. From this moment on, the psyche interprets (the cause of) the affect in terms of the generally accepted discourse. In this way, language becomes the organizing agent of bodily experience.

This shift that we have described from affect to feeling is, on Aulagnier's view, the essence of the subject itself, as an ego. The ego learns to qualify its own experience as, say, loving or hating, and identifies itself in this movement: the ego is a self-naming of the ego (*'une auto-appellation du je'*) (Castoriadis-Au-lagnier, 1975, 169). A project of identification can now unfold, in which certain signifiers are accepted by the subject, and others repressed. Using the accepted signifiers, the ego will retroactively reconstruct its own libidinal history, produc-ing a thread of continuity which ties together its previous, current and future affective experiences (cf. Aulagnier, 1992). In this way, the past becomes history.

In schizophrenia, this movement of historicization is a fundamental problem. The future schizophrenic subject, according to Aulagnier, cannot find in the mother's discourse any reference to a symbolic order of signifiers that is inde-pendent of her. The father, who would normally represent such an order, appears unable to carry out his function, and this hinders the child's access to the symbolic order. The relation to sound, to the voice, remains marked by the relation developed in the primary process between the persecutor and the persecuted. Words do not function within a universally valid order, but appear as enigmatic messages sent to the subject by a persecuting agent. Every form of autonomous thought is impossible: the subject is thought by the other (cf. Lacan's 'it speaks', *'ça parle'*). Nor does the parents' discourse offer any signifiers with which the subject might identify itself. The child persists in coinciding with its own bodily experience, and cannot find itself in anything outside itself. In such a case, the reflection of one's own body in the mirror does not offer the imaginary support that is so important in the development of identity. The investment in one's own (visual) body image, which for Lacan constitutes an essential moment in the construction of (secondary) narcissism (cf. the mirror stage), breaks down.

For Aulagnier, the essence of psychosis lies in the active manner in which the subject reacts to this impasse. On her view, the typical defensive strategy of the psychotic is to construct a *'pensée délirante primaire'* (primary delirious thought), an infantile delusional theory about the origin of one's own body, of the world, and of the genealogical order. The psychotic ego itself fills in the blanks in the parents' discourse about the libidinal origin of the child. The ego itself writes the first lines of its own history. In this way, an interpretive framework is created for affective experiences that invoke sensations of pleasure or displeasure and refer to the question of one's own origin and one's own desire. The delusional construction functions as an anchor for the ego's identifications, and makes a transition from affect to feeling possible. The affect that was threatening to overwhelm the subject becomes partially nameable. The schizophrenic thus makes his or her own code and language. Through this process the body becomes more or less inhabitable, but it has little or no interpersonal, relational significance. The entire construction remains fragile.

The delusional theory is initially present in the psyche as an encapsulated psychotic potentiality. In this form, it permits the person to speak a language that conforms with the dominant discourse, with the exception of the theme of one's own origin. However, when this person receives insufficient anchor points from his own surroundings which confirm his delirious truth (at least one person), or if too many situations are repeated that reactivate the first traumatic experiences, then there is a grave risk that psychosis will set in. This happens, for instance, when an intolerable interpersonal problem is resumed by the psychotic ego at the level of the originary, and the object then becomes a part of its own body (cf. diagram).

The fragility of the delusional construction set up by the ego means that the originary process retains its destructive power of attraction. There is always a risk of an eruption of an uncontrollable affect that plunges the ego into the abyss of fusion or murder (Castoriadis-Aulagnier, 1975, 68). Here, Aulagnier refers to certain forms of acting out performed by psychotics (some authors prefer the term 'transition to act', *'passage à l'acte'*), auto-mutilation, disintegration and fragmentation of the body image, and moments of confusion and fading of the ego. Even speech can be in the grip of the originary process: words are treated as objects that can be swallowed or spit out. According to Aulagnier, an ego that is completely absorbed by the originary process only occurs to a very limited extent in psychosis. After a while, the affect will be brought back into the scene by the primary process, in the form of feelings of persecution, and will acquire a new place within the secondary process via the delirious interpretation.

SOME REFLECTIONS ON AULAGNIER'S WORK

Aulagnier's theory gives us the ability to identify and situate a large number of clinical phenomena in psychosis: the psychotic's distancing from his own body, the impossibility to inhabit the body, the sudden upsurge of sensations causing anxiety and disintegration, and the function of delusions in the recovery stage. The schizophrenic's hypochondriac delusions of persecution can be seen, following Aulagnier's thought, as a dam erected by the primary process against a self-destructive process that cannot be represented.

Bearing in mind the current state of scientific research into schizophrenia, Aulagnier's etiological claims can be sharply criticized. For a long time, Aulagnier considered the parents' discourse to be a necessary condition for the emergence of schizophrenia. In her later work, though, she tempers this view somewhat (Aulagnier, 1984, 1986). Her statements on this point are rather crude and not developed in a very convincing manner. They are characterized by a linear, causalistic way of thinking in which the subtle interaction between a constitutionally vulnerable child and its parents are ignored. The rigid family organization that Aulagnier observes in practice is actually the result of a circular process carried out over many years between the child and its surroundings that is very difficult to reconstruct. It is improbable that these environmental factors play such a decisive role in the creation of schizophrenia. Aulagnier's etiological claims, then, have to be qualified. This does not mean, however, that her ideas about the functioning of the originary, the primary and the secondary processes in psychosis lose their value. Moyaert (1982 a, 1988), for instance, makes use of Aulagnier's theory without taking over the etiological, psychogenetic perspective. Concerning the ultimate reasons why psychodynamics assumes such a pathological form in schizophrenia, we can only venture a number of suggestions.

Vergote (1982, 1989) remains faithful to the psychogenetic perspective in his understanding of schizophrenia. Just like Aulagnier, he points to the importance of traumatic experiences of displeasure in early childhood, experiences which are activated retroactively at a later age. In his opinion, the child's inability to invest its body with pleasure causes a split between language and the body. Once language has lost its bodily roots, and hence its libidinal history, it can be controlled and manipulated in an arbitrary fashion, in sound associations, neologisms, etc. Vergote views the expulsion of the libidinal body as the crucial moment in schizophrenia. He is also much more cautious than Aulagnier regarding the origin of the experiences of displeasure, the reasons why they are so traumatic and why the ordering power of language falls short. He suspects that it has something to do with an exceptionally early attention to incomprehensible perceptions or observations, especially those of a sexual nature (Vergote, 1989).

Finally, it is interesting that Aulagnier's contributions to an understanding of the originary process have received a great deal of attention from authors inspired by Bion (MacDougall, 1990; Green, 1986, 1992). There are also striking connections with Tustin's theory of autism and child schizophrenia (Tustin, 1986; Castoriadis-Aulagnier, 1975). The author we now turn to, Andreoli, is inspired by the post-Kleinian thought of Bion and Meltzer. We will limit our discussion to a few core ideas.

THE PSYCHOSOMATIC ECONOMY OF SCHIZOPHRENIA, ACCORDING TO ANTONIO ANDREOLI

Antonio Andreoli, a Swiss psychiatrist, developed a theory of schizophrenic corporeality on the basis of his experience with relaxation psychotherapy. This is a form of psychotherapy inspired by Ajuriaguerra's psychoanalytic re-interpretation of Schultz's autogenic training, where interpretation takes the place of suggestion and transference takes the place of catharsis (Andreoli, 1981 a).

Andreoli believes that a certain number of striking invariants can be found in relaxation psychotherapy with schizophrenics. For instance, the patterns in the body's muscle tension (the tonic patterns) are quite characteristic. Schizophrenic patients answer attempts to mobilize their body experiences with a sort of plastic adaptation of their own tonus to that of the therapist (a mirror tonus: '*un tonus en miroir*'). In some cases, this can evolve into a situation of absolute obedience or imperturbable passivity (a thing tonus: '*un tonus-chose*'). Very often, the schizophrenic completely ignores or 'neutralizes' the lived body. Such an indifference to the body stands in pointed contrast to the bodily situation during an acute psychotic attack, when the therapist is struck by the violence of the psycho-motor excitation and the intensity of the internal neuro-vegetative disorganization, also known as coenestopathy (cf. Thiel, 1971). These experiences drag the person into a genuinely traumatic event where psychic experience is completely dissolved. In this dissolution, Andreoli sees the work of the death drive.

For Andreoli, the typical character of acute schizophrenia does not reside so much in the nature of the bodily excitation (cf. extreme situations of stress in normal people), but rather in the way that the psyche deals with this excitation (Andreoli, 1984). The schizophrenic is unable to link, to give form to, or to 'contain' the experience and the psycho-motor apparatus, with extreme bodily fragmentation as a result. The organization of elementary tonic discharges in emotions is problematic, for example the translation of sorrow and pain into a mimicry that gives form to these sufferings. In this way, the body loses its expressive, dialogical quality. Bodily fragmentation also means that the distance between subject and object is removed. The body fuses with the object, and the relation gets materialized. During the process of relaxation, one can then find 'a hollow belly — father' or 'cold arms — mother' in the patient's body (Andreoli, 1981 b).

The schizophrenic utilizes denial ('*le déni*'), dissociation and (excessive) projective identification as defence mechanisms against the situations of excitation just described. He shows himself to be a master in the 'disincarnation' of his psychic functioning. This disincarnation can clearly be observed in relaxation therapy. Some patients, for example, shake their arm to get rid of the heaviness induced by the therapist, while others attempt to remove painful affects through the eyes or the skin (Andreoli, 1984 a). Listening and speaking receive a similar material significance. The schizophrenic actively brings about a short-circuit in the changes of body tone, insofar as they form part of the rhythm of libidinal investment, for instance hypotonia in the presence and hypertonia in the absence of the love object. The tonic relation, on Andreoli's view, is the most primitive dimension of object relations. The process of actively disinvesting the libidinal relation also entails a paralysis of fantasmatic life. The body is 'purified' of all the bad things inside and acquires a sort of megalomaniacal character. Every possible movement of the drives is blocked, thus rendering the subject spaceless, timeless, immaterial and hyper-aware (Andreoli, 1976). Finally, it acquires the adaptive flexibility we have just described. This fragile adjustment comes about on the threshold of depersonalization and derealization. Andreoli (1976) stresses that the disturbances in bodily experience that characterize schizophrenia should not merely be considered as a defective condition, but rather as a defensive neo-organization.

Following the thought of Bion, Andreoli views schizophrenia as a problem in translating raw sensory perceptions, the beta elements, into meaningful content, the alpha elements. The psyche uses alpha elements in the formation of memory, in dreams and ultimately in autonomous thinking. The overwhelming presence of intolerable sensations in the body is the consequence of a defective containment function.

During treatment, Andreoli encourages the patient to re-establish contact with his or her own body. The images that then appear in the person's narrative are often very characteristic. They are imaginary perceptual representations or abstract intellectual constructions that escape any form of communication or dialogue ('my body assumes the shape of an eight', 'there are sparks in my arms', 'I feel waves in my stomach', etc.). These phenomena are the precursors of hallucinations and delusions, which always contain disorganized, confused bodily experiences at their core. Hallucinations and delusions are to be understood as an attempt to re-connect traumatic bodily experiences. In contrast to paranoia, the reconstructions in schizophrenia are confused and fluid.

For Andreoli, the effect of a somatic illness on psychotic disorganization is striking (cf. Freud, 1914 c; Lipper & Werman, 1977). A somatic illness can result in a dramatic modification of mental functioning: excitation and neuro-vegetative disorganization is tempered, bodily rigidity becomes more flexible and the persecutory violence of the affects fades away. The experience acquires more subjective qualities and becomes more accessible. Just like hallucination and delusion, somatic illness functions as a 'para-excitation' and a way of binding together previously confused and fragmented sensations. Some clinicians believe that neuroleptica, and more specifically this drug's extra-pyramidal side effects, can produce a similar effect (cf. Kapsambelis, 1994).

When the therapist finally succeeds in restoring contact between the schizophrenic and his or her body, the hallucinations and delusions move into the background and are replaced by extremely painful and violent affects (Andreoli, 1981 b). It is important to avoid too great an affective mobilization in the relation (cf. Moyaert, 1982 b). This may give rise to a paranoid-psychotic transference that is difficult to handle. Too brusque a reactualization of libidinal memories leads to psychotic decompensation. The schizophrenic rediscovers in this catastrophe the memory of his or her libidinal history.

Andreoli believes that the fantasm, as a defensive representation in the service of repression, fails to carry out its role as a mediator between the subject, the body and the external world. In psychosis, the psyche does not succeed in setting up a screen against the drive. The drive retains a crude, all too immediate character, appearing in the form of raw, unsymbolized and traumatic sensations. These are intolerable and are purged by the psyche. The traumatic event, according to Andreoli, has to do with the appearance of sexuality in the body and with its recognition and organization as the integration of differences into gender and generation (cf. the primal scene) (Andreoli, 1984). In schizophrenia, the drive is not inscribed in the symbolic register. It does not assume the form of an organized subjective experience. Ultimately, Andreoli reduces the entire problematic to a failure of the primal repression (and the formation of the pre-conscious). The function of primal repression is to metabolize the drive and to link it with representations so that an articulation in discourse becomes possible. This articulation is consequently a central problem in schizophrenia.

CONCLUSION

The uniqueness of psychoanalytic theory consists in viewing the diverse phenomena, symptoms and processes that make up the clinical image of schizophrenia as a comprehensible and structural unity of meanings (cf. De Waelhens, 1972, 23-24). Schizophrenia, however, is not easily grasped in a model. Indeed, it constantly seems to evade every model. The clinician nevertheless requires models in order not to become lost in the psychotic's alienating world, even though he knows that they can only bring to light a part of the truth. Much remains in the dark. Schizophrenia has been and still remains the sphinx of psychiatry (cf. Rümke, 1971).

In our opinion, the psychoanalytic models discussed above are an important counter-weight to the theories that view schizophrenia as the consequence of a sick neuro-biological organism or as the result of a defective information processing system. Within psychoanalytic thought, the psychotic's psychic functioning is taken as a particular organization which cannot be understood only in terms of a defect or a disease. The psychoanalysts we have discussed show us something of the internal drama that takes place in the lifeworld of schizophrenic patients. They show us the forced and often fruitless efforts these subjects make to stave off the drama, and they allow us to interpret the strange psychotic constructions as attempts to find meaning within an existence that is continually on the verge of losing all meaning. This is no mere epiphenomenon of a defective process in the brain, but rather the very essence of psychosis as a typically human mode of existence.

BODY, DRIVE, AND AFFECT IN SCHIZOPHRENIA, FROM THE PSYCHOANALYTIC PERSPECTIVE

Paul Moyaert

It is well known that Freud's interest in schizophrenia was not based on any psychotherapeutic process which he carried out personally and maintained over a long period of time. Freud himself never undertook the treatment of a schizophrenic patient. His rather scarce remarks on schizophrenia were therefore not based on reflection upon the therapeutic possibilities and difficulties of trying to engage a schizophrenic world of significance. His metapsychological reflections on Schreber, a case of paranoid schizophrenia with an explicit megalomaniac strain, rely on knowledge of the case-history, and more precisely on the study of Schreber's autobiographical writings. What Freud proposes in this study as possible hypotheses to understand the psychical mechanisms at work in schizophrenia, are thus not based on listening to what has been put into words in a relation of transference.

It is rather out of theoretical interest, and to meet the challenge of Jung, whose clinical experience was connected much more to the treatment of psychoses, that Freud addresses the psychodynamic aspect of schizophrenia in a number of metapsychological writings such as *The Unconscious* (1913), *On Narcissism: An Introduction* (1914), and *A Metapsychological Supplement to the Theory of Dreams* (1916).

In his reflections on schizophrenia Freud was not guided by the concept of a treatment of psychosis, but by his theoretical interest in conceptually-founded clinical distinctions. For the purposes of psychoanalytic praxis therefore, his hypothetical insights can only come to full fruition if they are reconsidered by psychoanalysts who do indeed have a direct contact with schizophrenia, and who, in the light of their personal findings, develop, reformulate and adjust certain aspects of Freud's hypotheses.

HYPOCHONDRIA: A DERIVATIVE OF NARCISSISTIC LIBIDO CATHEXIS

In schizophrenia, libidinal ties (connections) with reality fail in a radical and drastic manner: object cathexes are relinquished without this loss of interest making itself known by spectacular symptoms, such as heated arguments or histrionic behaviour. That this loss of interest can occur almost unnoticed partially explains why it is sometimes difficult to diagnose in a correct manner a first upsurge of schizophrenia during adolescence. From a diagnostic position, one will therefore have the tendency to await the further development of the condition.

Is it a temporary reduction of interest, a protest reaction of adolescents, or does the implosion of connections to the life-world permit us to suspect a more deeply seated personality disorder? It is indeed the case that provocative exchanges of words and noisy altercations between adolescents and parents or educators, the stakes of which turn around conflicting values, are often a decisive counter-indication of schizophrenia. By contrast, schizophrenia makes itself known by what one calls in classical psychiatry 'syndromes of poverty' or 'negative symptoms' (e.g. the dulling of affects, monotony in facial and bodily expression, reduction of personal commitment, a lethargic turn inward, decrease of alertness, etc.).

The loss of object cathexes inevitably goes together with a withdrawal of the libido into the self. The libido at work in the drives, which until then had been directed to the outside and divided over different objects and activities, returns to the inside and amasses in the corporeal self. This influx or upsurge of drives in the self turns into an unpleasurable and anxious oppression when the energy that has been amassed in the self finds no exit, that is to say, it finds no objects against which the tension of the drives can be abreacted. Strictly speaking, that the drives are withdrawn into the self does not yet mean that the self (one's own body, the body-image, and the representation of the self) becomes the object of a narcissistic libido-cathexis. It merely means that the libidinal drives are amassing in the self and are putting pressure on the corporeal self.

In the second chapter of *On Narcissism: An Introduction* Freud says that a narcissistic libido cathexis is the inevitable consequence of a withdrawal of the libido from objects in the external world (1914 c, 82). However, in order to arrive at a correct understanding of schizophrenia, it is necessary to make a distinction between two forms of narcissistic libido cathexis. In the broad sense, this concept only indicates that the corporeal self is the place where drives are concentrated and hold sway. In the strict sense, however, the concept indicates that the corporeal self and the image thereof become the object of love, care, or idealisation. The broad sense still leaves open whether the self can regard and experience itself as an object of love. The strict sense already indicates that the self is an object of love for itself.

However, it is the case that the withdrawal of libido into the corporeal self goes together with an *upsurge of hypochondria*. Hypochondria is the inevitable consequence of a narcissistic libido-cathexis (1914 c, 83), that is to say, of the fact that the drives are amassing in the self. In this connection, Freud speaks of "hypochondriacal anxiety as a derivative of the ego-libido." (1914 c, 84). Bodily sensations emerge in the foreground through the fact that the libido has been cut off from objects in the external world and has been withdrawn into the self. The horizon of existence is narrowed down to an over-sensitivity for corporeal sensations. (The more attention and libido are occupied by objects in the external world, the bigger the self-forgetfulness. In hypochondria all attention is taken up by the corporeal subject that one is, that is to say by the body out of which one lives, acts and loves). De Waelhens, in *La psychose* in this connection says the following: "Le reflux massif, sur le moi, des investissements objectaux abandonnés donne lieu à cette perception constamment pénible du corps propre que le psychiatre nomme l'hypochondrie." (De Waelhens, 1972, 96)[1] Lacan relies on the same observation when he says that a psychotic upsurge goes together with a withdrawal into the real body, that is to say into an experience of the body, the significance of which is narrowed down to the excitable carrier of innervations. In what it does, says and desires, the subject is always being thrown back upon, and captured by, the echo of its own sensations.

In order to understand correctly the *hypochondriacal aspect of schizophrenia* one has to take into account the double meaning of narcissistic libido cathexis. Hypochondria is indeed the correlate of a 'Stauung der Ichlibido,' (1914 c, 84-85) that is to say an upsurge of the libido in the self, but as such it is not yet a phenomenon of psychosis. Hypochondria testifies to an impoverishment and narrowing down of psychic life, but that is not necessarily the expression of a schizophrenic experience of the body. In a certain sense hypochondria is already a way to channel and to contain to some degree an otherwise unbearable amassing of tension of drives in the self; in a certain sense it is a mechanism of defense against an influx of energy of which it is at the same time the consequence. Furthermore one has to make a distinction between hypochondria which arises out of an anxious concern for bodily well-being and hypochondria which is not supported by a narcissistic cathexis of the body image.

When, then, is hypochondria the expression of a schizophrenic experience of the body? How does the affective relatedness to the self express itself in schizophrenia, and in which respect is it to be distinguished from other forms of hypochondriacal auto-affection?

These questions can also be introduced as follows. Freud makes use of financial and military metaphors in order to explain the dynamism of psychical processes. How far does the relinquishing of object-cathexes go, and behind which lines of defense does the self retreat in order to protect itself? Against what does one have to protect oneself, what is it that one attempts to shield oneself against, and by which means (for example: repression, projection, idealisation, etc.) does this defense occur? What is it that one can fall back upon once the ties to objects fall away? Does one find in oneself a reassuring support, perhaps smaller than the original interest, but enough to invest once more in reality? How far does regression go and what arrests it? What is this energy, which wreaks havoc in the self, used for, and in what is it re-invested?

In his study on Schreber, Freud says that the massive withdrawal of the drives into the self (that is to say narcissistic libido cathexis *sensu lato*) in dementia praecox is correlated to a falling back (regression) upon auto-erotism (1911 c, 77). A schizophrenic regression falls back *behind* a narcissistic libido cathexis, conceived of in the strict sense of the word. Auto-erotism cannot be called narcissism because it precedes the formation of a narcissistic self-image. On the level of auto-erotism, the experience of the body falls apart into an amalgamation of partial drives which are not kept together and unified in a bodily incarnated unitary image of one's self. For Freud, narcissism is the structural moment in the development of the ego in which the self breaks free of its confused perceptions and becomes an object of love for itself through an identification with a unified image of itself. In schizophrenia the narcissistic self-image is not capable of preventing the falling back into a scattered understanding of the self.

Because Freud defends a dynamic conception of psychoses, schizophrenia can never exclusively be understood from the perspective of auto-erotism. No matter how deep the regression might go, a dynamic conception entails, on the one hand, that an instance remains active in the subject that defends itself, and on the other hand, that there remains something in the subject that is worth the trouble of defense. In the return to auto-erotism a narcissistic libido remains active through which the subject attempts to surmount its disintegration. Without a tension between auto-erotism and narcissism one cannot even understand why the regression stops at some point, nor how the subject can strive to reconstruct the ties with the surrounding world, albeit through a world of fantasy.

I restate my question. Of what does the hypochondriacal kernel of a schizophrenic experience of the body consist? Via which affects and representations does a schizophrenic corporeality make itself known?

ACCESS TO SCHIZOPHRENIC CORPOREALITY VIA WORD-REPRESENTATIONS

Whoever is acquainted with schizophrenia is undoubtedly struck by the manner with which certain sentence structures and their possible significance are dealt. The linguistic phenomena to which I want to point here have indeed been known for a long time, but it seems to me that too little attention is paid to them these days. These phenomena, to which Freud also refers via a case study by Tausk, in *The Unconscious*, would not be much more than a linguistic curiosity were it not for the fact that they bring us on the track of the vicissitudes of the drives in schizophrenia at the same time.

Let me first recount Freud's example. "A patient of Tausk's, a girl who was brought to the clinic after a quarrel with her lover, complained that *her eyes were not right, they were twisted*. This she herself explained by bringing forward a series of reproaches against her lover in coherent language. 'She could not understand him at all, he looked different every time, he was a hypocrite, an eye twister [Augenverdreher], he had twisted her eyes; they were no longer her eyes anymore, now she saw the world with different eyes.'" (1915 e, 198). According to Freud: "Here the schizophrenic utterance exhibits a hypochondriac trait: it has become organ speech." (Ibid.) The young woman grafts the meaning of a word directly *onto* her eyes; the organ (the eyes), and more specifically, the innervations that she detects therein, represent the entire content of what she puts into words. The pronunciation of the thoughts contained in the expression 'Augenverdreher' throws the woman directly back upon her coenesthetic sensations. To come into contact with thoughts or words is equivalent to a physical touch. The meanings of her words are immediately transposed into a sensation of the body part concerned, and that in turn expresses the meaning of the linguistic utterance. According to Freud, this process can be compared to, but must at the same time be distinguished from, what happens in conversion hysteria. "A hysterical woman would ... have in fact convulsively twisted her eyes ... instead of having the impulse to do so or the sensation of doing so, and ... neither ... would she have any accompanying conscious thoughts, nor would she have been able to express any such thoughts afterwards." (1915 e, 198-199) In conversion hysteria, a painful content is repressed and eventually comes to expression indirectly. In Tausk's example, however, the content of the painful words immediately penetrates to the level of experience of the body. The understanding and uttering of thoughts does not rise above the detection of bodily sensations, with the consequence that bodily impressions exercise an increasingly oppressive power over the subject.

This example, which for Freud is paradigmatic, can easily be complemented by others. Pressing her hands to her head, a woman says that her head is 'broken' [kapot] (that is to say that it is falling to pieces). She immediately adds the following: "her mother had told her that she did not have to 'break her head over something' [the Flemish expression: 'zich het hoofd over iets breken' akin to the English 'to worry oneself sick about something' - Trans.]. And since she still remained worried ['bleef tobben' - worry, fret, struggle] her head was falling to pieces. This metaphorical expression 'to break one's head over something' is immediately transposed into vibrations that she feels in her head, and she experiences this bodily sensation as a falling to pieces of her head. The mental act of worrying affects her head after the manner of a physical force. The way in which her bodily innervations are experienced corresponds literally with what is expressed in the linguistic utterance.

Before he brings his daughter to the clinic, the father tells her that he has to 'pull the plug from the electrical outlet' ['dat hij de stekker uit het *stopcontact* moest trekken', where 'stopcontact' might also be rendered by the more archaic english term 'circuit-breaker']. For her this signified that the *contact* with her father [in line with 'stopcontact'] was *broken*. This same woman says that her hands have been '*cut off*' ['afgekapt' - 'kappen' meaning 'to cut']. Her father had told her during the weekend that she was a *handicapped* girl. This somatic hallucination is indeed not based on a reduction of figurative significance to a literal significance, but on the fact that the expression 'handicapped' is understood in a concrete manner that, furthermore, directly throws the woman back upon her bodily sensations - indicating that language is no longer capable of creating a distance with regard to bodily impressions. The loss of this distance comes to the fore most clearly in the case of word-representations (signifiers) that appeal to the body (for example: "a piercing gaze," "this hurts my eyes," "you are taking the words out of my mouth," "this cuts to the bone"). The manner in which the significance of words is understood allows the speculation that the schizophrenic experience of the body moves on a level on which the self, the other and language are entangled and interpenetrated.

These observations make it apparent that schizophrenia is characterized and caused by an unstable and fragile process of symbolisation.

Symbols stand for something other than themselves and posit something as present which is not actually at hand. The sensibility for symbols enables a person to maintain a minimal distance with regard to immediacy, so that he is not crushed by what he perceives. Thanks to this distance he is to some degree separated from himself and can relate to that which is not immediately present without this break in immediacy being experienced as a quasi-real attack on his corporeal identity. This sort of example, which demonstrates that the subject is thrown back upon *the echo of his corporeal affections*, is not the only expression of the existential consequences of an unstable capacity for symbolisation. Nor is this instability only shown in the strong attachment to obtrusive bodily innervations. A deficient capacity for symbolisation can equally *affect and undermine the ability of the imagination*. Imagination enables the subject to be affected by contents of consciousness such that it is not completely absorbed by them and does not lose itself in them. Imagination refers consciousness to an object whose manner of appearance differs radically from that of an object of a real perception; the object of imagination has the characteristic traits of a quasi-perception without being experienced by consciousness as a real perception. Imagination is an experience of consciousness that takes place within the subject, and by which the subject is affected from within, whilst at the same time maintaining an intimate distance to itself in this inner experience of itself. Normally, imagination presupposes, and indeed creates the possibility of a self-relatedness, without the concomitant non-coincidence with the self turning into an oppressive loss of self. The inner dispersion or splitting of the self is, in imagination, not experienced as a scattering of one's own self. The self moves in *the tension of an in-between*: it does not coincide with itself and at the same time does not lose itself in the dispersed images by which it is affected. In this way, it is not squashed by the contents that fill consciousness. "When this distance disappears, when the unconscious takes the place of reality, and the imagination poses as perception the subject falls prey to delusion." (Bernet, 1996, 71)

This is not the place to develop further the complex relation between language, symbolisation and imagination. In this respect, I merely wish to point out the following. The schizophrenic clings so firmly to his/her body that even the images and perceptions that arise in it *are too close to the skin, and as it were, break through it*. This permits us to understand why the act of imagination in schizophrenia is accompanied by an oppressive experience. Instead of keeping an inner distance from the content of imagination, the subject is caught up in it to such an extent that it loses itself in the imagination, and, just like in a nightmare, is swallowed up by it. Without distance, imagination is oppressive. This partially explains why a schizophrenic world of imagination is, on the whole, rather poor and barely diversified. Just as word-representations are oppressive because they shoot directly through to corporeal sensation, the subject is frightened by its imagination. It is not the content of imagination, but the act of imagining itself that is oppressive. The subject's fantasies of a scattered body are in a certain sense nothing other than the enactment (mise-en-scène) of the disastrous effects that the imagination, and even more broadly, the acts of thinking (mental-processes - Bion) cause in the subject: a destruction of the self. The schizophrenic does not have a rich imagination: rather, he exhausts himself imposing silence on the mental-processes and to destroy them, and in their destruction, attempts to defend himself against the pain and anxiety that these mental processes cause. One extreme consequence of this is autism. In counterpoint, the fact is that an important turning-point is reached in the therapeutic process when a schizophrenic person can speak about a dream as dream, and a fantasy as a fantasy.

In extreme cases a deficient faculty of symbolisation can undermine the act of speech itself. Speaking is after all, a sort of self-loss, because one exposes oneself to some extent and henceforth loses control over the words which have been spoken. A certain schizophrenic woman, for example, could only bear to speak by regularly verifying whether her face remained intact. After uttering disgusting words and thoughts, she anxiously asked herself whether her skin would not now be spoiled. Now and again she would run to the mirror to check that her eyes were still in their proper place. She used the reflecting lid of a tin of candy in which she could look at herself while she was speaking to me.

FROM THE PERFORATED BODY TO THE EXPULSION OF THE DRIVES

The skin is the quasi-natural embodiment of a border that constitutes the inside and the outside by separating them. It forms a thin membrane between both interiority and exteriority and it separates them in spite of their corporeal, intimate entanglement; the skin, in doing so, makes it possible that they touch each other without fusing into one another. In separating, enveloping and surrounding the inside, the skin permits a contact with Otherness or the (personal) other, without this contact turning into self-loss. In spite of its openness and in spite of its primordial and unremittable dependence on the other, the subject is able to retreat into itself, to withdraw itself from and close itself off to the other, in virtue of its skin. The awareness of self (that is to say the awareness of being separated from an exteriority that nonetheless has always already been lodged in me) arises from the experience (amongst others) that I am not simply accessible to the other, that the other cannot directly see and feel my thoughts. I, in spite of my visibility, remain invisible to the gaze of the other, which gaze at the same time has always already penetrated into me. But it is also the other way around: every understanding and interweaving between me and the other is based on a misunderstanding. However, in spite of its sometimes painful character, this discord is also a *felix culpa*. In the experience of misunderstanding, the other appears as someone who has his own life apart from me. *Disunity* assures me that I am not a symbiotic appendage of the other and that the other is more than the echo of the stirring of my soul. Without separation no space is freed for one's own life of consciousness, that is to say for thoughts and desires that are *my* thoughts and desires and not those of an other. That I can act secretly, that there are thoughts living in me that the other does not know, that I can lie to and deceive the other, creates in me the awareness that the other is not omnipotent and omnipresent, that is to say, that we are separated from each other in spite of our belonging together.

The skin, however, can only realize its quasi-natural role as a primordial limitation if this meaning is understood, respected and affirmed in personal contact with the other and is reinforced by him. In and of itself the skin is too weak to realize its role. Incestuous transgressions and traumatic experiences can undermine the kernel of the self and its integrity. The affirmation of the separation happens not only on the level of bodily touch, but must equally occur on the level of the word (speaking). By speaking to me as 'you' the other appeals to me to speak in my own name, and so, I can posit myself over and against the other without locking myself up in an idiosyncratic world of significance.

Without separation, no room is freed up for interiority, but this does not mean that what constitutes the interiority of the self belongs exclusively to the self. The kernel of the human subject, that which in a certain sense constitutes its intimate essence more than anything else, does not belong to the ego. The ego is not lord and master in its own home. Just as it can lose itself to the other, it can lose itself in thoughts that dwell within it, and in which it cannot recognise itself. Interiority bears the traces of an exteriority from which it cannot withdraw itself. The opposition of inside versus outside continues in interiority. The self is always being separated anew from within by confused contents that do not allow themselves to be identified or put into words, by contents in which the self does not recognise itself, and through which, in spite of its familiarity with itself, *it remains a stranger to itself.* It experiences the presence of an exteriority within itself, from which it has been partially separated with the support of the other. What Freud calls "den Kern unseres Wesens" [the kernel of our being] stands for the insurmountable tension within the self, for a never ceasing intrusion of the outside in the inside, which always dispossesses the self anew from within, and which cannot be appropriated by the self. Even by withdrawing into itself, the self takes the outside into itself. What the subject thinks, fantasizes and dreams, does not arise from out of an independent ego, but always goes back to what has slipped through between the gaps in the net of words and unspoken, confused perceptions. It finds its origin in the confused contacts and ambiguous experiences, the extent of which cannot even be illuminated completely in personal speaking. *I belong to the subject that I am but it does not belong to me and I can never fully identify with it. The subject that I am,* the subject that is more myself than whatever else, *is itself not an ego.* It is the bearer of words, impressions and thoughts, that lead their own life within me and without me. It generates desires of which I would rather know nothing, in which I do not recognise myself, that I can never express fully in my own name, and that I can never personally make entirely my own. Even feelings of pleasure and displeasure that testify to an intimate self-relatedness and make the self revolve back around itself remain surrounded and penetrated by an echo in which the feelings of the other reverberate. The universe of the other still *resounds* in what I say, think and feel. This reverberation is a resounding sound, a sound which no longer makes any noise, a sound which keeps resounding after the original noise has disappeared. Even when the other stops talking, he still continues to speak to me, in me. In auditory hallucinations this reverberation comes to the foreground explicitly and drowns out the resonance of my own speech. Auditory hallucinations are therefore always the continuation and expression of a *syncretic sociability* in which one's own words (thoughts) are perceived as the echo of the other.

So as not to be destroyed by the subject that I am, I must be able to protect myself against myself, that is to say, to shield myself against that which lives in me, and *to which I belong without it belonging to me*. That which Freud calls 'the ego' is a separated instance in the subject that I am, more specifically, a separated instance which has been constructed from a more or less stable kernel of representations in which I can recognise myself and with which I can identify. This self-identification makes it possible for me to relate to the foreign within me without the experience of self-loss that is accompanied by self-destruction. On the basis of this thought one can understand why psycho-analysts, such as Lacan and De Waelhens, have, following Freud, understood the "Urverdrängung" (Moyaert, 1983) as a temporally non-localisable psychical process that guarantees a primordial splitting of the subject. That is to say, it is the separation of an ego which can protect itself against that through which it has always already been withdrawn.

These general considerations concerning the constant tension between outside and inside must suffice to determine more closely the vicissitudes of a schizophrenic self-relatedness and its affective aspects.

THE PRESENCE OF AN IMPERSONAL OTHER IN THE SELF

In schizophrenia, the skin is too permeable and too porous. That which comes into contact, and which touches the schizophrenic subject as an incarnated subject is too close to the skin, and penetrates it. Words can enter his brain just like sharp objects. Incoherent thoughts and fragments of sentences keep reverberating in his head as an echo that simply does not want to die away. Titbits of words that survive themselves are wreaking havoc in his head and his body. Via rays, invisible threads, and ungraspable channels of communication whose power he experiences on his excited nerve-ends, he is subjected to messages that are sent out, and dumped on him. The other that resides in him does not direct itself to him as a person and does not address him personally; the other is an impersonal other. What goes around in his head are stereotypical phrases and unconnected words without a context, and which he cannot ascribe to anyone; they are the remains of a discourse without origin and without a sender. What resonates in his head are unfinished phrases that continuously provide a commentary on thoughts that he does not have and that deny him the possibility of speaking in his own name. It speaks in him. The schizophrenic has a body, but he does not inhabit it; his body does not belong to him. His body cannot shroud and defend itself against what forces its way inside. It is pure openness without defense.

Philosophical anthropology and cognitive psychology have been occupied with the question as to how a self that only has a direct contact with its own life of consciousness can come to understand an other to whose experiences it has no direct access. How can a monadic interiority, which is closed up in itself step outside, and break through its solipsistic universe? Schizophrenia confronts us with quite another problematic, namely: how do I get the other, who is always already in me, out of myself? With regard to schizophrenia, it seems that the point of departure of human intersubjectivity is not a solipsistic ego that wants to break out of itself, but a symbiotic entanglement where the outside is in the inside long before there can be any talk of an inside that can withdraw into itself.

AUTO-MUTILATION AND THE EXPULSION OF THE DRIVES

The erogenous zones (eyes, mouth, ears, anus, skin, reproductive-organs) are more or less localised points of contact on the body-surface which at the same time open and close themselves, and where the corporeal ego is forced to turn itself inside out. There, in the erogenous zones, the tension of the drives can be felt and the confused entanglement between self-impression and hetero-affection takes place. In coming into contact with what is pleasurable, the subject enjoys itself, and the life-force of the body marked by drives (*corps pulsionel*) is reinforced. That which is experienced as pleasurable is incorporated by the corporeal pleasure-ego, that which is a source of unpleasure is rejected by it. In *Negation*, Freud expresses this in the following manner: "Expressed in the language of the oldest - the oral - instinctual impulses [Triebregungen], the judgement is: 'I should like to eat this' or 'I should like to spit it out'; and, put more generally: 'I should like to take this into myself and to keep that out'. That is to say: 'It shall be inside me' or 'It shall be outside me'. As I have shown elsewhere, the original pleasure-ego wants to introject into itself everything that is good and to eject from itself everything that is bad." (1925 h, 237)

What happens in schizophrenia with the affects that together with repre-sentations are the psychical representatives of the body marked by drives? How does the primordial pleasure-ego express itself, and what happens to the body when this pleasure-ego does not rise above itself?

Let me address once more one of Freud's observations, the extent of which I shall deepen on the basis of my clinical experience, as supplemented by insights of Aulagnier and Vergote. A patient observed by Freud loses all interest in life due to the bad state of his facial skin. "He declares that he has blackheads and deep holes in his face which everyone notices. Analysis shows that he is playing out his castration complex upon his skin. At first he worked at these blackheads remorselessly; and it gave him great satisfaction to squeeze them out, because, as he said, something spurted out when he did so. Then he began to think that a deep *cavity* [Grube] appeared wherever he had got rid of a blackhead, and he reproached himself most vehemently with having *ruined* [verdorben] his skin for ever by 'constantly fiddling about with his hand.'" (1915 e, 199-200; Author's emphasis) To my mind the schizophrenic aspect of these observations mainly expresses itself in the fact that the hypochondriacal self-relatedness goes together with an affective conviction that his skin had been ruined for good. This connection is even more apparent in the following clinical examples: a woman, who scratches and cuts her breasts until they bleed, tells me that they are 'oil-tits' [olietetten] full with puss and filth. She burns little lumps and scabs out with cigarettes, and the 'refuse' in her body spills out of them. Another woman tries with malignant obsession to master her delusion of being poisoned; she is being poisoned by the mixing of words and disgusting thoughts into her food. Amongst the words was also the name of a child to which she had never given birth. In eating she crushes the name between her teeth; the words lie in her stomach and in swallowing them she is infected by them. In order to protect herself against infection she forces herself to throw up. In contrast with anorexia nervosa, the malignant obsession of this woman is not supported by a preoccupation with the body image. It has always struck me how the erogenous zones, centres of ebullient vigour, are conceived of in schizophrenia as rotting wounds and ripped open sores that are experienced from within as bad. It is as if the drive is experienced only as a source of destruction and not as a source of enjoyment.

On this point, schizophrenia differs radically from paranoid psychosis. The paranoiac has pushed out and projected to the outside the unpleasurable which, together with the pleasurable, constitutes the affective representations of the drive. He has split himself off from the unpleasurable. What is bad is maintained outside of his body; that which threatens him lies outside and can be localised in an other that does not reside in his body. By splitting himself from it, he can place the malignant over and against himself. Good (the pleasurable) and evil (the unpleasurable) are radically separated from each other and, furthermore, this difference coincides with the opposition, inside versus outside, and it is exactly this opposition that allows him to separate good and evil from each other. In schizophrenia, on the contrary, this inner splitting has not occurred. *The outside, that which is evil, resides in him.* What is threatening comes from within. In paranoia, on the contrary, it comes from the outside. The schizophrenic is perforated by evil. The paranoiac is persecuted by it.

The paranoiac is protected by the walls of his room and his house, a symbol of the secure limits that his body provides. In schizophrenia the body offers no safe place in which to dwell. The schizophrenic has not introjected or invested his body libidinally. "Everything indicates... that in psychosis [that is, schizophrenic psychosis] the pulsional body has shown itself to be essentially a source of displeasure and that the "I" has accordingly expelled it, rather than introjecting it to inhabit it libidinally." (Vergote, 1980, 29-30) The drive as drive is experienced as a source of displeasure and destruction and is therefore expelled by what Freud, in *Negation*, calls the original pleasure-ego. On the one hand one can, on the basis of this hypothesis, understand why libidinal ties with reality are being severed. How can the subject invest in reality and experience pleasure from it when the libidinal body cannot be experienced as a source of pleasure? On the other hand, one can understand why the withdrawal of the libido into itself cannot be called narcissism in the strict sense of the word, that is to say that it does not go together with a libidinal cathexis or re-cathexis of one's own body. The body does not offer itself as a loveable object. When Freud says that in schizophrenia a regression to auto-erotism takes place, and when De Waelhens, adding to this, claims that schizophrenia does not rise above 'le corps morcelé' (the scattered body), then this claim is, even though it is not incorrect, too weak. It is too weak because it neglects the *affect-aspect* of drive representations and the repercussions thereof on corporeal self-relatedness: *the drive as such is characterized as the 'kakon' - the evil.*

On the level of the original, undifferentiated pleasure-ego, the erogenous zones, the drive that puts pressure thereupon, and the representations of the objects from which pleasure is experienced, form an indivisible unity. In *Violence de l'interprétation* Aulagnier calls the synaesthetic base of the original pleasure-ego the *pictogram*. (Castoriadis-Aulagnier, 1975, 59) We have indeed no direct experience[2] of this synaesthetic base, the echo of which can be heard in some linguistic expressions (e.g. "This cuts to the bone," see above), but it breaks through in schizophrenic auto-mutilation and the aggressive fantasies of a libidinal body that reacts self-destructively. This synaesthetic base entails that the unpleasurable adheres so directly to the body that the expulsion of the unpleasurable inevitably goes together with the destruction of the object-representation and the corresponding erogenous body-part. "This is why every pleasurable experience reproduces the coalescence of the sensible organ and the perceived phenomenon, and why every experience of displeasure implies the desire for self-mutilation of the organism, and for the destruction of the object which excites the organ" (Ibid., 77) Freud probably points to this in *Negation* when he characterises schizophrenia as 'allgemeine Verneinungslust' ['the general pleasure in negating' (1925 h, 239)] that is the work of Thanatos that is directed against Eros. The schizophrenic says no to the drive and in extreme cases he can only express this by the destruction of the drive and thus of himself. The regression to catatonia is probably also an expression thereof. The catatonic body approaches a life without drives and is the enactment [mise-en-scène] of a body that can only survive by identifying itself with a dead body.

VIA EXCAVATED WORD-REPRESENTATIONS TO AN IDIOSYNCRATIC UNIVERSE OF DE-INCARNATED SYMBOLS

The process of de-metaphorisation by which meanings which appeal to the body are reduced to organ-speech is only one aspect of the schizophrenic use of language. Another important aspect is that the mutual correlation between pre-conscious word-representations and unconscious thing-representations is severed.

In schizophrenia, word associations prevail over thing associations. This does not only mean that words are combined with each other on the basis of a marginal agreement of content, but also and mainly that they are put into sequence with each other on the basis of formal similarities, and of formal sound-associations that produce surprising combinations, bizarre sentence structures and all sorts of neologisms. Of words, only an empty shell remains. Their cathexis no longer seems hindered by unconscious thoughts. In normal free association, on the contrary, the free flow of the words is obstructed. Thoughts which are defended against, and which keep insisting from the margins emerge on the surface now and then, for example, via slips of the tongue. Someone who makes a slip of the tongue expresses more of himself than he wishes to say and is surprised by thoughts that he would rather not pronounce and which overtake his meaning-intention. A slip of the tongue (for example: 'Famillionair') is the effect of an interference of two chains of signifiers wherein the one, which expresses what one wishes to say, is intercepted by another which, is the vehicle of a meaning that one does not want to express. Schizophrenic 'Wortneubildungen' [neologisms] appear to be the funny or annoying results of slips of the tongue but are not consequences of slips of the tongue. What happens in a schizophrenic word-formation is rather to be ascribed to the fact that words, as pure content-less signifiers, lead their own lives apart from a conscious meaning-intention. Words can rearrange and reform themselves freely because they no longer experience resistance, either from a thought that wants to communicate itself, or from unconscious thought-contents. It is as if a schizophrenic is submerged in a universe of *pure signifiers.*

In schizophrenia words are treated as thing-representations are treated in dreams (for example by the addition or omission of letters, the deformation of word-forms, etc.). In dreams they are handled in the manner in which the primary processes of the unconscious condense, deform and transform memory-images and thing-representations (that derive from memory-traces) *in order to* provide an access to the preconscious for unconscious thought-contents. The interpretation of dreams follows the course of the dream-work via free association and pursues the ways that lead the latent thoughts towards dream elements and the manifest dream content. Free association goes along with active attention to what appears in the preconscious unwillingly and allows itself to be guided by unexpected verbal ambiguities: words and pre-conscious thoughts come under the sphere of influence of the mechanism at work in the unconscious. Because consolidated thought-constructs and the meaning-intentions of the speaking subject are being undermined, free association may give "an impression now of a joke, now of schizophrenia." (1916-17 f, 229) In a footnote of *The Unconscious* Freud says the following: "The dreamwork, too, occasionally treats words like things, and so creates very similar 'schizophrenic' utterances or neologisms." (1915 e, 199, note 2) However, this noticeable similarity must not make us forget that what happens in dream-work and free-association is radically different from what occurs in the schizophrenic hyper-cathexis of word-representations. (1916-17 f, 229) In schizophrenia the words themselves become the object worked upon by the primary processes. Because, in the dream, thing-representations are connected to words, these are subjected to the workings of the primary processes. In contrast with schizophrenia, the dream knows only a topological regression. All verbal operations that take place in the dream *are a preparation, form a fertile-ground, or are an incentive* to arrive at unconscious thoughts via a return to the thing-representations. The dream-work, as well as free association upon which the interpretation of dreams is based, are permeated by a *tension* between the unconscious thing-representations and pre-conscious word-cathexes. Free association guides words to the direction in which they are drawn by the unconscious.

In schizophrenia, on the contrary, the traffic between word-representations and unconscious thing-representations is blocked ('abgesperrt' – 'cut off'). (Ibid.) Words lead their own life and form an independent universe apart from any tension with unconscious contents. Normally, the force of significance of words is over-determined by the interaction with unconscious contents and the resulting ambiguity can never be completely clarified by any form of interpretation. Every dream interpretation, for example, adds new traces of meaning to points of connection and at the same time disentangles them. Schizophrenic word associations, in contrast, are *not over-determined in their meaning but are empty of meaning*: the free play of words no longer clings to object-representations (since the libidinal object-attachments have been cut), it no longer connects to the personal life-history of the subject that speaks and it has lost its anchor in the body. Words glide over everything and hang in empty space. In a certain sense the schizophrenic feels more at home in a *system of purely formal, de-incarnated symbols*, than in symbols which appeal to his corporeal existence.

The freedom enjoyed by word-formations and combinations is the consequence of the fact that words are no longer supported by a meaning-intention that in turn rests on the libido that aims to realize itself in cathecting objects. In *The Unconscious*, Freud asks whether schizophrenia can at all still be understood in terms of repression. (1915 e, 203-204) Certainly, schizophrenia too protects itself against that which is unbearable. The question is, however, whether the mechanisms of defense still correspond to what one calls repression. Repression, after all, entails that what is pushed out of consciousness maintains a cathexis in the unconscious from out of which it keeps working upon the preconscious. Is it not rather the case that the withdrawal of object-cathexis in schizophrenia goes together with *a dis-investment of the unconscious representations* that derive from memory traces? The only thing that remains and is being cathected are words that have become empty shells. Words that no longer refer to anything have become the last remainders of connection with a reality that makes itself known as an emptiness. In this empty world of words the schizophrenic maintains himself as a subject without a body, as a subject that has become a pure, meaningless signifier. Therefore it is wrong to compare schizophrenic language with poetic activity. True enough, certain procedures in poetry coincide with the manner in which the schizophrenic deals with language. But this coincidence does not go further than a formal similarity. The poet, after all, turns words inside out and is hyper-sensitive to the form in order to evoke the unspeakable and allow it to resonate in the speakable. A poem borrows its power of expression from the tension with an ungraspable point of flight that is at work in language itself. The schizophrenic, on the contrary, connects words so as not to have to speak and so as not to have to hear the emptiness; language here does not circle around a symbolically articulated emptiness but looks for protection against a real emptiness.

In schizophrenia no new world of significance is founded and the limits of the traditional code of language are not breached in order to allow a new order to emerge. Or might this perhaps be the case after all?

The schizophrenic stands, in a certain sense, at a new beginning, at the origin that precedes the beginning. He stands at the origin of a new language, a language that shall create order for the first time, an order that shall arise from nothing and is therefore completely arbitrary. He stands at the point where an order shall originate in the chaos that surrounds him. But he is alone on that point, and he can only speak a language that others cannot share with him. And from out of this defenceless solitude, he speaks.

(translated from the Flemish by Jo Köhler. Edited and proof-read by Jo Köhler and Brendan Maloney in cooperation with the author.)

NOTES

1. Cf. also p. 96, footnote 16: "On pourrait trouver une confirmation de la thèse freudienne dans le fait qu'on n'observe jamais un accès psychotique aigu sans symptomes hypocondriaques, le plus souvent massifs."
2. P. Castoriadis-Aulagnier, 1975, 78: "C'est cela que nous appelons 'le fond représentatif' (i.e., the pictogram) forclos au pouvoir de connaissance du Je. Mais les effets sur le Je se manifesteront hors champs de la psychopathologie, par ces sentiments indéfinissables que le langage traduit par des métaphores dont l'usage a emoussé le sens profond: 'se sentir bien dans la peau', 'être en forme', 'être mal à l'aise', 'porter le monde sur ses épaules', 'sentir son corps en morceaux', et d'autres encore. Dans le champ de la psychose ce fond représentatif par moments occuper l'avant de la scène."

FREUD AND LACAN ON NEUROSIS AND PSYCHOSIS

Antoine Vergote

In 1954, in his *Séminaire* given at Saint-Anne, Lacan invited Jean Hyppolite, the famous specialist on Hegel's philosophy, to comment on Freud's short text of 1925, *Negation* (1925 h, 236-239). That year, the whole of Lacan's seminar was consecrated to Freud's technical writings.[1] As he himself states in his introduction to Hyppolite's comments, Lacan's interest in this seminar was especially directed towards Freud's concept of resistance. This indeed was a key concept in the thought and practice of the *Société psychanalytique de Paris*, from which Lacan had been forced to separate. Readers familiar with Lacan know that for him "there is only resistance on the side of the analyst himself". Freud's study *Negation* should serve to support Lacan's harsh criticism of analytical practice centred on resistance. More essentially however, Freud's considerations on pulsion[2] and language allow Lacan to develop his very personal psychoanalytical theory. Indeed, this does away with Freud's conception of repression and the unconscious, and consequently dissipates the question of resistance itself.

As is well known, from 1934 to 1937, Lacan attended Alexandre Kojève's seminar on Hegel's *Phenomenology of Spirit*. So, Lacan was especially attentive to the function of negation and he felt he could use Hegel's philosophy in interpreting Freud. Moreover, in the ten years before starting his seminars in the newly founded psychoanalytical association, Lacan had been studying philosophy intensively - Plato, Aristotle, Kant, Hegel, Heidegger - in order to be able to re-think the fundamental psychoanalytical concepts. His deepest conviction, restated in endless polemics, was that medical positivism and ego psychology had degraded contemporary psychoanalysis. In this context, Hyppolite's invited comments were meant to be a liberating return to the truth, speaking through Freud's words, above and beyond Freud's clear personal consciousness of what he was revealing.

Lacan himself 'answered' Hyppolite's commentary very extensively,[3] 'answer' here obviously meaning a laudatory expression of agreement, along with an interpretation that conducts Hyppolite's interpretation further astray.

Hyppolite, says Lacan, presents an exegesis worthy of Freud. He applies a critical method, which is faithful to the very principles of the Freudian message. Lacan, of course, pursues the elaboration of this 'authentic' comprehension. Yet for the reader trained in exegesis and in psychoanalysis, Hyppolite's commentary is an anti-psychological Hegelian parabola constructed out of Freud's words.

I will not follow the texts step by step, but I will successively consider Freud and Lacan, eventually together with Hyppolite, concerning the two main topics: first, expulsion and negation, and second, the intellectual function and reality. In order to complete the discussion of psychosis, I will add some notes concerning

Lacan's idiosyncratic reading of the Wolf Man's hallucination. In my conclusion, I will evaluate, with respect to psychoanalytic observations, Lacan's highly original 'return to Freud'. For a better understanding of Lacan I would also suggest a look at the theoretical sources of his ideas, sources cutting across Freudian thought and language.

EXPULSION AND NEGATION

Freud

Following the *Standard Edition* (SE), I will translate Freud's *Die Verneinung* by 'negation'. The *Standard Edition* justifies this translation by the necessity of distinguishing 'negation' from 'denegation', the true translation of Freud's term *Verleugnung*. As a matter of fact, *Verleugnung* (denegation) of castration (in fetishism for instance) does not express itself in a negative proposition. It is the psychoanalytical interpreter who converts the negative symptom of denegation into a negative proposition. The authoritative Sachs-Villatte German-French dictionary also gives the grammatical form 'negation' for the substantive *die Verneinung*. For the verb *verneinen* it gives *désavouer* (disavow) and *nier* (negate). Now, Freud obviously starts from the observation of negative propositions within the analysand's associations. He further examines the general importance of the linguistic symbol of negation. Therefore the proposal made by the *Vocabulaire de la psychanalyse* of Laplanche and Pontalis to translate by *(dé)-négation* and to preserve in this way 'the ambiguity' of Freud's text, seems to miss the point. The ambiguity is not inherent in the linguistic formulation, but in the meaning the interpreter acknowledges when placing the proposition in the context of the analytical setting. The negation there is a grammatical form loaded with a repressive force that rejects the content of the proposition.

Freud begins by interpreting different examples of negation, which may occur during an analysis. As he had already previously demonstrated in various contributions, negation is often a way of repressing the idea coming to mind. In the present text Freud explicitly insists on the other aspect: the negative propositions under consideration partially suppress this repression itself. They indeed bring the repressed idea to the mind. In some cases the analyst can even undo the negation and bring the analysand in a second moment to accept the repressed content. Nonetheless, the repression may not be really removed. Intellectual acceptance is not necessarily a therapeutic achievement. There should be a working-through process and an acceptance by the whole ego. The ego is more than the conscious mind. Freud, however, does not elaborate here on this last element.

What interests him are the theoretical, not the technical implications of the dissociation between mental statements - negation or acceptance - and affective resistance. The analysand who negates an idea is at least already entertaining it.

In this sense, the mind gives the content of the entertained and negated idea some kind of presentability, so that the subject can have the content at its disposal. This does not mean that before this time the words of the negative proposition were lacking. The subject who says of the figure in his dream, "this is not my mother", already had, of course, an idea of his mother, and of the words to describe her. But the very particular idea occurring as a dream association had been repressed and it was not yet available to the mind for pursuing the analysis of memories and feelings concerning the mother.

Freud draws an important theoretical insight from this observation. The ambiguous function of the negation in question manifests the link and the difference between mental functioning and the affective process. In its capacity as a substitute (*Ersatz* or *Nachfolge*) for the repression, negation to some extent continues repression (*Nachfolge* meaning that which pursues) and yet liberates the subject from it. The term 'substitute' here clearly identifies the linguistic symbol as characterized by the continuity and the discontinuity in the affective process. Stressing one aspect, Freud speaks of the psychological origin of the intellectual function (1925 h, 236); stressing the other, he deals with the creation of the linguistic symbol.

It is well known that Freud sought to derive language and the whole of culture from the vicissitudes of pulsions. We are thinking here of his linguistically dubious theory of the origin of language signs in the sexual cry, and his adherence to Karl Abel's theory of the original ambivalence of words.

In *Negation*, he focuses his view on the successive fitting of the different negative processes into one another. The work of every negative process is accomplished with the energy of a positive force. By intervening negatively with this force, the negative processes gradually construct the psychic organism. By this expression Freud precisely designates the personality, as structured by the analyzed processes.

The first structuring process is the process of introjection of what is felt to be good, and of ejection of what is felt to be bad (see 1915 c, 136). At the very origin, Freud posits an original reality-ego. We should think of this as a fictional moment, for there is neither ego nor reality at this hypothetical first moment. Actually Freud posits a biological organism that is adapted to its milieu, as is the animal with its pre-programmed instincts. Human psychic formation follows from this moment. It is characterized by the *Triebe,* which Freud in his *Three Essays* of 1905 distinguished from animal instinct. *Triebe* are the human psychic modalities of forces in the lived body. As mentioned already, in order to avoid all confusion, I follow Freud's proposal to distinguish between instincts and *Triebe* and I translate this last term by 'pulsion', using this word as the metaphorical psycho-analytical term. As soon as the psyche is human, actually as soon as it is born, it is thus regulated by the positive and the negative workings of the pulsion obeying the pleasure-principle. In the oral stage for example, the psyche takes in and spits out. We should note that even before the narcissistic action through which the ego posits itself as ego for itself, introjection and ejection preserve and construct a kind of ego. This primary ego already has a narcissistic character, for it is identical with that which it feels to be good, and it rejects as the other that which it feels to be bad.

Investment and repression are the second major forms of dissociating simultaneously, good from bad, and ego from non-ego. Investment and repression are also under the command of the pleasure-principle. Otherwise they would not even be possible, for the idea of a conscious repression into the unconscious is a contradiction. At this stage, the psyche is already a complex organism formed by narcissism and by the construction of the ego ideal. The other that is the effect of repression is the inner other, the unconscious. This new 'ejection' within oneself into the unconscious of course presupposes a kind of unconscious which exercises an attraction on the representations to be repressed. Freud only qualifies original repression as having attractive force. Similarly, I would say that original repression evolves simultaneously with an original investment. This investment attracts the subsequent ones made by the narcissistically formed ego. I thus would identify the first introjection-ejection with the formation of the original unconscious.[4]

Language introduces the third and newest form of positive and negative movement. These two movements are no longer dominated by the pleasure-principle, at least, not completely. Negation during analysis ("this dream figure is not my mother") already effectuates a partial suppression of the repression, which is to some extent regulated by the pleasure-principle. Of course this is only partially so, for, as has been mentioned, the ego ideal is also partly the assimilation of prevalent cultural ideas in the social milieu. Consequently, repression presupposes a cultural world, which is not the mere product of the pleasure-ego. Although distinct from the pulsional process, the intellectual function, because it operates by attributing qualities, good or bad, to the designated object, pursues the aim of the pleasure-principle. Ultimately, the judgments of existence and non-existence are the most free from the pleasure-principle. I will come back to this point.

Lacan

Lacan immediately concurs with Hyppolite's thesis that the creation of the symbol of negation effectuates a level of functioning that is different from affirmation (*Bejahung*) (1966, 382). And for Lacan, after Hyppolite, in Freud's mind the creation of the symbol of negation is beyond the scope of psychological genesis. Freud's intention is not so much to describe the constitution of objects in the world, but to describe the relation of the subject to Being. Freud, says Lacan, anticipates here the philosophy of Heidegger. Freud contests, as does Heidegger, the whole tradition of western thought, which confused Being and being.

Lacan's elusive way of talking may have impressed listeners and readers not familiar with Heidegger, as an 'exegesis' faithful to the mysterious depth of Freud's text. However, insofar as there is a connection between Freud and Lacan his interpreter, it should first of all be sought in the massive polemics that pervade all Lacanian reflections on Freud and on Hyppolite, Lacan's own choice for an interpreter of Freud. Lacan forcefully battles against some prevailing conceptions within the Parisian Institute of Psychoanalysis, from which he now had to break. These conceptions stress the importance of fostering the patient's 'object-rela- tionships' (*relations d'objet*), and of the analysis of affective experiences in transference. It is however an ironic fact, that both these topics, reality and affectivity are central in Freud's study *Negation*. The progressively structured psyche, we read, evolves through different stages of internal-external splitting into the reality-testing of the object present in the representations. And this structuring process is also a progressive liberation from the dominance of affective processes.

Hyppolite's explanation of Freud's text was made from a Hegelian perspec- tive. As is well known, in the *Phenomenology of Spirit*, negation and later the *Aufhebung* (suppression and preservation at an elevated rank) through the nega- tion of negation, compose the active principles constructing the successive phenomenological forms of the conscious, the self-conscious and ultimately the rational subject.[5] Without a doubt, there is some similarity in the way Hegel and Freud conceive of the subject, or the ego in Freud's terminology, as growing in the normal case towards a rational, objective disposition. The differences, how- ever, are great. Freud does not share Hegel's optimistic view of civilisation as evolving, through tightly woven sequences towards the status of a rational subject. Lacan too has a strong distaste for this rational optimism. For him, the idea of a progressive, self-conscious mastery in fact represents the most self-de- ceptive loss of the true relation to Being. In this respect, Lacan is a disciple of Heidegger. This can help us to understand his 'exegesis' of Freud, now under consideration. Lacan takes over Hyppolite's idea that the core of Freud's text is the negation that transforms the *Bejahung* (affirmation). But for Lacan this means that the 'subject' (a Hegelian, not a Heideggerian term) can truly relate to Being. For Lacan, as for Heidegger, this precludes Hegel's finalistic philosophy of history. For Lacan, this also opposes the idea, common in contemporary French psychoanalysis and, in my view, also to be found in Freud, of the progress towards object-relationships. For Lacan, the concept of object-relationship falls into the primordial confusion of Being with beings (1966, 382).

We can now clarify, I hope, the first and the most basic idea Lacan attributed to Freud's *Negation*. At the very origin, at the 'mythical' origin of the subject (i.e. before any psychological development), the negation-symbol lifts the subject out of the primary confusion of Being and beings, thus producing the 'subject' as such.

In the first place, this recalls Freud's fundamental doctrine according to which the negation-symbol, and more generally all language symbols, do not exist in the unconscious. They rather belong essentially to the system Pcs-Cs. Secondly, in Freud's text the first structuring moment is both negative and positive, the splittings good-bad, interior-exterior being produced by the pulsion, operating according to its own law, namely the pleasure-principle. We can already observe here Lacan's projection of language-symbols into the unconscious. It is not by chance that this happens under the influence of philosophy, for philosophy has never been at ease with the psychoanalytical theory of the unconscious. Other psychiatric and literary sources also influenced Lacan in his rethinking of the unconscious according to the model of mental automatism.

Lacan's comment (1966, 383) on Freud's short passage on 'the affective process' (1925 h, 236) pursues the same idea I just summarized. In Freud's text, as we have seen, the negation being considered is the negation of a particular proposition within an analysis, which partially separates the intellectual function from repression. Repression is called an affective process because it is effectuated by the pulsion under the dominance of the pleasure-principle. Lacan understands "the affective... in this text as the effect of primordial symbolisation within discursive structuration". Primordial symbolisation according to Lacan, we said, consists of the negation lifting the subject out of the primary confusion. Here this negation is also called death; a reminder of Heidegger's consciousness of 'being towards death', the fundamental ontological experience revealing the difference between Being and beings. The 'discursive structuring' (*structuration discursive*) to which Lacan refers in the text I quoted and translated, at first sight means the proposition of a negation ("this is not my mother"). But Lacan generalized what for Freud is a particular type of negative proposition occurring in analysis. For Lacan the affective process is, most generally, the repression that deforms all human speech (discursive structuring). For the original symbolisation, the differentiation of Being-being, normally accomplished by negation and 'death', can only manifest itself in the discursive structuring, in the form of a failure to recognize it (*sous forme de méconnaissance*).

According to Freud the negative proposition is a liberation from the affective process. It partially suppresses (*aufheben*, in a non-Hegelian sense!) the repression. Lacan understands the negative proposition as the partial retrieval of the primordial symbolisation by negation. What is proper to the negative proposition is that it simultaneously manifests and hides the primordial symbolisation. Lacan applies to the 'discursive structuration' Heidegger's philosophy of truth as the tension between manifestation and hiding; this is the biblical conception of God's revelation translated into ontological terms.

For Freud, the affective process is the activity and the unfolding of the affect, the pulsion working according to the pleasure-principle. Negation considered in an analytical context is the procedure the intellect uses to free itself from the dominance of the affect. Lacan interprets this affective process as a mixture of the primordial symbolic negation and of the conscious, necessarily deceptive way of expressing the original symbolic structuration. This is what Lacan generally calls *l'imaginaire* (the imaginary). No doubt, Lacan uses Freud's terminology here to articulate a theory, which is not at all Freudian. This observation does not yet mean either, that Freud is right and Lacan wrong, or that we are dealing with two formulations of equal value.

THE INTELLECTUAL FUNCTION AND REALITY-TESTING, NEUROSIS AND PSYCHOSIS

Freud

Freud's main interest in this text, as is the case generally in his metapsychological contributions, is to understand how the individual comes to an objective disposition towards reality. We are not yet introducing a philosophical criticism of these terms, but first of all trying to understand Freud's inquiry. His clinical observations impose this question upon his thought. Using normal language shaped in Western civilisation by philosophy and science, Freud observes that there is a "loss of reality in neurosis and psychosis" (1924 e, 183-187). For him, that loss results from a disturbance in the process through which the individual would normally conquer reality. To be sure, Freud posits a reality-ego (*Real-Ich*) at the origin. But as soon as the individual manifests itself as a human psychic being (i.e. at the first moment of his personal history), the reality-ego is lost through the effect of the pulsion and the pleasure-principle. In the first part of my contribution, I exposed the stages of the structuring of the subject in correlation with the conquest of reality. Both processes are intrinsically interwoven.

The intellectual function, which is the locus of reality recognition, must be separated from the pulsions. From the beginning Freud was acutely aware that in neurosis, judgment can be under the sway of the affective process. In *The Interpretation of Dreams*, for example, he distinguishes between *Verwerfungsurteil* (judgment shaped by affective rejection) and *Urteilsverwerfung* (judgment which rejects on the basis of intellectual insight).[6] The separation between the affective process and the intellectual function is a long, complex process menaced by neurotic or psychotic failure. What endangers the process is that the intellectual function constructs itself through affective processes, whilst using the aid of linguistic symbols. Underlying the intellectual function there remains the affective process, whose characteristics Freud repeats: "the original pleasure-ego wants to introject into itself everything that is good and to eject from itself everything that is bad" (1925 h, 237). When, after being perceived, things are present in inner representations, the pleasure-ego still experiences the good things represented as being things, which fulfil the pulsional desires. This happens in dreams, when they are not nightmares. Therefore dreams are a kind of hallucination. Affective idealisations work the same way.

The most important intellectual function is the judgment of existence. To be sure, attribution of the qualities good and bad also belongs to judgment. This attribution follows perception and the inner representations of the pleasure-ego. The judgment of existence is a completely new, typically intellectual function. However, it should fit in with the affective process. Freud indeed uses terms which clearly insist on the unavoidable and even necessary link between the pleasure-ego and reality-testing. The latter consists in examining whether the content of the presentation (which has been introjected) can be *rediscovered* in perception as well, whether what is internal is *also* outside (never merely outside), and whether the ego can rediscover the object and convince itself that the object is *still* there. This process of reality-testing proceeds by sending out a certain amount of cathexis into the perceptual system (1925 h, 238). This is only possible of course because the inner representation is already a pulsional cathexis oriented by the pleasure-principle.

I could discuss here Freud's conception of reality; undoubtedly, it is a rather simple, positivistic conception. Despite Hyppolite's Hegelian fervour, nothing in Freud's text hints at the cultural transformation of 'reality' as philosophers and cultural anthropologists have steadily thematized it. Precisely here lies the whole problem of sublimation in Freud. His theory requires this concept but prevents its articulation.

My critical remarks should not prevent us from recognizing Freud's acute clinical questions and his genial insights. Working with a common-sense, rather positivistic concept of reality, Freud is addressing the major clinical problem of loss of reality. In neurosis this loss can be surmounted by analytical therapy. Negation is a first way of regaining for the mind those contents (i.e. the representations) which had been repressed by the complex narcissistic pleasure-ego. In this way, through negation and the subsequent affirmation, the mind can re-discover the objects of its pulsional desires. I would complete Freud's text in the direction of his thought: an object, which the subject held to be bad and whose representation it repressed, can be judged as existing and good. And an object whose representation had been transformed into an idealised good object, can be recognized for what it really is.

Obviously, a more fundamental loss of reality characterizes psychosis. And it is not by accident that Freud ends his study by briefly considering this problem. The ejection and repression by the normal pleasure-ego only explains the neurotic loss of reality, not the psychotic one. Therefore Freud had to go beyond the pleasure-principle as he conceived of it. Yet, before the introduction of the death-pulsion, Freud already had an illuminating insight into the basic failure causing a psychotic loss of reality. In the last chapter of the metapsychological paper *The Unconscious* (1915) Freud reflects on the fact that in schizophrenia words are treated as things. In the context of the tortuous discussion on the dynamic and/or economic conceptualisation of the topical unconscious, Freud suddenly understands what is lacking in schizophrenia: the thing-representations of objects (*Sachvorstellungen der Objekte*). This refers to those representations which are of the nature of the thing, not of the nature of words (*Wortvorstellungen*). Word representations are of a linguistic nature. We can identify them with what the linguist Saussure calls *les signes*, composed of signifier and signified. While not using the Saussurian vocabulary, Freud had held the same conception since his pre-analytical work on aphasia. In order to understand the structure of neurosis and the psychology of dreams he elaborated at that time his theory of unconscious, non-linguistic representations. But this new psychology was not appropriate to psychosis. He observes that in schizophrenia, language is also used as sign (i.e. signifier and signification). But the signs no longer function in the normal way of referring to objects: they are treated as if they were in some sense things. In this case, what are lacking are the normal components of the unconscious, namely the thing-representations. This lack opens a void where words come in to re-establish what is lost. However, not being rooted in thing-representations, words are treated as if they themselves were things.

Freud does not ask here why the thing-representations are lacking. Considering that the thing-representations are inscriptions in the psyche of the first experiences of perceived objects, which fulfil the pulsional desires, we can propose a hypothesis. In psychosis, some first bodily pulsional experiences, which normally bring about introjection in the form of thing-representations, are so disturbing that they are ejected. In the case of Schreber, for example, we can see a confirmation of this conception in the fact that pleasure became torture inflicted by the external persecutor, God.[7] The problem then is not to confuse the primordial normal vicissitude of pulsion - introjection-ejection - with the psychotic ejection. I surmise that the latter ejection is the process accomplished by the already narcissistic ego. In this way, we can understand both phenomena of schizophrenia: the self-centred inflation of the ego and the delirious treatment of words as things.

In his paper on *Negation* Freud is not so much questioning the loss of reality as examining the procedure by which the ego conquers and recuperates it. Negation is an important element in suppressing a neurotic repression. Negation is also working in the intellectual procedure that tests the real presence of represented objects. Without saying so explicitly, Freud considers negation to be a hypothetical tactical exercise of doubt, necessary for differentiating what is merely subjective from what is both subjective and objective. Freud then asks which pulsional force is working within negation. At the primary level, it is the pleasure-principle which is working within an ejection that is not yet negation in the formal linguistic sense. "We never discover a 'no' in the unconscious" (1925 h, 239). There, the law of the normal pulsion (the pleasure-principle) is sufficient. But reality-testing requires a liberation from this principle. Freud consequently invokes, as he had previously for similar reasons, another force which is no longer of the same nature as the erotic pleasure-principle: the pulsion of death or of destruction. In "some psychotics" he thinks he observes the naked manifestation of this pulsion in their *Verneinungslust* (pleasure in negation). Freud interprets it as the manifest defusion of *eros* and *thanatos* resulting from "the withdrawal of libidinal components". These last words of course remind us of the lack of primary cathexis (and thing-representations) due, in my view, to the ejection of too-painful experiences.

Why this enigmatic expression *Verneinungslust*? The *Standard Edition* translates it as "general wish to negate, the negativism..." (1925 h, 239), dropping the word *Lust* (pleasure). I think the translation should stress the paradoxical combination of pleasure and its contrary, (self-) destruction. We can understand this if we pay attention to the link between narcissism (and its pleasure), and psychotic negativism. The withdrawal of libidinal components cannot be the simple lack or destruction of them. Megalomania and autism show that the libidinal components are withdrawn within the ego. The destructive consequences for the ego should then be further analyzed. In view of this process, the nature of the death pulsion should be considered anew, but that is not my topic here. At any rate, the death pulsion is not a force that is symmetrically antithetical to eros; otherwise Freud's term 'defusion' would have no meaning. Besides, Freud does not think that the theoretical step beyond the pleasure-principle means the theoretical suppression of this principle.

We can now understand why strictly analytical therapies do not work with schizophrenic psychotics and why they do not come to reality-testing. The negation in their case is not the lifting and preservation of the repression of unconscious representations. These latter are lacking, as far as these subjects are psychotics. Their negations are manifestations on the level of linguistic expression of a fundamental compulsion to eject and destroy libidinal experiences. We hear in them the pure voice of the death pulsion, with which narcissism is in tune.

Lacan

Recall Lacan's idea that at the very origin - mythical and not psychological - the symbolic creation of negation works out the primary symbolisation. At that primary moment, the differentiation between the real and the symbolic takes place (1966, 383). These ideas, which he believes it possible, to discover in Freud's text, are first illustrated by Lacan with his analysis of the psychotic phenomenon of hallucination. The case he refers to is the castration hallucination of the Wolf Man. Lacan thinks Freud's paper *Negation* has the power to explain psychotic hallucination. For him, this application of Freud's text to hallucination functions as a reality-testing of Freud's ideas as he, Lacan, reads them in *Negation*. Two questions are thus at stake here: Lacan's 'Freudian' theory of psychotic hallucination and the psychotic nature of the Wolf Man's hallucination. I shall treat them in turn.

Affectivity, writes Lacan, makes the subject fail to recognize primary symbolisation. In Lacan's French text *mé-connaître* (mis-recognize, as in mis-take...) is way of recognizing, which at the same time fails to grasp *adequately*. This is the natural effect of affectivity (Freud's 'affective process'). Being-towards-death can only fail to fully grasp the symbolic, while recognizing it in some dubious way. To express it from another, ontological point of view: Being manifests itself while hiding itself.

Hallucination, rather than being a case of *méconnaissance*, attests rather to the patient's incapacity even for this misrecognizing. It is psychotic, says Lacan, and the analysis of hallucination takes us to the core of psychosis and, by way of contrast, reveals the true function of symbolic negation. Lacan first denounces the gross simplification of psychoanalysts who try to conceive of hallucination by using the concepts of Husserl's phenomenology. They still reason within a philosophy of consciousness. They apply to hallucination the phenomenological scheme of intentionality structured as the relation, noesis-noema. They complement it with Freud's pleasure-principle and they interpret hallucination as the eruption within consciousness of the pleasure principle (1966, 384). They do not see, says Lacan, that the hallucinatory content (the noema) cannot be understood at all in terms of pulsional satisfaction.

Instead of reasoning within the phenomenological scheme, Lacan returns to Freud's 'structuralistic' thought. Following the line of Freud's *Negation*, he will make "a really scientific reconstruction" of the hallucination problem (1966, 385; all quoted passages my translation).

The Wolf Man's hallucination occurred quite out of context, in his fifth year. According to Freud's interpretation, says Lacan (1966, 386), the initial traumatic experience of the subject (the sight of the original scene, during which the subject adopted the feminine position according to Freud), "makes it impossible for him to accept genital reality without the unavoidable castration menace" (1966, 386). According to Freud, says Lacan this castration representation is not repressed (*verdrängt*) but rejected (*verworfen*), a term for which Lacan proposes 'cut off'. What is rejected, cut off, can no longer return in symptoms, as do the repressed representations in neurosis.

Lacan then pursues this idea of rejection, believing that Freud opposes it to repression. This rejection has taken place in the primary moment as the movement opposed to the *Bejahung*. Lacan obviously means by *Bejahung* the first introjection as Freud analysed it in *Instincts and Their Vicissitudes*. According to Lacan, the primary negation of human *Bejahung* normally constitutes the primary symbolisation that could not happen with psychotics, for instead of the *Bejahung*-negation, they reject, expel, cut off.

Rejection consequently "cuts short all manifestation of the symbolic order, i.e. the *Bejahung* (affirmation)... which is the primordial condition in order that something of the real offers itself to the revelation of Being..." (1966, 388). This latter event can only take place once, as we already know. After the primary *Bejahung* "it [the *Bejahung*] can only be renewed through the veiled forms of unconscious words, for it is only through the negation of the negation that human discourse permits a return to it" (1966, 388). We should note here that in Lacan's conception, the unconscious is composed of words (*paroles*). Lacan interprets repression as an absolute universal process, which has the nature of the negation of the first symbolisation. All human conscious speech is only a veiled (negated) manifestation of the primary affirmation of these original words. Man can only return to this primary revelation of Being to some extent, through the negation of that negation which is identical with the universal repression of the primary revelation. Hegel's idea of the negation of negation is taken up by Lacan, not in the Hegelian perspective of a progressive accomplishment of the rational subject, but in the Heideggerian perspective of undoing the progressive deceptive confusion of Being and being.

What happens to that which has been rejected (*verworfen*), cut off? Lacan answers: "what did not come to the light of the symbolic appears within the real" (1966, 388). This is the way Lacan interprets Freud's statement about the primary split, through introjection-ejection, between the internal and the real, or external.

Again, I would insist on the fact that in Freud's mind, this primary pleasure-commanded process is the universal pre-linguistic construction of the pre-subject and its pre-objects. This process is not even neurotic. It is the basis of further reality-testing, when narcissism and language have transformed the structure of the ego and the meaning of reality.

In his commentary on the Schreber case, Lacan will repeat the idea found in the text I just quoted. Lacan even 'translates' in this way Freud's proposition *von aussen wiederkehrt* (1911 c (GW VIII), 308), "returns from without" (1911 c, 71). Freud explains paranoia as a projection and interprets the delusion of persecution as the return from the outside of what has been projected. Lacan's 'translation' of Freud's text is in the same spirit as his reading of the metapsychological paper *The Instincts and Their Vicissitudes*. Lacan does not take into account the active element of the paranoiac process thus formulated: "comes back to the ego from the outside". Lacan explains ejection as the non-assumption of the real within the symbolic order of language. So for him, the ejected is there outside the ego, for it is that which remained outside his first assent to the Being-revelation. The real has been and remains there, reappearing as the real in hallucination. "For if the judgment of existence functions, ... it is at the cost of a world [the real, A.V.] from which the cunning of reason twice deducted its share" (1966, 388-389). Here, 'twice' means through the negation of negation.

The subsequent texts of Lacan add nothing either to his interpretation of negation nor to his conception of the unconscious and of psychosis. I will therefore limit myself to the text already considered, and examine Lacan's reference to the Wolf Man's hallucination. Is it really psychotic?

First, I would remark that nowhere else does Freud give the term *Verwerfung* the specific meaning of a fundamental rejection which should be distinguished from repression (*Verdrängung*), and which would produce psychosis. To be sure, discussing psychosis in one of his earliest texts (1894 a, 58) he writes: "Here, the ego rejects the incompatible idea together with its affects and behaves as if the idea had never occurred to the ego at all." However, this does not mean that Freud uses rejection as a specific technical term. Freud only stresses the active process working in psychosis, and he is aware that this process is not the same as repression in neurosis. Often in his later texts, rejection has this meaning of an unspecified active defense process.

As for Freud's text on the Wolf Man, Lacan writes "... how striking the formula is, without any ambiguity, the subject will *know nothing of it in the sense of the repression*" (1966, 388; Lacan's emphasis). 'It', meaning here the castration representation, which, being cut off, "reappears in the real". However, Freud's text can and should be read in quite another way. I quote: "*Er verwarf sie*" [*die Kastration*]. And Freud explains: "*so ist die nächste Bedeutung dieses Ausdrucks, dass er von ihr nichts wissen wollte im Sinne der Verdrängung.*" (1918 b, 117). The *Standard Edition* translates: "When I speak of his having rejected it, the first meaning of the phrase is that he would have nothing to do with it, in the sense of having repressed it." (1918 b, 84). Obviously to reject (*verwerfen*) and the will to have nothing to do with something, are the descriptive terms Freud regularly uses for the active defence process. In this particular case Freud specifies the process as being one which is already well known: repression (*Verdrängung*). Freud's whole commentary makes this interpretation manifest. The young boy had accepted the new representation of vaginal coition, but afterwards he rejected it out of castration anxieties (1918 b, 79). Thus, nothing had been definitively cut off in him! Freud is quite clear about this: "We may therefore assume that this hallucination belongs to the period in which he brought himself to recognize the reality of castration and it is perhaps to be regarded as actually marking this step." (Ibid., 85). Besides, after the sudden hallucination, the boy very quickly proceeds to reality-testing and perceives that his finger has not been cut off (Ibid.).

Lacan is correct in that not all hallucination can be understood as an intense wish fulfilment, comparable to the dream-satisfaction. But Lacan is wrong when he interprets the hallucination of the young Wolf Man as psychotic and thus not as an effect of the pleasure-principle. Far from being psychotic, this hallucination is the perception of the traumatic representation of castration as real. It is comparable to a nightmare. As such, this hallucination is still the product of the work of the pleasure-principle. For the subject governed by that principle rejects and represses what is unpleasant.

CONCLUDING REVIEW AND REFLECTIONS

There is no doubt that from the start, Lacan's Seminars, forcefully proclaiming the program of a return to Freud, use Freud's texts in order to construct a wholly new theory. I would not say that Lacan did this with conscious intent. Lacan's merit has been that with his philosophical passion, he commented extensively on Freudian theoretical texts which very often were neglected by the rather pragmatic and theoretically less cultivated contemporary analysts. This distinguished merit of Lacan aside, the question should be asked whether his theory sheds light on the essential Freudian concepts and the clinical facts and practice which pertain.

First of all, do we better understand neurosis with Lacan's theory? I do not think so. The Heideggerian philosopher may think that the veiling of primordial signifiers is a universal repression. I doubt whether Heidegger would agree with this psychoanalytic formulation of the 'forgetting of Being'.[8] But this Lacanian idea of repression (the first 'negation') does not at all permit us to take into account and to understand the secondary repression, which in Freud's mind is responsible for neurosis. Besides, this category is completely absent from the whole volume of *Ecrits*. I myself agree completely with Freud. In order to make neurotic repression understandable, we must conceive of unconscious representations as thing-representations and not as word-representations.

Lacan's conceptualisation clearly takes manifest psychosis as a model for understanding psychic reality and its structure. In psychosis, as Freud argues, word-representations are substituted for thing-representations. But conceiving as he does of the psychic structure according to the model of psychotic verbal machinery, I fear that Lacan can neither explain psychosis nor give secondary repression its proper place. For psychosis, as Freud insists on, can only be understood as the result of a double active process. It would tend ultimately towards psychic death, if there were not implicit therein the positive attempt to reconstruct lost reality with the remaining word-representations.

Lacan's reference to structuralist thought gets its full meaning in this context. The signifying order, the symbolic order, is there, pre-given from the origin, organised as language. Normally the human individual, the 'subject', immediately grasps the structure of the elementary 'signifiers'. From the real, the pre-given Being, he introjects immediately the most important signifiers. When he does not, when he 'rejects' some important ones, especially the castration-idea, or the function (the 'name') of the father, these signifiers will impose themselves in hallucinations, in the 'real' that lies outside the subject.

And what happens to those who introject the essential original significant givens? They lose them as soon as they try to conquer them consciously in their intentional language. The introjected significant givens, the symbolisation of the real, are necessarily 'repressed' by the entrance into conscious language. They are negated a first time. In all their thoughts and philosophy, people are deceiving themselves naively. Lacan, along with Freud, came to reveal the unavoidable self-deception which is the happy effect of culture, this collective neurosis. Psychoanalysis brings the innocent self-deceiver to effectuate the negation of negation and to rediscover some semblance of the original, definitively lost truth of Being.

Of course, the reader who knows Heidegger's philosophy is immediately aware that Lacan borrowed some conceptual schemes and some terminology in order to say something which is not to be found in Heidegger's ontology. Where do Lacan's ideas come from then? I am convinced that they stem from the combination of three main sources: from the social philosophy which heavily influenced Lacan's pre-psychoanalytical thought and his doctoral thesis.[9] Secondly, he draws from the French Surrealists who were convinced that thought and language automatism is at work within the universal 'unconscious' structure of the mind; consequently, for the surrealist, psychosis was a particularly revealing phenomenon of the hidden structure of the mind. Third, he takes from Jung. This is surely the most hidden, because it is the most suspect, source of Lacan's thought. Lacan not only considered Jung to be 'a great mind'[10]; he undoubtedly also sympathized with the questions Jung asked and the ways he tried to answer them. Indeed, Jung had been the one, so intimately acquainted with psychoanalysis, who very early on opposed Freud's reductionism in matters of mythology, art or religion. And, Jung elaborated a theory of the 'subconscious' as conveying original mythical or archetypal structures which man expresses in symbolic language and rituals. Psychosis for Jung is the breaking through of these archetypal structures which have not been integrated in thought and feeling, which have been projected and appear outside the subject as delusions. Some similarities with Lacan's thought on these points cannot be denied. I fear my views may scandalize some people. If so, evil to him, who evil thinks!

NOTES

1. *The Seminar of Jacques Lacan, Book I, Freud's Papers on Technique 1953-1954.* John Forrester, trans. Cambridge University Press, 1988. From *Les écrits techniques de Freud,* Paris, Seuil. Text established and published in 1975 by J.A. MILLER.

2. Although in the authoritative dictionaries this term does not occur as a psychological term for human instincts, I will adopt it as a metaphorical word for translating *Trieb,* which Freud distinguishes from instinct.

3. Jacques LACAN, *Introduction au commentaire de Jean Hyppolite sur la 'Verneinung' de Freud,* in *Ecrits,* Paris, Seuil, 1966, p.369. Jean HYPPOLITE's 'spoken' commentary, pp. 879-887; LACAN's 'answer' in the main text, pp. 381-399.

4. I elaborate this thesis in a work on *Sublimation* (1997).

5. An excellent study seems to me to be Joseph L. NEVICKAS, *Consciousness and Reality: Hegel's Philosophy of Subjectivity,* The Hague, Martinus Nijhoff, 1976.

6. 1900 a, 140-141. See also 1909 b, 144-145 and 1916-17 a, 294.

7. I developed this interpretation with reference to Freud and also to Lacan, in my study *La folie de Schreber,* to be published in an ensemble of Schreber studies by Peeters, Louvain.

8. I recount a personal confidence from Lacan. In 1956, after meeting Heidegger, he told me, with some regret, "Heidegger is not interested in psychoanalysis".

9. *De la psychose paranoïaque dans ses rapports avec la personnalité,* reprinted: Paris, Seuil, 1973, pp. 337ff, *inter alia.*

10. 'Un grand esprit', I heard him say, at the Binswanger Symposium in Zürich 1962, just after the death of Jung. Although disagreeing with most of Jung's ideas, I would surely agree with Lacan in calling him 'a great mind'.

THE ELDERLY PARANOIAC IN FRONT OF THE MIRROR
Reflections on the current relevance of psychoanalytic and phenomenological criteria of psychosis for the clinical psychiatrist

Jan Godderis

PSYCHOTIC DISORDERS AND THEIR EXPLANATION

Since the early 1970s, psychiatry - especially biological psychiatry - has made extraordinary leaps, and has been able to claim some remarkable successes, particularly with respect to affective disorders, and in the field of experimental pathology of the psychoses. Much information has accumulated from a number of laboratories, both psychiatric and psychological, with regard to the underlying brain mechanisms of psychotic disorders, especially of schizophrenia. Neuropsychological evidence and clinical observations have repeatedly, directly or indirectly, implicated specific brain regions (the limbic system, the temporal lobe and particularly the prefrontal cortex), as a locus of dysfunction in schizophrenia, providing some empirical support for the 'frontal-lobe' hypothesis of the disorder (Weinberger, 1991). This hypothesis dates back at least to the German neurologist Aloïs Alzheimer (1917) and to Emil Kraepelin, in whose view the basic behavioral deficit in this disorder, namely the destruction of the mainsprings of volition, was secondary to physiological pathology of the frontal cortex. In fact, we may be reminded that although Kraepelin himself focused more on the nosography than on the etiology of dementia praecox, he generally assumed that "there is a definite disease process in the brain, involving cortical neurones", whether resulting from constitutional anomaly, autointoxication, metabolic derangement, or other causes (Kraepelin, 1910, 1919).

There is general agreement that the profound disturbances in thinking, cognitive organization, perception, sustained attention and vigilance, information processing, motivation, reasoning, and affect regulation that accompany psychotic disorders of the schizophrenic type must indicate that something is wrong in the brain of at least some of our psychotic patients (Goldberg et al. 1987; Goldberg & Weinberger, 1988). This is less obvious with those disturbances which traditionally have been classified as paranoiac disorders. In any case, it is no longer sufficient to say merely that schizophrenia is a disease of the brain. Nor is it sufficient to determine the site of brain lesion; one must also take into account what might be called the level of brain events -anatomical, physiological, and biochemical.

Research, on brain mechanisms, and also in the field of developmental study, are most promising. By means of gathering physiological data, direct behavioral observations, or specialized laboratory procedures, several longitudinal samples of children have been followed from infancy to late childhood, researchers have tested the hypothesis that the amygdala and its projections to motor, autonomic, cortical and brain stem targets are important participants in temperamental vulnerability to a state called 'fear of the unfamiliar', (Kagan, J., 1996). Also, the study of psychotic thinking ('schizophrenic cognitions') by cognitive scientists, by means of experimental observation in controlled conditions, and, last but not least, the advances in understanding the genetics of some psychotic disorders, show plainly that psychopathology has finally joined the ranks of the 'mature sciences'. The standard of scientific evidence, and the ingenuity of experimental design found in the field attest to this (Matthysse et al., 1996). So say rather boastful biological psychiatrists, at least.

But where does all this leave the clinical psychiatrist? Where does it leave the psychiatrist, who believes in the psychogenesis of at least some forms of psychosis, such as Kretschmer's *sensitiver Beziehungswahn*? We are referring to that class of psychosis, which can be understood in terms of an event in the sufferer's world, or by virtue of the patient's premorbid personality, which Kretschmer called a particular predisposed "sensitive personality" (Kretschmer, 1927). We want to stress this distinction, even though this class of psychoses is very frequently (following Kurt Kolle, 1931 a, 1931 b) subsumed, together with less evidently psychogenetic forms, under the categoric heading 'schizophrenia', which unfortunately has become a label for almost any psychosis. In their reductionistic zeal for diving ever deeper into biological mechanisms, the majority of scientists forget to cast an upward glance at the complex and intriguing phenomena of psychopathology. This holds not only for those who have been exploring the correlations between psychotic phenomena and prefrontal lobe structural abnormalities, but also for those who have been assiduously investigating the various neuropsychological deficits in psychotic disorders (e.g. deficits in delayed-response task performance as a symptom of prefrontal damage). And it holds also for those who have been studying the smooth pursuit eye movement dysfunction and its connections with thought disorder and genetics (Matthysse et al., 1996) - using sophisticated techniques, such as Positron Emission Tomography and electronic devices for examining the relation of eye movements and attention. They surely lose touch thereby with some of the clinical phenomena that prompted their research study. In their efforts to coarse-grain, they try to reduce one or another set of psychotic phenomena to the 'basic' processes they have been studying, and in this effort they exemplify a simplistic and rather erroneous reductionism.

If one aims to be fully informative about schizophrenia and other psychotic disorders (such as paranoia), should one not explore phenomena which, like Janus, face in two directions at once? Should one not address the psychology of the disorder, and, at the same time, the known processes in the brain? A superficial glance at the different journals that inundate our desks monthly suffices to show that today, in psychiatry, the emphasis is on research, the experimental manipulation of variables, and the amassing of new facts. Where once in psychiatry we stood at the crossroads of theory and empirical investigation, today experimentation commands the resources of research funding and journal space, while theoretical excursions, especially meta-theoretical ones, are all but forgotten. It is rather amazing that the broad theories that dominated the past play but a very minor role in contemporary research efforts. Contemporary psychiatrical research seems quite indifferent to dynamic or psychoanalytical theories, which previously were very influential. In our opinion, psychiatry is none the better for it. Even though one cannot deny that biological research has lead to the development of powerful drugs, useful in relieving the sufferings of the mentally ill, it should nonetheless be mentioned, that much in these matters is due to serendipity.

PARANOIA: A LOST SON

Another astonishing fact is that the treatment of delusional disorder, or paranoia, which is a delusional state without other psychotic phenomena such as those seen in schizophrenic patients, and which shows signs of being understandable in terms of the pre-psychotic personality of the individual, has benefited almost not at all from the great advances in the neurobiology of psychoses. Indeed, an entry for 'Paranoia', or even its recent DSM IV-equivalent, 'Delusional disorder' is conspicuously absent from the subject index of *Psychopathology. The evolving science of mental disorder*, a recent volume issued by Cambridge University Press (Matthysse et al., 1996), where a pleiad of biological-psychiatrical coryphees celebrate the coming of age of their field. The same goes for Bolton and Hill's *Mind, Meaning and Mental Disorder* (1996), a remarkably well-written book on "the nature of causal explanation in psychology and psychiatry". Delusional disorder seems to be badly served, compared to schizophrenia, in J. Cutting's *Principles of Psychopathology: Two Worlds - Two Minds -Two Hemispheres* (1997), which nonetheless is partly meant to be a comprehensive reference book on psychopathology. Must one consider these silences as silences that speak? Must paranoia be considered a lost son?

These remarks may seem to have a bitter undertone, and could be considered as ruminations on the part of someone who is not well versed in biological psychiatry, or who did not have enough flexibility to attune himself to "the coming of age of psychiatry" or would not submit to the hegemony of DSM-psychiatry. Yet, a clinical psychiatrist, even one with a main interest in both geriatric and organic psychiatry, who should naturally have a strong interest in the progression of biological psychiatrical insights, will not always take his lead from these new approaches. This holds especially for one confronted with specific problems, such as the task of determining, for example, an elderly patient's testamentary capacity, or his ability to give or withold consent for medical treatment.

We take as the point of departure for our considerations concerning the relevance of psychoanalytic and phenomenological criteria for psychosis in geriatric psychiatry the detection of the possible influence of a paranoiac disorder on a patient's cognitions; this is a rather complicated issue for the gerontopsychiatrist, as we will show. Here, one should first compare the value of the two possible approaches, which might lead to a better understanding, and consequently, a better detection of the peculiar thinking and decision-making processes in elderly paranoiac patients.

The first approach is the account of the formation of psychotic symptoms, especially those of the acute phase (e.g. delusions and hallucinations) given by recent neuropsychological theories. Although these theories focus more on schizophrenic thought disturbances or disorders of cognition than on paranoia, they eventually might be applied to elderly paranoiac patients. The second approach will be the psychoanalytical interpretation of paranoiac disorders.

NEUROPSYCHOLOGICAL THEORIES OF PSYCHOSIS

Neuropsychological theories of schizophrenic psychosis aim to provide an explanation of the sometimes disordered, chaotic, overwhelmed, and unpredictable thoughts and behaviours of these patients, which are triggered either by anomalous sensory or perceptual experiences or by a primary feeling of mysterious significance. By contrast, delusions and hallucinations are, according to neuropsychologists, clear, unambiguous, and relatively or absolutely uninfluenced by evidence. Let us consider further contrasts. The experience of self predicted by the neuropsychological theory is fragmented and discontinuous in time; the experience of self in relation to delusions and hallucinations is likely to be coherent, and to have continuity. The experience of external reality where stimuli require constant reassessment, and where context is indecipherable, is likely to be one of uncertainty in which a high level of vigilance is required. The experience of external reality through delusions and hallucinations is likely to contain substantial predictability. Furthermore, the neuropsychological theory predicts a deficit in information-processing which renders action impossible or at best fragmented and inconsistent; delusions and hallucinations will often have clear implications for action.

For these reasons, the symptoms of at least some patients may be seen as the outcome of coping strategies which restore coherence to representations, and provide a basis for action and even for making decisions. They are possible attempts to restore the integrity of intentional-causal processes (Bolton & Hill, 1996). Several sources give evidence for this proposition.

Studies of the attributional style of deluded and hallucinating patients have shown that, compared to non-psychotic individuals, they make use of less evidence in coming to conclusions, and when making causal inferences they ascribe more global, stable, and external origins to events, as has been shown by Bentall et al. in *Paranoia and social reasoning: an attribution theory analysis* (1991). This is evident in relation to tasks that have nothing to do with their abnormal beliefs. It seems possible therefore that they are using a particular strategy for making inferences; that they have a characteristic set of internalized rules for the interpretation of events. This may be considered as a style which restricts attention to incoming stimuli and creates certainty. The attributions, at first glance, have much in common with the depressive (global, stable) cognitions that have been described in depressive patients (Beck, A.T., 1976), but they favour externality over internality, and therefore provide a better basis for action.

In *Delusional belief systems and meaning of life: a preferred reality?* (1991), Roberts compared currently deluded patients, with patients who had recovered from delusions, and with psychiatric nurses and Anglican ordinands, on measures of purpose in life and depression. The groups with the highest purpose in life scores were the deluded and the ordinands, with the nurses slightly lower, and those who had recovered from delusions substantially (and statistically significantly) lower than all other groups. The recovered patients were also the most depressed. The explanation could be in part that the delusional content of more of those with persistent delusions was grandiose or erotic, although persecutory delusions seemed to be detected with an equal frequency in both groups. One might conclude then that the delusions, although in some respects maladaptive, also provided coherence and meaning. These findings are consistent with the notion, coming from other sources, that delusions, as reparation, wish-fulfillment, defence, or compensation, may be reinforced and persist because of benefits they confer on the individual, including relief from previous defects and deficiencies. Furthermore, loss of delusion (i.e. recovery) may be resisted by some of these patients, through fear of the pain of re-entry into a realistic appraisal of life, with its awareness of compound loss, and the deprivations of chronic illness.

The introduction of experimental method and measurement from cognitive psychology clearly represents a new and welcome direction, and has gone some way in furthering the development of a model of delusion as based on abnormal thinking. Still this research, however promising, has several flaws. For the time being there has, unhappily, been little consideration of what might predispose, inaugurate, or perpetuate these abnormalities, or what the relationship may be between the contents of these thoughts and the antecedent history and experience of the patient. Besides, it seems unlikely that delusion may be considered a single entity. Attempts to dissect out its component parts, such as the one made by Brett-Jones et al. (1987), have indeed demonstrated that these vary, with considerable independence, from each other over time and during the progression of a delusional disorder. Finally, much of the recent research, most unfortunately, continues to lump together, not only different delusional types but also delusional disorder (paranoia) and schizophrenia. Definitely, more research is required on specific delusions.

PSYCHOANALYTICAL INTERPRETATION OF PARANOIAC DISORDERS

Whereas neuropsychological theories focus on defects or difficulties in thought processes, psychoanalysis has emphasized the specific contents of pre-psychotic life. Psychoanalytical theories on psychosis see delusions as resulting from conflicts between desires and drives concerning people or objects in the external world, which are unacceptable and cannot be assimilated. "Dread of an instinctual wish initiates the process of symptom formation", so said Freeman in his publication *The psychoanalyst in Psychiatry* (1988).

Following in the footsteps of Freud's influential hypothesis concerning paranoid delusions, a hypothesis formulated in his *Über einen autobiographisch beschriebenen Fall von Paranoia*, and based on his study of the memoirs of Judge Daniel Schreber, psychoanalytical theories still employ the projective defense mechanism to explain paranoid delusions (Freud, 1911 c). Projection is the attribution of one's own feelings, qualities or wishes to others on the basis of one's inability to recognize the presence of such perceptions and aspirations in oneself, and as one's own. Paranoiac delusion is therefore the reflection of unconscious impulses, desires or anxieties, which are expelled from the self and, stored elsewhere, (i.e. located in another person, group or thing). This mechanism of projection, which is one of the most primitive defense mechanisms, providing an outlet for aggressive desires on the part of the subject, and which supports his stability, would function in accordance with the rules of the mirror stage (*le stade du mirroir*). The mirror stage is an original concept derived from Henri Wallon (1931), and has been empirically validated through observations of children by Charlotte Bühler, Elsa Köhler, and the Chicago school in the thirties. The idea has been further developed and interpreted by Jacques Lacan (1948) and Alphonse De Waelhens (1972). The mirror stage is regarded by most psychoanalysts as an important category in the constitutive history of subjectivity (Wilden, 1968).

In accordance with psychoanalytical theory, the mirror stage is considered, from a psychodynamic-genetical angle, as an essential structural moment. It is the critical phase in the development where the helpless child or infant, who is *infans* (not yet capable of speech) and who cannot yet command its own body nor has any experience of being a psychic unity, receives its identity as a gift from the other, when it discovers itself in the mirror. This experience of the mirror image gives the child, who has not yet entered into the symbolic or discursive order, an experience of itself for the first time as a corporal and spiritual unity in the shape of another of the same species (the image, or *Gestalt*), another who is perfectly similar, and submissive. As a matter of fact, the mirror image faithfully follows all the movements of the child before the mirror. It lays its little hands on the mirror at the very same place, where the child lays its own hands, it smiles when the child smiles, sticks out its tongue when the child sticks its tongue out; it disappears when the child makes himself disappear. But this benificent 'gift' is also a 'poisoned present', because it is at the same time thoroughly alienating. This basic aspect of alienation consists in the radical impossibility of coïnciding completely with the mirror image, the ideal image of one's self, and can therefore unleash a violent and even fatal aggression against this image of oneself. One needs only remember the myth of Narcissus. Indeed, this aggression may turn against whomever (or whatever) confronts the subject with the non-convergence with, and therefore the inexistence of, the ideal image (De Waelhens, 1981).

In this period, the mirror image structures experience, and grants an imaginary identity to the child. The child, who has become identified when it is told one way or another, "that's you!", is inclined to treat his real counterpart (*'le semblable'*) as a mere copy of his own mirror image. This means that the other is the same as the mirror image, and vice-versa (De Waelhens, 1981). The mirror stage in the first instance concerns the mirror image of the subject itself. It is ideally finished and complete. And in that sense, the evolving person wants to coincide with it, even believes, in conformity with the logic of this stage, that he wholly commands and possesses the ideal image of himself, inasmuch as he restlessly sees it.

In the case of a fixation at this stage (that is, of a fixation of the subject in the imaginary order), this relationship to oneself and the similar other is perpetuated; one wants to preserve the coïncidence with an idealized image, held up as a mirror image. This is what a person is pursuing and anxiously protecting in the development of a paranoid personality, or in the eruption of a paranoiac psychosis. The aggressive reactions manifest in these developments are acts of regression, against both internal doubts and external challenges. Indeed, the possibility of experiencing oneself as a unity, and henceforth of having a sense of identity, relies absolutely upon it. Through the mirror stage, a person gains direct contact with, and insight into, the truth, conceived as what is immediately present and seen. Accordingly, one understands that the truth, as seen by the paranoiac patient, cannot and may not be doubted. To see is, for him, to enter an open and ready plane of self-evidence. In this context he might remind us of the well-known fact that "I know" (οἶδα) in Greek, from which "idea" is derived, is the present perfect of "I see" (ξιδῶ). In this particular view, it is clear that the truth must not be sought, or construed in dialogue with another, contingent interlocutor. In the mirror relationship, one *is the other* who is *the same*, and one is one's own absolute witness of what is to be seen.

It is clear that not only persons who are fixated at the mirror stage, but many others as well, will experience any undermining of the foundations of their bodily being, such as aging, "when the mirror image breaks as it were, or gives a deformed picture" (Messy, 1992) as barely tolerable and absolutely reprehensible. Perhaps they will react like André Gide, who at eighty wrote in *Ainsi soit-il*:

"Oh! It is important, by the way, that I do not meet myself in a *mirror* : ...
pouches under the eyes, those sunken cheeks, this faded look in the eyes.
I am just terrifying and this burdens me with a terrible melancholy".

When they perceive the inexorable crumbling seen in the material face, the anxiety about the fantasm of *le corps morcelé*, the image of the not yet unified scattered body, which was experienced retroactively by the child in the mirror stage, will rear its head again. They retreat, we hypothesize, in an act of regression, back into the mirror stage, if indeed they ever came out of their fixation. Together with their fear of becoming dependent, the spectre of the threatened fragmentation of the body again moves to the forefront of the imagination.

As one knows, this regression, through which the components of a possible latent paranoiac constellation are activated, is not as emphatic as in paranoid schizophrenia. Although the regression and withdrawal show evidence of the features of the paranoid constellation, the regression in schizophrenia is deeper still, as more primitive phases and more regressed aspects of the psychotic process come into play. The ego defects are more severe. There is evidence of psychic desintegration, with a more pronounced disappearance of the distinction of self and non-self, and a more radical distortion in the relation to reality and objects.

To the neurobiologically-oriented psychiatrist, this short and simplified psychoanalytical exposition will likely provoke some opposition, moreso than would neuropsychological approaches, which may be better articulated with neurobiological and neurophysiological data. It might likely be dismissed, in fact. Kraepelin did as much in the third volume of the 9th edition of his *Psychiatrie*, after giving a brief account of the attempts of Freud, Jung, Bleuler and Abraham to understand schizophrenic experiences and to regard them as psychogenic developments:

> I have to confess frankly, that with the best will I find myself unable to go along with the ideas of that 'metapsychiatry' which, like a complex,[1] soaks up every kind of sober clinical method of examination. As I usually tread the firm ground of direct experience, my philistine scientific conscience keeps stumbling with every step over objections, reservations and doubts, which, however, are no obstacles for the winged imagination of Freud's Followers (Kraepelin, 1923).

THE ASSESSMENT OF COMPETENCE IN THE PARANOIAC ELDERLY PATIENT

Having thus made a rough sketch of the neuropsychological and psychoanalytical perspectives, and lacking a model incorporating both perspectives, let us now turn to the important and aforementioned issue of the assessment of competence in psychotic or virtually psychotic elderly patients.

The evaluation of the competence or incompetence of a paranoid patient poses more problems than the case of depressive elderly patients, and also seems to be more difficult than with patients suffering from Alzheimer's, where primarily cognitive criteria, which can even be easily appraised by a layman (e.g. a notary in a case of testamentary competence) have to be applied (Haekens, 1998).

How is the non-expert to detect abnormality, when a pathological suspiciousness, or even a delusion lurks beneath the surface, even though the person being examined appears to be clearly conscious, without immediately recognizable formal mental disorders (for instance, paleological or pre-Aristotelian thinking) and without conspicuous behavioural disorders? A paranoiac elderly person may be imagined to make certain decisions, for instance concerning his will, or health care options, according to a deluded disposition. The pitfall for the interviewer, however, is that the patient may seem justified in his disposition, even while delusional. After all, he does not deviate from normal Aristotelian thinking and does not present any noticeable formal mental disturbances in his reasoning, in the course of a normal interview. Indeed, the world of the paranoiac patient is, at first glance, a world of coherent meaning, to such an extent that his delusions can be understandable, or *einfühlbar*, and often difficult to distinguish from a normal affective disposition. Of course, a florid and recognizable psychotic-paranoiac syndrom will always be more pronounced than the understandably vindictive or suspicious attitude of a frustrated, upset older person towards relations who are truly lacking in their affection or care, or of one who suffers from a serious loss, or faces a real threat. Nevertheless, if it concerns a manifest pathological condition, for example a delusion patently coupled with a disturbance or distortion of the patient's cognitions or interpretations, one must proceed cautiously. In such a case, it remains possible that the patient is or was not under this influence at the moment of his decision. It is not enough to show that such a condition could influence his will in principle; it must be demonstrated, by means of a careful evaluation, that such is *in concreto* the case (Haekens, 1998).

Although this is by no means a simple matter, the answer to the question of competence or incompetence can in our view be answered with a considerable degree of certainty by applying the following criteria, which must be considered in conjunction:

First of all, there is the question of the comprehensibility of the meaning given to relevant context data by the patient. Although an expression of will, for instance a testament, can give the impression of having been guided by a pathological affect, it is probably wrong to draw conclusions automatically with regard to competence. Hate or fury, dissatisfaction with society, a feeling of being rejected by everyone, can indeed exert an influence on a person's decision-making process without any need to refer to manifest dysfunctional schemes that might point to paranoia.

Secondly, attention must also be paid to the perceptual and behavioural aspects of the *status praesens* as indicative of the level of functioning. One can speak of a pathological affect, compatible with an *affekt-laden Paranoia* when a patient's negative attitude towards persons who figure in their decisions (for example, the potential heirs in a case of testamentary competence, or the physician and nurse in health care decisions) is expressed in an uncommon tone, a seemingly bizarre manner, or takes an unusual form (e.g. frantic searches for possible heirs who may have hidden themselves in the house or hospital, or refusal of food or medication for fear of poisoning).

Third, there is an even tougher criterion, weightiest of the three, for which one must take into account the patient's capacity, in an interview, to distance himself from the paranoid affect (which threatens to guide his decisions), or at least consider his ability to indicate the basis upon which the affect and/or his particular perceptions have developed. Indeed one must in this connection remember that the patient's subjective evaluation is not merely gratuitous, or without motivation. It still requires some justification. Although the paranoid patient does not owe a special justification to others, in particular to the inter-viewer or clinician, they will nevertheless in a way have to derive their legitimacy indirectly from others. Like everyone, they must appeal, at least implicitly, to the so-called 'third as witness' (*le tiers témoin*), who is ideally present at each encounter. For in a conversation one always wants to be a true, not a false, witness (unless the falsehood is intentional). If one really wants to bear witness truthfully, one should in principle always try to be in concord with this third party – the imaginary, absolute witness, who acts as an impartial 'arbiter' with regard to the truth of what is said.

However, every healthy person knows that it is impossible to coïncide with the third witness in practice, because the truth always has a necessarily intersub-jective character. This implies that one does not experience the observed as an exhaustive datum or as a flat presence, as is the case in the mirror stage. The logic of this stage is indeed, as has been emphasized by De Waelhens in his *Le duc de Saint Simon*, dependent on a vision that has an immediate and exhaustive grip upon perceived reality (De Waelhens, 1981). Phenomenology rightly emphasizes the perspectival and time-bound nature of any perception and its essential inexhaustibility. In normal cases, one will therefore assume the position of a potential observer of a reality alongside other possible observers. This means that one is willing and able to listen to others, that one acknowledges the other's right to speak, that one assumes a respectful or at least open attitude towards tempo-rality and historicity (Corveleyn, 1984). Indeed, the truth must be sought, dis-cussed, and must grow in consultation with others.

And it is precisely here that the paranoiac patient goes wrong. Presumably guided by dysfunctional schemes, to be regarded as resulting from a fixation at the mirror phase, which lead to paranoid interpretations, he has a particular conception of a truth directly given to him, in a peculiar inner attitude, just as in a flat visual perception. The perspicacious interlocutor soon notices this in the way such a patient instantly, with a glance (*augenblicklich*) understands, reads and unmasks the other in his intentions. In this, the patient has a sense of infallibility. He has an unshakable confidence in the accuracy of his perception; nothing escapes it, certainly nothing of what the other wants to hide. The eye of a paranoid patient, when one wants to question him with respect to particular affects or cognitions, seems as keen as an eagle's, his gaze as deep as a crystal ball. The truth is there, open and unconcealed to the gaze of one who can see all. Accordingly, the truth for him has no intersubjective nature at all. To him, his vision - or gaze - is the same as the perception of the truth. And so, he is incapable of listening to others. One cannot be on both sides of the mirror simultaneously. What is more, as far as listening goes, he needs it not, for he *knows* (again, the Greek οἶδα). The other who is normally called upon as witness or interlocutor to check an opinion is for him completely unnecessary. And even if he himself acts as a witness, he will be a very particular sort of witness. For a witness in the full sense of the term, as De Waelhens says, is one who, while speaking in the dialectical movement of the dialogue, is himself conveyed, together with his interlocutor, toward the truth (De Waelhens, 1981). He is someone essentially able to acknowledge that he may have been mistaken, or at least he remains willing to listen to the other and if necessary try to prove his truth.

In the paranoiac patient all this appears to be totally out of the question. He talks, even a lot, but he by no means intends to lead the other to a real conclusion of the dialogue, to a truth that issues from the dialogue (De Waelhens, 1981). In fact, this type of patient deprives the other of the right to his own expression. All this is clearly coupled with a particular attitude towards temporality and historicity. The truth unveiled to the patient in one glimpse is inalterable. His opinion is unchangeable, not subject to possible doubt. In this way, time (genesis, evolution and history) is compressed and reduced to a single spot (*rendu punctiforme*, De Waelhens, 1981). His view of the other, of reality, is therefore atemporal, ahistorical. As for the intentions of others he has always known better. He knew them early on and knows that they will never change, except perhaps under the pressure of representatives of the symbolic order, such as the police, and other authorities.

The pathogenetic mechanism just described, which can often become active in some older people, especially in those who show a clear fixation at the mirror stage, is easily recognizable enough, if the interviewer has an ear for the cadences of the condition, and takes sufficient time to unmask or break through the sometimes strikingly effective dissimulation by the patient.

With such a pathogenetic mechanism, in those elderly people who develop a reactive, circumstantially evolved paranoia, the disorder is often only temporarily present, namely during the phase of regression to the dynamics of the mirror stage. In such cases the individual's will need not yet be definitively eliminated. In this, they are unlike chronic paranoia, with its fixed and typically systematized delusions. But anyway, the integrity of the working of their free will (i.e. competence) must at least however, be questioned the moment this morbid mechanism is demonstrably present or active.

PARANOIAC PATIENTS: GOOD DISSIMULATORS

A concrete difficulty in the application of the aforementioned criteria of competence in paranoiac patients is the fact that they often dissemble their symptoms. This dissimulation can be so perfect that the less experienced interviewer will only diagnose the pathogenetic mechanism after long observation, if indeed at all.

One must make sure that every discourse (*discours*) -which in French has other connotations than in English, and means 'talk', 'conversation', 'speech' (*parole*) - is a reflection of, and is supported by more than merely conscious and rational intentions. A second discourse, speaking from the unconscious desires inevitably interferes covertly with the conscious colloquy. This second discourse is situated on another stage, which Freud has called *die andere Bühne*, and can betray itself in a number of formal splittings and distortions in the content of the manifest discourse. Take for instance, a gap in speech, which hides an important motive, which nevertheless must be presumed to understand why the patient acts one way and not otherwise in a given course of events. Indeed, as the psychiatrist or psychoanalyst knows only too well, the patient in his discourse frequently does not tell everything. Often something seemingly innocent is omitted.

This unsaid will, in the first place become clear from subtle discrepancies in content which are often barely noticeable. Much more important in this connection are the formal signals in which the unconscious motives of the patient are revealed in his discourse. In such a case, as Corveleyn emphazised in a commentary on De Waelhens's book *Le duc de Saint-Simon*, one has to listen to the patient's story, as a psychoanalyst listens to the stories of the analysand (Corveleyn, 1984). In disentangling the discrepancies, one has to appeal to references outside the patient's text, namely to the context or heteroanamnesis. But the interpretation of the formal indications must in principle be intratextual, meaning that attention will be devoted especially to two formal characteristics: the explicitness, or insistent elaboration with which the patient speaks of certain persons and their intentions, and the tone, the affective colour of the text, the rhetoric, so to speak, of the more or less conscious affective involvement. To measure this tone the interviewer will have to listen very closely to the way certain things are related. This means that one must pay attention both to the overall structure of a part of the discourse, and to the literal text (*"Il faut écouter le récit jusque dans la littéralité de ses mots"*, as De Waelhens puts it), listening for the one word that will sometimes reveal the patient's emotional position vis-à-vis another person. This may be, for instance, a word in which ironic disapproval resonates (De Waelhens, 1981). These two formal characteristics can be regarded as giving indications of the unconscious. As psychoanalytical theory rightly emphasizes, the context of the unconscious may be seen not only as a collection of fascinating curiosities, but also as a possible, coherent whole. This coherence is of course never a given, but can be traced after the fact (*nachträglich, après coup*) be and reconstructed through a careful interpretation of the body of data (Corveleyn, 1984).

It is to be expected that in such cases, specific expertise and often a good deal of time is required. As well, an evaluation of competence involving paranoiac affects or cognitions cannot always be made by means of a simple Attributional Style Questionnaire, such as the one developed by Kaney and Bentall (1989). Nor, in the framework of a cognitive-psychological examination of paranoiac patients will other tests, such as the *Emotional Stroop test* (Bentall & Kaney, 1989), necessarily be adequate. The only remaining possibility is to show that the patient is unknowingly dealing with a certain part of reality in a selective way, and that as it were, he wears magic glasses, allowing him to see certain parts of the objective world no longer as they are, but in a peculiarly changed or subjective way to suit his needs. At present, phenomenological psychiatry and the insights provided by psychoanalysis still offer a better clinical footing than those of cognitive psychology and neurobiology. In this, I agree with the psychoanalytic and existential criteria of psychosis, especially regarding the characteristics of paranoia, given by De Waelhens (1972, 1981).

NOTE

1. Kraepelin means Jung's autononomous *Gefühlsbetonter* , or 'feeling-toned' complex.

GAZE, DRIVE AND BODY IN LACAN AND MERLEAU-PONTY

Rudolf Bernet

My 'gaze' is one of those givens of the 'sensible', of the brute and primordial world, that defies the analysis into being and nothingness, into existence as consciousness and existence as a thing, and requires a complete reconstruction of philosophy.[1]

The phenomenology of Husserl has as its aim to disencumber the phenomenon from all metaphysics of a world behind appearances. This approach, however, carries with it the danger of flattening out the phenomenon into a pure given. This given may be incomplete or it may even be 'cancelled out' for the sake of another given, but the imperfection of its givenness is without mystery and without depth. Similarly, there is the danger that the subject, which holds out such a phenomenon as its correlate, will receive this givenness as what is rightfully due to it since it is the subject which is the source of its appearing. The appearance of the phenomenon neither surprises nor disconcerts the subject, who sees only what it has foreseen and receives the given armed with all its categories and doxic modalities. The flat phenomenon and the subject to which nothing ever happens form a pair.

It goes without saying that the work of Husserl contains resources other than this phenomenology of a flat and symmetric correlation between noesis and noema. Our intention, however, is neither to criticise nor defend Husserl but to direct our attention to the phenomena for which a static phenomenology and a phenomenological reduction of the epistemological kind are unable to account. These phenomena, rather than being given instantaneously in the harsh light of evidence, contain their share of obscurity, and have already travelled far before reaching the subject, whom for the most part - they only pass over in order to continue further on their way by themselves. These phenomena require a genetic phenomenology which has the task of articulating their silent genesis, maturation, and decline. These phenomena engender their own mode of appearance and give birth to the subject whom they address. And it is by their very manifestation that they distinguish themselves from the facts of the world and accomplish a phenomenological reduction to which they alone hold the secret. The suspension of the economy of natural life is thus due to a radiance of the phenomenon itself and not to a subjective decision, and thus this phenomenological reduction amounts to an abolition of the power of the subject over the phenomenon.

There are many phenomena endowed with such a revelatory power, phenomena which suspend or destroy the correlation between the subject and the world.

It is enough to think of the phenomena of the unconscious which, while directing their manifestation to the consciousness of a reflexive subject, simultaneously assert their incompossibility with the laws of that consciousness and so upset the power of the conscious subject over its own life. The unconscious is not, therefore, a noumenal substance existing in itself and manifesting itself under the form of a phenomenon of pure semblance (*Schein*), but rather it is a phenomenon *sui generis* which, while manifesting its irreducibility to consciousness in the midst of that consciousness, asserts its difference and suspends the dogmatism of so-called 'normal' consciousness.[2] Without a doubt, the same applies also to the theological phenomenon of the revelation of God in the Law, in the testimony of the prophets, and in the incarnation of his Son. One could therefore say that man's conversion to a new life through the effect of the Word of God, also has the value of a phenomenological reduction.

If we have chosen to illustrate this revelatory power of a phenomenon wending its way between obscurity and light, between truth and semblance, by an analysis of the gaze, it is principally for the two following reasons: Firstly, to demonstrate that those phenomena which upset the order of worldly appearance and our usual mode of being, are not confined to experiences of the extraordinary, but rather arise everywhere, even in visual perception, which we tend to consider as the standard example of a flat phenomenon. The second reason is that we would like to demonstrate the central place the analysis of the gaze occupies in French phenomenology and psychoanalysis, passing from Sartre to Levinas and Lacan via Merleau-Ponty and Freud. This will allow us not only to define more precisely our conception of the movement of the deep phenomenon, but equally to comprehend better the circular path of the scopic drive, which runs from the eye to the gaze and back again to the eye. A more attentive examination will be reserved for the gaze in the consideration of anamorphotic painting and psychosis, and this will afford us a better estimation of the effect of the deep phenomenon of the appearance of the invisible upon the emergence or abolition of the subject.

THE INVISIBLE GAZE OF THE OTHER (SARTRE AND LEVINAS)

The analysis of the gaze in Sartre's *Being and Nothingness*[3], well known as it is, deserves a close re-reading. It is first of all a decisive contribution to the phenomenological analysis of intersubjectivity, bringing out the fact that the presence of the other already dwells within my most secret feelings well before appearing under a recognisable form in the phenomenal world, or lending itself to a transcendental constitution. If one can still speak of a constitution with reference to this experience of shame before the gaze of the other, then the primary subject constituting it is the other and not me, and the other's power of constitution is so strong as to deprive me of mine. The other, by negating my freedom, alienates me from myself, forces me to accept as mine something alien, something in which I cannot recognise myself. Even more remarkable and more significant for our purposes, is the fact that in the midst of this experience we encounter at the same time both notions of the phenomenon that we distinguished at the beginning. The manner in which I appear to myself under the gaze of the other is undoubtedly a 'flat' phenomenon, since I am nothing other than the correlate, the end point, the object-in-itself of his gaze. But this gaze which flattens me and negates me is in its turn a phenomenon, even if it does not belong to me and I do not exercise any power over it. I apprehend this gaze as a 'deep' phenomenon, the secret and disconcerting power of which I am unable to fathom. Sartre says explicitly that this apprehension of the gaze as phenomenon implies "the pheno-menological reduction prescribed by Husserl" (1958, 258), that is to say, the bracketing of the eyes of the other as a worldly object of my perception: "if I apprehend the gaze, I cease to perceive the eyes" (Ibid.).

Accepting these premises, one cannot avoid the conclusion that the gaze of the other is an *invisible phenomenon*. The gaze is, moreover, invisible not only for me but also for the other himself. That does not mean that he is blind; he is quite on the contrary seeing, but is a seer affected by a blind spot. The gaze that sees me is attributed by me to the other, but that does not mean that it really belongs to the other. Not seeing his own gaze, the other is like myself incapable of appropriating it. It is thus more correct to say that the gaze is, or rather moves, between us. The gaze is thus really an invisible phenomenon *en route*, its manifestation is in movement, as it travels a path. A phenomenon in movement, the gaze does not always appear in the same manner at each point along its way.

But it must be admitted that we are still completely ignorant of the way in which the invisibility of the gaze is nevertheless able to phenomenalise itself, as well as of the path travelled by this phenomenalisation. We know only that this appearance of the gaze is to the detriment of the eye and of its manner of seeing or of representing worldly objects.

How can we learn more about the appearance of the gaze and the manner in which it disqualifies ordinary vision and flat phenomena? French phenomenol-ogy and psychoanalysis of the last fifty years offer us at least three different approaches which bring out phenomena which transcend the objectifying or representational power of the vision proper to the eyes. Firstly, there is the Levinasian description of the manner in which the Face of the Other — irreducible to its visible form — appeals to my ethical responsibility. Secondly, there is the Merleau-Pontian analysis of the interrogative gaze of things and of the manner in which, for example, the painter responds to this gaze in creating a work of art. Finally, there is the approach common to Sartre and Lacan which situates the gaze in the path of the scopic drive, especially as it manifests itself in voyeurism. In what follows we will draw freely from these three sources with the sole aim of better defining the deep phenomenon of the gaze and without being too greatly concerned to do justice to the detailed analyses of the authors mentioned.

It could be shown in more detail how much Levinas's thought concerning the appearance of the Other (as an untouchable Face and not as a recognisable form or figure, as a traumatising command, as an event outside the economy of the world, as a source of an infinite desire, etc.) owes to Sartre's analysis of the gaze and of its irreducibility to the eye.[4] But then it would also be necessary to demonstrate what it is that differentiates the subject according to Sartre, a "for-itself" animated by a *conatus essendi*, from the subject according to Levinas, a receptivity and a response originating in the Other with whom it maintains a "relation without relation". But this is not our purpose here. All we wish to retain from these descriptions is simply the fundamental incapacity of representational, intentional and objectifying consciousness to account for the appearance of the Other. It can be said that no-one has more relentlessly denounced the pretensions of intentional consciousness than Levinas, but it would be more just to say that no one has worked harder to give a positive sense to the appearance of the Other as 'mystery', 'height', 'trace', 'infinity', 'appeal', etc. It is not Levinas, but the epiphany of the Face of the Other which destroys and negates intentional consciousness, and its way of perceiving things and of transforming them into controllable objects. It is the rising up of the Other which creates at once the conditions of its own appearance and those of the subject capable of responding to its commandments.

Accepting that the Face of the Other is, just like his gaze, a deep phenomenon, that which must most of all be kept in mind about its mode of appearance is the circular path in which activity and passivity are intimately intertwined. In effect, one cannot separate the response aroused by the appearance of the Other from the appearance itself, and in this response the passivity of the submission to a commandment necessarily prolongs itself in the activity of giving oneself to the Other. Rather than speaking, as Sartre does, of an objectifying and petrifying negation of the subject by the gaze of the other, Levinas makes us attentive to the profound transformation of the subject by the appearance of the Other. The response to the gaze of the Other thus cannot consist in paying him back in like kind, that is to say, in negating him in his turn; the response, for Levinas, is not symmetrical to the appeal. Similarly, the 'vulnerability' of the subject with regard to the gaze of the other does not at all have the same sense for Sartre and Levinas, since for Levinas the trauma of the violent intrusion of the Other into the secret of my intimacy gives birth to a new sensibility which is the expression of my 'essance' for the Other. In the deep phenomena, the appearance of the Other comes from the Other and returns to the Other, alter-ing everything as it passes by. That which, on the other hand, Levinas takes over from Sartre and which reveals itself to be of the highest importance, is that the gaze of the Other, as unfathomable and invisible as it is, is not the sign of any interior richness nor of an overflowing glory. If the gaze of the Other takes hold of me in so poignant a manner, it is because it testifies to a lack and a destitution, it commands by supplication, it is more worried than dominating, and is never self-sufficient.

What is peculiar and even paradoxical about the manifestation of the Other is that it imposes its own mode of appearance, which puts an end to the egoic power of apprehension and even to the subjective openness to a phenomenon, and yet, for all that, is not satisfied by this appearance, but looks for something in return and demands a response. The gaze of the Other is invisible in the sense that it is measureless, that is to say without a stable measure by which my response could regulate itself. That which is invisible to the eyes is thus visible in its own way; the gaze of the Other gives birth to a gaze which is other than that of thematising contemplation. The gaze of the Other thus truly accomplishes a phenomenological reduction of vision since it leads the perception of worldly objects back to the invisible gaze which dwells in the Other and perhaps even in things.

THE GAZE OF THINGS AND THE INVISIBLE FLESH OF THE WORLD (MERLEAU-PONTY)

The analysis of the gaze and of the Face of the Other in Sartre and Levinas leads us logically to the analysis of the invisible gaze of things which never ceased to haunt the thought of *Merleau-Ponty*.[5] One can perhaps say that for Merleau-Ponty the exchange of gazes between subjects is but a particular case of the exchange of gazes between things and the subject or even between the things themselves. However, claiming that this approach leads to an attribution of subjectivity to things would be to mistake totally the intention of Merleau-Ponty, since he is concerned, quite on the contrary, with a primitive and anonymous intercorporeity which precedes the division between subject and object, between the gaze and the visible. That which interests Merleau-Ponty is a perception without subject or, more precisely, the genesis or emergence of vision among things, of a vision which sees 'according to' (*selon*) wild essences" (*essences sauvages*) or according to the 'invisible flesh' (*chair invisible*) of things, and not according to the subjective categories of the understanding, or the existentials of Dasein. Thus the Sartrean opposition between the gaze of the other and my perception, by which Levinas was still greatly inspired, disappears in favour of one single gaze, which in a universal 'narcissism' of vision circulates tirelessly between the body and things, their common essence being that both are at once seeing and seen. Contrary to Levinas, who proscribed all relations of symmetry or of reciprocity between subjects, Merleau-Ponty celebrates a universal sensible reversibility which takes hold of all bodies and binds them together.

Does this mean that the Levinasian notion of separation finds itself abolished in favour of a notion of fusion and ontological in-difference? Not at all. According to Merleau-Ponty sensible reflexivity is, in effect, a reflexivity that is always incomplete, a unity of 'incompossibles'. As for Levinas, the proximity of which Merleau-Ponty speaks does not do away with either difference or distance. Merleau-Ponty even radicalises the Levinasian idea that the appearance of that which appears always addresses itself to the other rather than to itself, by insisting upon the fact that what appears does not appear from itself but from a common ground which it shares with that to which it appears. This common ground of appearance, which escapes the visibility of representational consciousness, is precisely that which Merleau-Ponty calls 'the invisible' or, more exactly, the invisible 'flesh of the world'. This invisible flesh of the world is inhabited by an incarnate logic of the sensible, which unites the multiple dimensions of sensing, yet does not recognize the principles of identity and non-contradiction. Before being expressed in the language of literature or philosophy, before offering itself to the gaze in painting, this invisible flesh of the world makes itself felt in the silent experience of a 'perceptual faith' (*foi perceptive*) which, questioning itself about its gaps and lacks, sets about a search for an equilibrium or order while completely rejecting any pre-established order.

According to Merleau-Ponty, the invisible thus inhabits every body and even every part of the body; it nestles itself in the interstices between that which is seeing in that body, and that which is visible. It is that empty space and that absent time which prevent the body totally curling up into itself. But the invisible is also the abysmal emptiness, straddled, but not filled-in, by the vision which passes from one body to another. Insofar as it is the invisible source of the visible, this invisible is unable, in principle, to make itself visible, and insofar as it is at any time a particular invisible it adheres to the surface of the visible as the reverse side of something adheres to the facing side. It is thus not simply the gaze which is invisible (to the gaze of another as well as to itself) but also the being in its entirety from which this invisible gaze arises. Thus the gaze is an invisible *in actu* or, more precisely, in movement, which, wandering about in the midst of visible bodies on an endless quest, takes on different forms, all the while remaining immersed in the elemental matter of the invisible flesh of the world.

It is without a doubt the phenomenon of *painting* which provides this philosophy of the invisible gaze with its clearest illustration.[6] Painting has in effect the "magic" power to make the invisible visible (1964, 166). It puts itself at the service of being in order to make to appear its 'dehiscence', its multiple and 'incompossible' 'dimensions'. It assembles these dimensions and establishes between them "systems of equivalencies", it confers on a flat and immobile image, the power to let the 'depth' of things and the 'movement' of bodies be seen. Manipulating light and shadow, colour and line, juxtaposing brushstrokes in order to reveal the thickness of things, making bodies 'encroach' upon one another in a tremendous "deflagration of Being", painting makes visible the invisible as invisible, that is, while preserving all of its 'enigma'. It unfolds a space which is neither the focal space of thematising consciousness, nor the space of perspective such as geometry understands it, but the 'vibrant' space with which the thing surrounds itself in order to join up with another thing while "eclipsing it".

Keeping to our intention, we want to pay special attention to the part played by the gaze in this Merleau-Pontian understanding of painting as the sensible phenomenon of the essence of the flesh of the world. For Merleau-Ponty, the appearance of the thing, to the degree that this appearance testifies to the invisible of the thing, is quite equivalent to a gaze (1964, 166, 167). The mountain of Sainte-Victoire 'looks' at Cézanne in showing itself to him in its unfathomable mystery, its startling visual incoherencies, in the texture of its mass composed of motley elements. This gaze of the thing is thus at once an interrogation and an invitation directed at the painter and more precisely at his body, at his hand. It gives 'birth' to the painter (1964, 181) who "restores to the visible through the offices of an agile hand" that which has moved him (1964, 165). The appearance of the thing under the form of a deflagration, sets on fire the hand which, in the act of painting, restores to the visible world the invisible by which it has been touched. Or to say the same thing with a phrase of Klee's that Merleau-Ponty liked to cite:

> "[A] Certain fire pretends to be alive; it awakens. Working its way along the hand as its conductor, it reaches the support and engulfs it; then a leaping spark closes the circle it was to trace, coming back to the eye, and beyond." (1964, 188)

The appearance of the thing under the form of an invisible and dazzling gaze thus follows a circular path: the gaze of the thing invests the body of the painter with its interrogative force and arouses in him that which Merleau-Ponty, in Proustian language, calls an 'internal equivalent' (1964, 164), something which, expressed in the form of painting, restores to the thing its enigmatic gaze. It is unnecessary to add that this circle, travelled by the appearance or the deep phenomenon of the thing, never quite closes, and that no painting of Cézanne is identical to the gaze of the mountain of Sainte-Victoire.

It is necessary, on the other hand, to emphasise the fact that here the subject or, more precisely, the eye and the hand of the painter, play the secondary but nevertheless essential role of a relay-station or mediator in the circuit of appearance which runs from the thing to the painting. The thing appears "in the midst" of the things of the world and reverberates in those things; its invisible, instead of holding the thing captive to itself, on the contrary, relates it to the other things of the world in the form of an 'encroachment' (*empiétment*) or of a chiasmatic 'interweaving' (*entrelacs*). The painting magnifies this mode of appearance of the thing, it is a "visible of the second power"(1964, 164) because in it the gaze of the thing addresses itself to a body capable not only of reflecting and sensing, but also of expressing the invisible 'wild essence' of the thing. One could as well say that the thing itself cannot apprehend its own gaze, and that the painting allows this gaze to be seen only in the form of an equivalent, which is, however, never to be confused with the invisible of the thing. This does not exclude that the picture is a true equivalent of the thing, since the picture, in its turn, interrogates the gaze of the spectator. The gaze or, more exactly, the multiple *gazes of the picture* arouse and conduct the gaze of the spectator who, displaced from his central point of view and his frontal and thematising vision, from now on sees "according to the picture" (1964, 164). What we have said concerning the relation between the *thing* and the picture, thus applies as well to the relation between the *spectator* and the picture: the gaze of the spectator which replies to the gaze of the picture is invisible in and to itself; only within the picture, and transformed by the picture, can the gaze recover itself. But this return to itself is at the same time an exile, since the gaze of the spectator always bears with it the trace of the gaze of the picture. In contrast with the gaze of the other which, according to the description of Sartre, negates the subject, the gaze of the picture (like the gaze of the thing) reverses the subject like a glove pulled inside out, exposing the inside while at the same time internalising the exterior of the picture (or of the thing).

THE GAZE OF THE PICTURE AND THE CIRCUIT OF THE SCOPIC DRIVE (FREUD AND LACAN)

A most striking illustration of this transformation of the spectator by the gaze of the picture is provided by the canvas by Holbein entitled *The Ambassadors*. Taking his inspiration to large extent from Baltrusaitis'[7] famous work, and having just completed reading Merleau-Ponty's *The Visible and the Invisible* and *Eye and Mind*, Lacan pauses at length before this canvas in his seminar of 1964[8]. This picture by Holbein is in reality a double picture, the expression of two different gazes which impose upon the spectator two incompossible modes of vision. First, there is the gaze of the picture viewed from the front representing two persons richly attired and surrounded by objects, the refined symbolism of which evokes the different forms of human vanity. But there is also in the foreground of the painting the gaze of the anamorphotic object which only strikes the spectator at the moment he turns away from the picture. Only then does the distortion of the perspective correct itself, such that the unusual object becomes upright and shows itself to be a Death's Head. If the first gaze of the picture confirms the good conscience of the spectator, the second shakes him to the foundations of his being since it reveals his own being-towards-death. This makes one think of a phrase in Heidegger's *Sein und Zeit* [9] that can be read as a commentary on this gaze of death which strikes the spectator at the very moment he turns away from the contemplation of the picture:

> "But just as he who flees in the face of death is pursued by it even as he evades it, and just as in turning away from it he must see it none the less..."

There is no need to go into a detailed analysis of this picture overloaded with symbolic meanings, in order to understand the phenomenological reduction that its double gaze effects. This reduction is in the first place directed to the subject and consists in displacing the distant and impartial spectator from his position in order to force him to enter into the picture and to allow himself be contaminated by what is seen. The gaze of the picture comes up on the subject from behind, it takes him by surprise and leads him back to his authentic mode of being as a finite *Dasein*. But one could also say that through its double gaze the picture exhibits the phenomenological reduction itself: indeed it shows how a thematic vision gives way to a vision which allows the invisible face of the world to be seen. It is remarkable to note that in the anamorphosis, which is the result of clever geometric calculation, the laws of perspective turn against their own pretension to represent faithfully the reality of the visible world. In the anamorphosis one witnesses the self-destruction of the flat phenomenon of subjective perspective in favour of the deep phenomenon of the invisible gaze of the picture and the thing.

Lacan pursues these reflections on the phenomenological reduction carried out by the painting, even if he does not himself employ the term 'reduction'. In describing how the 'gesture' of the painter lets a rain of touches of colour fall from his brush, he does however use the word 'suspension'. Painting, just like the gestures of the dancers in Chinese ballet, also mentioned by Lacan, is a movement made up of 'suspended' acts, that is to say, of acts which rather than being directed to worldly things with the intention of transforming them, want only to "allow something to be seen" (donner à voir). This is why Lacan repeatedly says that a suspended act is something other than an interrupted act (1981, 114-116). What is it, then, that the picture allows to be seen? The response of Lacan is perhaps surprising: it lets the drive or the desire to see be seen. But then, by what sleight of hand or short-circuit can Lacan end up identifying the manifestation of the invisible "flesh of the world" according to Merleau-Ponty with the appearance of the scopic drive according to Freud?

The Lacanian theory of the drive such as it is laid out in Seminar XI (1981, 65-200) is presented as a long commentary on Freud's text *Instincts and their Vicissitudes* (1915 c)[10]. As is well known, this difficult and dense text by Freud deals with, among other things, the essential characteristics of drive - the 'pressure', the 'aim', the 'object', and the 'source' of the drive, as well as those vicissitudes of the drive that Freud terms 'reversal into the contrary', 'turning back against one's own person', 'repression' and 'sublimation'. Besides this, Freud also deals with the 'pleasure principle', 'love' and 'auto-eroticism', as well as the opposition between subject and object, between pleasure and un-pleasure, between activity and passivity. Freud especially emphasises the fact that the reversal into the contrary and the turning against one's own person, rather than excluding each other, are vicissitudes which can occur at the same time within one and the same drive. This is why the study of such multifaceted phenomena as sado/masochism and voyeurism/exhibitionism takes up such a large part of the text. The result of this is that a drive such as the 'drive to see' (*Schautrieb*) combines at once an active form (seeing), a passive form (being seen), and an intermediary form (letting oneself be seen). Similarly, its object can be either a 'foreign object' as in voyeurism, or 'one's own object' as in exhibitionism, or even both at once, as in primitive auto-eroticism which precedes the differentiation between voyeurism and exhibitionism. In insisting, firstly, upon the fact that these forms of voyeurism and exhibitionism ought not to be confused with the sexual perversions bearing the same name and, secondly, upon the fact that 'seeing', 'being seen' and 'letting oneself be seen' are vicissitudes of one and the same drive, Freud thus confirms Merleau-Ponty's intuition that vision travels in an open 'circle' which brings into play different bodies and gazes. For Freud, as for Merleau-Ponty, it is the case that to see is to move and that this movement is the movement of a 'drive' (Freud) or of a 'desire' (Merleau-Ponty) which precedes and destabilises the subject of inten-tional consciousness.

What we have called Lacan's 'short-circuit' is thus not as arbitrary as it first seems and is, very precisely, the development of a theory of the 'circuit' of the drive which draws its inspiration conjointly from Freud and Merleau-Ponty. Without going into the details of this theory, one can retain from it at least the idea that the drive travels in a circular path which has its source in an erogenous zone of one's own body, turns about an irremediably lost object (called the *objet a*) and - unable to find satisfaction in this elusive object which moreover depends on the other - turns back on itself and passes through the surface of the body whence it came. The inaccessible object around which the circuit of the scopic drive turns is none other than the gaze. Seeking to see that which cannot be seen, namely the invisible gaze of the other, the scopic drive retraces its steps, but without ever completely catching up with itself. Thus the exhibitionist is not content with the fright of his victim, but he derives pleasure from the victim insofar as he or she is given over to his gaze, he enjoys his own gaze such as it manifests itself in the being-gazed-at of his victim (1981, 182). It is only at the moment in which the gaze, set in motion by the drive to see (that is, to see the gaze of the other) returns to its bodily source, thus to the eye as an erogenous zone, that the scopic drive gives birth to a subject Lacan calls "the acephalic subject... of the drive" (1981, 181). Under the pretext of a commentary on Freud, Lacan actually places himself in the wake of the Merleau-Pontian conception of a pre-subjective narcissism of vision to which the invisible flesh of the world holds the secret. And there is nothing to prevent us from going a step further and understanding the circuit of the scopic drive as the path of the appearance of the invisible gaze; something we have described as a 'way' in which the 'deep' phenomenon comes to appearance.

Is there thus nothing to be learnt from Lacan that we do not already know? In order to persuade us of the contrary, it is enough to mention the manner in which Lacan, in another of those astounding shortcuts with which he is familiar, ties the sort of phenomenological reduction performed by the painting to the sublimation of the scopic drive. In making the invisible gaze appear, the picture at once forces the desire to see "to lay down its weapons" (1981, 101). This is explained, above all, by the fact that for Lacan the picture manifests the gaze as a 'lure' (*leurre*) or as a nothing which owes all its power of fascination to the imaginary or symbolic veil which covers it. For Lacan this veil is torn as soon as the picture allows itself to be seen as the *trompe-l'oeil* that it is; that is to say, as a veil which represents nothing other than a veil, such as the celebrated painting of Parrhasios (1981, 103 and 111-112). The phenomenological reduction, allowing the appearance to appear 'as appearance', and thus depriving the scopic drive of all, even illusory, satisfaction, then turns this drive towards another aim, i.e. to that aesthetic pleasure which Lacan terms 'Apollinian' (1981, 101). This sublimation which 'pacifies' the desire to see by revealing to it, through the (indispensable!) mediation of the picture, its illusory support, is thus a phenomenological reduction which puts desire out of play while bringing to appearance its secret mechanism. The gaze of the picture unmasked as a *trompe-l'oeil* and yet preserved in a sublimated pleasure is, moreover, for Lacan the very model of the position of the psychoanalyst in therapy.

But what becomes of the subject in this reduction-sublimation performed by the gaze of the picture? It seems that Lacan would agree with Sartre in saying that, outside of the picture (or outside of the situation of psychoanalytic therapy), the gaze of the other can only annihilate the subject. In order to better understand what it means for the subject to be seen not directly by the other as a voyeur, but by the gaze which comes from a picture, Lacan employs the example of mimetism, which amounts to the "subject being inserted in a function whose exercise grasps it" (1981, 100). From this he concludes that the picture takes hold of the subject and that under its gaze, the subject in its turn becomes a picture. It is enough to think of the example of the anamorphosis and to remember what Merleau-Ponty called a seeing "according to the picture", for the Lacanian definition of the picture as "the function in which the subject has to map himself as such" (1981, 100) to lose some of its obscurity. Mapping itself in the lure of the picture as being nothing, the subject comes the closest to the truth of its being, and this is in any case something other than allowing itself to be negated by the other (Sartre) or sacrificing itself for the other (Levinas). But it is true that in this Lacanian conception of the invisible gaze of the picture, the path of the gaze is blocked as it is brought to a halt before the manifestation of the authentic non-being or of the 'lack' of the desiring subject. For Merleau-Ponty, by contrast, this gaze only passes through the subject, it rushes into its constitutive divergence (*écart*), only in order to rebound far away from the subject. In such a conception, the invisible gaze is not susceptible to being brought to a rest or being suspended, since it straddles the gaps, and circulates in a universe where, despite all the incompatibilities or 'incompossibilities', everything holds together. For Lacan, on the other hand, nothing holds together with anything else except by the arbitrary and conventional force of the law of the signifier.

THE GAZE IN PSYCHOSIS

What could this analysis of the appearance of the gaze and its impact upon the genesis of the subject teach us about psychosis? What difference is there, on the one hand, between the gaze of the other described by Sartre, Levinas, and Lacan, as well as the gaze of the thing and of the picture that we have encountered in the analyses of Merleau-Ponty and Lacan, and, on the other hand, the gaze - hallucinated or not - such as a psychotic subject experiences it? Pretending that we have never encountered a psychotic patient and that we have only a very vague idea of the difference between schizophrenia and paranoia, and pretending also that we have only heard it said that psychosis is characterised by a basic difficulty in accepting the subjective lack which results from all absence, what can we then say about the nature of the gaze in psychosis? What could we reply to the psychiatrist who, proud of his experience, asserts that the fact of feeling oneself to be gazed at by a mountain points to evidence of a persecution delirium, and that Cézanne, great painter that he was, must have been paranoid?

Actually, we could already make the essential point that someone who rejects absence cannot acknowledge the gaze. And we could develop this assertion with the help of each of the analyses of the gaze to which we have referred. Relying on Sartre, we could, without fear of error, claim that the psychotic confuses the gaze with the eye. Referring to Levinas, we could add that the eye, deprived of all personal alterity, does not exercise any sort of appeal on the subject. With Merleau-Ponty, we could insist upon the fact that without either appeal or interrogation, the invisible gaze can only be a blind eye and that this eye is incapable of stimulating a response which would form a restitution. Merleau-Ponty would certainly like to add that without the reversibility set in motion by the *invisible* flesh of the *world*, there can be no equivalence between things, no communication between people, and no vision the path of which would follow the trace of desire. The vision of an eye deprived of the invisible would be like a voyage interrupted before departing, and psychotic delusions would be nothing other than a desperate and impotent attempt to reconstitute the lost reality of the common world.[11]

Turning now to the experts in this matter (i.e. Freud and Lacan) the inexperienced philosophers whose hesitant progress we have pretended to follow, are not greatly disoriented. Despite their distrust of Freud's overly mechanistic or economic explanation of the processes of psychic life, they would willingly recognise that the psychotic, deprived of access to the alterity of the other and his reality, can only find himself in that position of primitive auto-eroticism, which, as we have seen, precedes the active and passive form of the drive. They would have no more difficulty in understanding that in this auto-eroticism, which is characteristic of psychosis for Freud, the source, object, and subject of the drive, must remain confused. In the case of the scopic drive, this means that the eye (erogenous source) is confused with the gaze (object) and that the subject is confused with the other: this withdrawal into a position this side of the distinction between seeing and being-seen, between myself and the other, as well as between the word and the thing, leads quite logically to the feeling that the seductive gaze of the other (of which it has been said that he is an '*Augenverdreher*') is inside one's own eye ('*verdrehte Augen*'). (1915 e) One can thus easily understand why a patient of mine scrutinises his own eye in the mirror at length, intensely, to the point of vertigo.

Our philosophers, beginners in the field of psychoanalysis, would even more willingly follow in the footsteps of Lacan. They would experience no difficulty in understanding that the circuit of the drive, having to be supported by an elusive and irremediably lost object, cannot even get underway when it is deprived of such an absent object. Rather than returning to its source after having passed around the *object a*, as required by the narcissistic essence of the drive, the drive has no other alternative but to *stay* with itself. Does this mean, as Aulagnier suggests, that the object, the subject and the subject's own body are dissolved into the same primitive fog she terms the '*pictogramme*'?[12] Nothing is less certain for Lacan. Lacan would say rather that an object detached from the circuit of the drive, and a fortiori from the network of signifiers, nevertheless remains an object, even if this object belongs to what he calls the *réel*. If the drive and desire live, as Merleau-Ponty claims, from the "invisible flesh of the world", then such an object can only be an extra-terrestrial one. Indeed, is this not the way in which the voice and the gaze appear in the hallucinations of the psychotic, that is to say, as impersonal objects, without sender or addressee? And do not these 'objects' traverse the psychotic's own body in the way that a wave traverses a radio receiver or a photographic plate? Is this to say that the psychotic subject is to be identified with this mechanical receiver? Certainly not, since he or she is able to give an account of these messages and complains of the exhaustion and derangement that this incessant bombardment by missiles from beyond the world causes him or her. This presupposes that instead of placing him- or herself within the message, the psychotic escapes from it in order to account for it. In other words, he or she is totally incapable of recognising in the murmur of this continuous commotion of voices and gazes, the work of a drive which has its source in his or her own libidinal body.

Our philosophers, inexperienced but not stupid, may now ask what becomes of the drive in psychosis? In effect, what becomes of the scopic drive when the invisible gaze becomes the eye of a dead fish, when the other, rather than living in the same world, is a mere machine, and when one's own body no longer responds to the siren song of pleasure? Remembering the Freudian explication of the origin of anxiety, our philosopher friends may be tempted to put forward the hypothesis that a drive deprived of an object exercising an attraction or expressing an appeal, and deprived of an erogenous zone upon which to return in order to console itself for its necessary failure, can only *poison* itself. Instead of a pictogram, there would therefore be only a wound. And this is indeed what psychotics say when they agree to talk to us. In the place of an erogenous zone, they have holes which leak and ooze, the secretions of which are at most a matter of practical concern. As regards the drive, they recognise nothing that attracts or motivates them, but only that which compels them. And when they speak of themselves, they employ the language of the judge or of the scientist, and often express relief at the idea of getting rid of this undesirable and indignant companion. The psychotic thus has something in common with the pervert who refuses, in Lacan's words, his condition of being an "acephalic and split subject of the drive". Both consider themselves as subjects-outside-drive, the one the better to enjoy himself and the other the better to suffer. In both cases, the circuit of the drive is fragmented or interrupted and not suspended as in sublimation. But it is true that the proximity of sublimation, perversion, and psychosis makes one think....

Our philosopher friends, impatient to return to what they are more familiar with, press us not to go any further with this interrogation of the sort of gaze found in psychosis and urge us to come to a close; that is, to close the circuit of our reflections. This circuit has lead us to better understand that the power of the deep phenomenon is commensurate with the phenomenological reduction which brings it to appearance, and is commensurate also with the destruction of the power of a subject who behaves as the master of phenomena. We have also come to realise that it is not only philosophy that is concerned with the phenomenological reduction, and that painting - rather than limiting itself to the accomplishment of the phenomenological reduction - even has the power to make it appear as such. It is true, however, that the painting does not *say* what the phenomenon is, nor what the phenomenological reduction is. Our elucidation of the deep phenomenon in the light of the invisible gaze, as well as our borrowings from Sartre, Levinas, Merleau-Ponty, Freud and Lacan, have also allowed us to better understand that the deep phenomenon is continually in movement and lacks any specific content. The gaze of the other, the Face of the Other, the appearance of the thing on its invisible ground, and the scopic drive as the search for an inaccessible and illusory gaze, all deserve to be called deep phenomena. Finally, we have also at least glimpsed how the deep phenomenon brings about a subject while taking away from it any stable and complete hold it has upon the phenomenon and upon itself. This genesis of the subject by the deep phenomenon has revealed itself to be a radical transformation of the egoic subject of intentional consciousness and a sublimation of its desire to see. In the case where this transformation is both experienced and rejected by the subject, that subject risks falling into psychosis. When in psychosis the tension between the flat phenomenon and the deep phenomenon, between the conscious subject and the split subject of the drive is abolished, then the appearing confuses itself with that which appears and this too simple apparition is the apparition of the inhuman.

(translated from the French By Paul Crowe and the author)

NOTES

1. M. Merleau-Ponty, *The Visible and the Invisible*, trans. A. Lingis, Northwestern University Press, Evanston, 1968, p.193, transl. mod.
2. Cf. R. Bernet, "Husserls Begriff des Phantasiebewusstseins als Fundierung von Freuds Begriff des Unbewussten", in Ch. Jamme (Hrsg.), *Grundlinien der Vernunftkritik*, Suhrkamp, Frankfurt a.M., 1997, pp. 277-306.
3. J.-P. Sartre, *Being and Nothingness, An Essay on Phenomenological Ontology*, Trans. Hazel E. Barnes, Routledge, London, 1958, pp. 252-303.
4. Cf. E. Levinas, *Totality and Infinity. An Essay on Exeriority*, trans. A. Lingis, Duquesne University Press, Pittsburgh, 1969; *Otherwise than Being or Beyond Essence*, trans. A. Lingis, Martinus Nijhoff, The Hague, 1981.
5. Cf. M. Merleau-Ponty, *The Phenomenology of Perception*, trans. Colin Smith, Routledge, London, 1962, pp. 81-86, 213-215, 317-327; and above all "The Eye and the Mind", trans. Carleton Dallery, in *The Primacy of Perception*, ed. James M. Edie, Northwestern University Press, Evanston 1964, pp.159-190; as well as *The Visible and the Invisible*, trans. Alphonso Lingis, Northwestern University Press, Evanston, 1968.
6. Cf. M. Merleau-Ponty, *The Eye and the Mind* ; op cit also "The Doubt of Cézanne", in *Sense and Nonsense*, trans Hubert L. Dreyfus and Patricia Allen Dreyfus, Northwestern University Press, Evanston, 1964, pp. 9-25.
7. J. Baltrusaitis, *Anamorphoses ou Thaumaturgus opticus*, Flammarion (coll. "Champs"), Paris, 1996, pp.125-160.
8. J. Lacan, *The Four Fundamental Concepts of Psycho-Analysis*, (Seminar XI) trans. Alan Sheridan, Norton, New York and London, 1981, pp. 79-90. (hereafter S XI)
9. M. Heidegger, *Being and Time*, trans. J. Macquarrie and E. Robinson, New York, Harper and Row, 1962, p. 477.
10. Cf. also the helpful commentary by J. Laplanche, *Vie et mort en psychanalyse*, Flam-

marion, Paris, 1970, p. 150-160.

11. Cf. R. Bernet, "Délire et réalité dans la psychose", in: *Etudes phénoménologiques*, 15, Ousia, Bruxelles, 1992, pp. 25-54.

12. Cf. P. Castoriadis-Aulagnier, La violence de l'interpretation. Du pictogramme à l'énoncé, P.U.F., Paris, 1975.

ETHICAL ISSUES IN THE SCHREBER CASE

Zvi Lothane, MD

Whether mentally healthy or mentally ill, we live with persons in groups (families, societies, nations), ruled by laws of nature or biology, laws of the mind or psychology, and laws of conduct or morality (i.e. the laws of the ascending hierarchy of body, mind and ethics). Whereas the body, as the condition of biological life, and the mind, as the instrument of psychological functioning, are beyond good and evil, the same cannot be said of the conduct of persons (Lothane, 1994, 1997 a). The evolution of mankind culminates in the ethical, which gives a normative definition of human conduct as what ought and ought not to be: good or bad, right or wrong. Apart from ethics, walking away with a book from a store is the same conduct whether you pay for it or not; likewise, in behavioral terms, lying is nothing but speaking, but morally, it is speaking falsely with the intent to deceive. Such misconduct is labeled by psychiatry as illness, by religion as sin, by law as crime, by ethics as vice, and by psychoanalysis as neurosis.

The normative criterion in psychology is embodied in perception, which helps us tell truth from error, reality from illusion, delusion, and dream (Lothane, 1982 a). The normative criterion in ethics is assured by conscience, or moral consciousness, which helps us to choose the morally right form wrong. Both perception and conscience are forms of knowledge. In French, *conscience* is the word for both consciousness and conscience, while the German *Gewissen* is related to *Wissen*, i.e. knowledge or awareness. While knowledge of things is assured by perceptual and cognitive intelligence, knowledge of persons is aided by emotional intelligence (Goleman, 1995) which fuses cognition, feelings, and instinctual drives into the compound emotions of pleasure (love, happiness) and unpleasure (anxiety, depression, rage), the motivators of social conduct. The most important emotion or conduct is love; but it is more than an emotion, it is a way of life, a mode of knowing, being, doing, and having (Lothane, 1982 b, 1983, 1987 a, 1987 b, 1987 c, 1989 a, 1998 b).

By 1917 Freud realized that, in contradistinction to symptoms of medical illness, "psychical (or psychogenic) symptoms and psychical illness are *acts* detrimental, or at least useless, to the subject's life as a whole" (emphasis added). I have used Freud's definition to underscore the following differences:

There are both monadic and dyadic facts in human physiology and psychology. ... Thinking — and the subspecies imagining, remembering and dreaming — occur as a monadic, self-contained activity. But here a momentous and radical change takes place: the tools of thinking, that is words, are learnt in the course of dyadic, or interpersonal, development. Therefore thinking always oscillates between being a monologue and a dialogue. ... *A fortiori,* speaking and listening as human situations — the analytic situation included — cannot but be inherently dyadic (Lothane, 1997 d, 176).

Symptoms considered as dyadic are acts of communication: gestures and speeches transmitted from actor to audience, from speaker to listener, from sender to receiver.

Since love is a dyadic (or relational), and not a monadic phenomenon, it follows that sexuality is necessarily a relational phenomenon as well (Lothane, 1992 a). And since love is also a supreme moral value, cognitive and emotional intelligence should also include moral intelligence, the fully developed capacity to judge right and wrong, to practice the virtues of love, wisdom, justice, and compassion, in short, good character and good conduct. I have applied these principles to my reading of Schreber (Lothane, 1992 b, chapter 9; Lothane, 1992 c).

Psychiatry and psychoanalysis are ruled by ethics extrinsically, as is seen in the rules governing confidentiality, the exchange of sex or money between doctor and patient, in the ethics of drug use, and commitment procedures. However, since the relation between conduct and morals is an intrinsic one, classification and the diagnosis of disorders in psychiatry, and the assurance of quality of life need to be complemented by an understanding of the evolution of the moral sense in the individual and in society. As well, we need insight into the ethical structure of emotional disorder, especially in view of the current advances in neuroscience, and the trend to remedicalize psychiatry, and to redefine the diagnostic system.

Psychiatry and psychoanalysis, then, as therapeutic, investigative and philosophical disciplines embody two methods: the historical one, which includes growth and development, and the ethical one. As the search for the Socratic ideal of self-knowledge and the examined life, *the historical quest* seeks to ascertain a patient-validated biography. As an *ethical quest,* it strives to understand how emotional conflict becomes pathogenic because it is also a moral conflict of *conscience*, and how it is resolved through psychotherapy, whose older name was moral treatment.

In founding psychoanalysis (a method meant to be complementary to psychiatry, and the fountainhead of psychotherapy), Freud argued that there was a dynamic continuum between health and disease, a revolutionary feature of his paradigm. Beginning with the investigation of the cause and cure of psychopathology, psychoanalysis evolved into a general psychology of the individual and society. One bridge across this continuum was the dream: both healthy and sick people dream, both healthy and sick dreams have meaning. Another bridging idea concerned the unconscious mental processes: all people are moved, more or less, by unconscious drives and processes and are more or less aware of the unconscious motives of their actions. The third concept was the ubiquity of psychological conflict, in everyday life, in neurosis and in psychosis. It will be argued that psychological conflict is moral conflict par excellence.

A psychiatric or psychoanalytic case study should reflect the following aspects of method:

106

(1) *descriptive*, consisting of a detailed, and accurate presentation of the historical facts and events in health and disease and a careful observation of the person, including his/her moral character and conscience;

(2) *diagnostic*, derived from a longitudinal and cross-sectional view of the history;

(3) *dyadic*, the conception of symptoms of mental disorder as relational, as a discourse, consisting of gestures and speeches for the purpose of communication of interpersonal meanings;

(4) *dynamic*, following from an understanding of both external and internal moral conflicts, not only as a clash of opposing forces but as the patient's moral character and conscience, in addition to his/her identifications, dreams and fantasies;

(5) *dialectical*, the debate that ensues as a result of conflicts between the person and others in his social orbit, and among the various commentators on the case, stemming from different theoretical or ideological positions. These aspects are traditionally pursued by clinicians striving to arrive at a comprehensive assessment of the person, the situation, and a rational treatment plan assuring therapeutic success and quality of life.

To the above I should now like to add two more aspects:

(6) *deontological/axiological*, to be applied to the foregoing four aspects, to ensure an accurate description, diagnosis and dynamic formulation, derived from the data, and not imposed on them, in order, first to meet the needs of the patient, and second the needs of society. This means that the patient's story, his feelings, and his interpretations have to be believed and accepted explicitly and implicitly before any other valid judgment can be reached. This moral stance is possible in a good analytic situation, as it is among true friends. It is not possible in a psychiatric ward, in a police or prison setting, or in a political system based on despotism. Judged by these standards, the only reliable source about Schreber is his own story as told by him in his *Denkwürdigkeiten eines Nervenkranken*, mistranslated in English as *Memoirs of My Nervous Illness* (Schreber, 1903), rather than reflections of a nervous patient. All the secondary sources on Schreber have been self-serving to a greater or lesser extent, including my own;

(7) *doctor-patient dialogue*, which is the principal arena where symptoms and ethical issues are played out, both as reality and as transference discourse.

SCHREBER ON HIS OWN TERMS

The Schreber literature as a whole can be divided into two parts. The first part is historical, small in size, and comprises Schreber's *Memoirs*, written in Sonnenstein between 1897 through May 1901, the writ of appeal (Schreber, July 1901), excerpts from Schreber's hospital chart and other contemporaneous sources (cited in Baumeyer, 1955, 1970; Busse, 1991; Israels, 1989; Lothane, 1989 a, 1989 b; 1992 b, 1992 c, 1993 a, b), texts and statements of his psychiatrists Flechsig and Weber (Flechsig, 1882, 1888; Weber, 1894; 1895; Weber, 1899,

1900, 1902, 1905), and Schreber's personal file (Devreese, 1981). This first part deals with Schreber as agent and author and the people who had direct interaction with him. The second part is interpretive, built on Schreber's *Memoirs*, is vast in size and still growing. It started with a forgotten article by Otto Gross in 1904 (cited in books by Jung, 1907, and Bleuler, 1911) and was followed by the trail-blazing interpretation of Freud (1911). This interpretive literature, feeding upon itself, has fabricated 'new' historical facts about Schreber derived from unfounded premises and assumptions (e.g. in the writings of W. G. Niederland, who created a secondary literature of its own). Within the interpretive literature, a unique place is occupied by the valuable hermeneutic approach of Devreese (1989, 1996 a, b), whose aim is to disclose meanings embedded in Schreber by a detailed *explication du texte* of the *Memoirs* and comparing Schreber's text with similar *topoi* in literary texts, an approach which I have pursued as well. Similar efforts were made by Prado de Oliveira (1997).

Seeing that in this vast secondary literature, Schreber has been appropriated by commentators projecting their ideas *upon* him, the basic ethical question that leaps to mind is: who owns Schreber? My answer is: Schreber belongs to himself and he is the ultimate authority about himself, and my method has been to give Schreber back his own voice. For Daniel Paul Schreber was himself an interpreter, and like his biblical namesake, the prophet Daniel, he both encoded his story in cryptic language and interpreted it himself, by the act of writing his *Memoirs*. His immediate goal was to rescind the incompetency ruling hanging over his head, to secure his release from Sonnenstein and, in addition, to bequeath important reflections, *Denkwürdigkeiten*, to present and future generations of readers. He succeeded on both counts.

THE HISTORY

Here is Paul Schreber's story in a nutshell. He was the middle child of five, born into an upper class family in Leipzig. The father, Moritz, made history both in his lifetime and posthumously. The mother, Pauline, came from a wealthy family of professors and doctors. Paul came between firstborn brother Gustav, who died, mentally ill, of suicide by gunshot, and elder sister Anna, the forbear of all the descendants, and two younger sisters. As a nine-year-old, Paul appears darkly brooding in a family portrait painted in 1851. An excellent student in school and gymnasium, he chose his grandfather's profession and studied law at Leipzig University, earned a doctorate in law, and entered the service of the Saxon Ministry of Justice, advancing steadily in his career. He married late, at age 36, to a daughter of opera director Heinrich Behr -a mésalliance in the eyes of the family-, a diabetic woman who suffered several miscarriages. In 1884, he failed in his bid to be elected to the Reichstag, and subsequently had his first depressive episode. After an unsuccessful water cure, he turned for help to Paul Flechsig, Professor of psychiatry and director of Leipzig University Psychiatric Hospital. After spending six months under Flechsig's care, Schreber left improved, completed his convalescence at another spa, and resumed his judicial duties in 1886. Seven years later, he became depressed again, this time more seriously, with intractable insomnia, agitation, profound depression, and suicidal gestures. Instead of seeking outpatient therapy, persuaded by his wife and Flechsig, he was readmitted as a *voluntary* patient to Flechsig's *Nervenklinik*. In his *Memoirs* he described the events preceding and during that hospitalization, and other lived experiences (*persönliche Erlebnisse*) in lucid narrative prose. I disagree with Antoine Vergote and Jacques Lacan that the *Memoirs* in their entirety are delusional, let alone schizophrenic, texts. Interwoven with hallucinations and delusions is a fantastic, fantasmatic, magical, mystical text. The assorted poetic, psychological, and philosophical *memorabilia,* in the sense of the term used by Swedenborg (a *Geisterseher*, or seer, with whom Schreber identified), are thus not memoirs, the English mistranslation of *Denkwürdigkeiten*, but a treatise on various worthy subjects, in a tightly woven text. Schreber's *memorabilia* are closely argued, with such a richness of detail, often maddeningly demanding, that it must be patiently studied. An integral part of the *Memoirs*, but one so far neglected by Schreber's commentators, is his lucid writ of appeal from 1901, (*Berufungsbegründung*), as are the documents of the court case to regain his freedom.

Schreber divides the nine years of his second illness into two periods: (1) The prodrome, in the summer of 1893, (2) The manifest illness, which can be divided into three stages, the first of which has two phases and the third of which has four, and (3) The epicrisis.

(1) The prodrome takes place in the Summer of 1893 as Schreber reports:

"after recovering from my first illness and I spent eight years with my wife, on the whole quite happy ones, rich also in outward honours and marred only from time to time by the repeated disappointments of being blessed with children. In June of 1893, I was informed (in the first place by the Minister of Justice Dr. Schurig in person) of my impending appointment as *Senatspräsident* to the Superior Court in Dresden (Schreber, 1903, 36, here and henceforth the pages are as in the original)".

The repeated disappointments refer to his wife's repeated miscarriages and still births, the last one, a boy, in 1892. During that time, Schreber had two premonitory dreams. First, he "dreamt several times that [his] former illness had returned." Second, "one morning while still in bed (still half asleep or already awake) [he] had a feeling which struck [him] as highly peculiar. It was the idea [*Vorstellung*] that it really must be rather pleasant to be a woman succumbing to intercourse" (Schreber, 1903, 36). The idea was "so foreign to [his] whole nature" that he "would have rejected it with indignation," attributing it, retrospectively, "to some external influences [that] were at work to implant this idea in me" (Ibid., 37). Were he in possession of Freud's dynamic ideas, he would have said that the idea represented a return of the repressed, from the unconscious. On Schreber's testimony, it meant the identification with woman (Lothane, 1993), and did not, as Freud held, imply homosexual desires. The prodrome ends in the eruption of the second illness, in Dresden, in early November, after six weeks on the job as *Senatspräsident.*

(2) The manifest illness runs its course in three locations, from November 21, 1893 until 1902:

(a) at Flechsig's asylum,

    i. from admission until March of 1894, there is a phase of sleeplessness, anxiety and agitation, suicidal depression, and nihilistic delusions, but without the element of the supernatural or of contact with God;

    ii. from March or April until June 14, 1894, is the onset of contact with God, soul murder, and the experience of *Weltuntergang* (end of the world), and therewith the beginning of a dream life in an unreal, imaginary world.

(b) at Pierson's asylum, which covers two weeks, he sees himself as dangerously ill and he questions his transfer.

(c) he is transferred to Sonnenstein, June 29, 1894 until December 20, 1902. The four phases of this third stage are as follows:

    i. 1894 — 1896 he continues to see himself as sick, leading a passive existence in a dream world and being visited by 'miracles,' his euphemism for maladies, and then begins to wake from his dream state;

    ii. 1897 — 1899, he wakes up from the dream state of unreality, seeks contact with the outside world, considers himself well enough to be discharged, and is blocked by his wife and his incompetency status, which he starts to challenge legally. He is busy writing notes and drafts for the future *Memoirs*, has attacks of anxiety and rage over the continuing incarceration and calls this the *Brüllwunder*, or bellowing miracles;

    iii. 1900 — 1901, completes the *Memoirs*, composes the writ of appeal and wages the legal fight to have incompetency rescinded;

    iv. victory for Schreber on Bastille Day 1902. Completes his recovery and preparations for discharge.

(3) The epicrisis. Just before publishing his *Memoirs*, in March of 1903, Schreber adds the "Open letter to Professor Flechsig" in which he retrospectively accuses Flechsig of "having committed soul murder ... a malpractice" (Schreber, 1903, viii-ix). After a stay with his mother in Leipzig he moves with his wife to a newly built house in Dresden and lives there quietly until his third and terminal psychotic depression in 1907 (Lothane, 1992 b).

SCHREBER'S DIAGNOSIS AND TREATMENT

Paul Schreber clearly and consistently described his depressive moods and diagnosed his second illness, even though more severe than the first, as a return of the former one (i.e. of depression, a mood disorder, not a psychotic thought disorder). Unable to cope with conflicts about career, marriage, sexuality, and childlessness, he took flight *into* depression rather than *from* his wife and job, both of which made him anxious and despondent. He made a Faustian pact with psychiatrists and they made him pay dearly for the consolations of psychiatry. In Flechsig's asylum, he was "completely cut off from the outside world, without any contact with my family, ... left in the hands of rough attendants, ... and at times [treated] with the utmost brutality. ... sometimes the attendants ... ducked my head repeatedly, and then while making all sorts of rude jokes forced me to come to the surface again, and finally leave the bath" (Schreber, 1903, 57-58). He had nobody to complain to, for "Professor Flechsig, ... on his medical rounds, ... of course denied all knowledge of these matters" (Ibid., 59). Flechsig clearly couldn't be bothered, because he needed his attendants, who had the run of the place, more than Schreber, who was merely a wretched "Schreber-soul." It was worse still at Sonnenstein. There, after having recovered in 1897 after three years of hospitalization — twice the time he had needed to get over the first illness — he was robbed of five more years of life as a free man. He was kept in "almost prison-like isolation, separated from contact with educated people, excluded even from the family table of the Director [to which the class of patients called boarders of the asylum were admitted, Z. L.], never able to get outside the walls of the Asylum" (Ibid., iv) of Sonnenstein. Here he was held without proper treatment and kept for two and a half years running in darkened solitary confinement. To this was added the stigma of an incurable disease, labelled as paranoia, and the doom of life imprisonment, sealed by the imposition of incompetency status (which reduced his civil rights to those of a seven year old), and by his wife's reluctance to take him back because she was afraid of his bellowing.

Weber based his decision to keep Schreber confined against his will (as stated in the title of Schreber's forensic essay and in the usually omitted subtitle of the *Memoirs*), and to make Schreber's temporary incompetency permanent, more on the content of Schreber's manuscript of the future *Memoirs* than on his actual conduct, or on what Schreber said. The outcome of Weber's policies and reports to the court, in his capacity as forensic expert and Advisor to the Court, was that Schreber was not allowed out of Sonnenstein on trial home leave even though his social functioning improved steadily. The added irony is that Schreber offered the manuscript as proof of his sanity.

Because of this I have viewed Schreber as a victim of psychiatric persecution under the primitive conditions of German psychiatry of the time, from which he emerged victorious. Weber was vehemently opposed to the publication of the *Memoirs*, which he considered indecent trash, and would not relent even after Schreber's release, acting the sore loser in a 1903 presentation to the Forensic-Psychiatric Society of Dresden. My predecessors in the task of commenting on the Memoirs have not considered the repercussions of the conditions of incarceration on the content of certain delusions. Some delusions, such as are portrayed in the various *Wunder* of chapter 11, can only make sense as delusional day-dreams in response to reality stimuli, or, as Freud said, they constitute Schreber's *Wahnarbeit,* or delusion-work, on an analogy with *Traumarbeit,* or dream-work. However, the first to overlook this was Freud himself.

Far be it from me to deny that some of Schreber's productions were delusional, and even that residual delusions persisted in his writ of appeal. But what if the latter ones, too, were merely a show of defiance? For these delusions did not constitute the core of his illness, or his morbid conduct, certainly not of Weber's forensic extrapolations. For me the emotions are the core. "Gefühl ist alles, Name ist Schall und Rauch" (feeling is everything, name is noise and smoke), says Goethe, and, à la Merleau-Ponty, I submit that it is a matter of the primacy of emotions over ideas. I do not mean just feelings, but *emotions* as modes of acting in the world, through the positive emotions of love and the negative emotions of frustrated love: jealousy, envy, hatred, revenge. These are the emotions that overwhelmed Schreber; these are the emotions that he transmogrified into the phantasmagoria of the *Memoirs*. This indeed is its spell on the reader. But no more should Schreber have been jailed for his ideas than should Isaac Newton have been committed to the madhouse because, in suffering from distemper and dotage, he dabbled in the occult and the miraculous, writing tracts on divinity and works with titles such as *Observations on the Prophecies of Daniel* and the *Apocalypse of St. John, A History of the Creation, Paradoxical Questions Regarding Athanasius*, and many others. More charitable and enlightened than the nestor of Saxon forensic psychiatry, the judges in the Oberlandesgericht (Superior Court of Appeals) agreed with Schreber that:

> "Whatever one may think of his belief in miracles, no one is entitled to see in it a mental defect which makes plaintiff [Schreber] require State care. One does not usually and without further reason declare the adherents of spiritualism mentally ill and put them under a guardian, although their way of looking at things supernaturally is also neither shared nor comprehended by the vast majority of their fellow men (Schreber, 1903, 481).

I do not know if the judges were familiar with the definition given by St. Thomas Aquinas: "those things are properly called miracles which are done by the divine agency beyond the order commonly observed in nature" (*praeter ordinem communiter observatum in rebus*). Nor do I know if they were conversant with Spinoza's attempt to reconcile his concept of *Deus sive natura* and the authenticity of the miracles in the Bible by claiming that there are less miracles than meets the eye, because people read the poetic idiom of Bible too literally. But Spinoza's caveat is helpful for reading the *Denkwürdigkeiten* as well. I have pointed out that many *als ob* (as if) expressions in the original have been omitted in the English translation. Rather than offering a new kind of Christian apologetics, Schreber resorted to "images and similes" (Ibid., 2) in order to explain "how, owing to [his] illness, [he] entered into peculiar relations with God — which were in themselves contrary to Order of the World" (Ibid., 4). Schreber's miracles are indeed signs, or *semeia* of divine intervention, both *terata* (wonders and prodigies) and *dynameis* (powers). As miracles against the Order of the World, which is meant to be constructive and not destructive, as words used in the special language called *Grundsprache*, or basic language, these were wonders in reverse, miracles as maladies and other afflictions. Only later did they become, in the language of St. Paul, *charismata hiamaton* (graces of healing), and idea echoed by Freud (1911 c, 71).

One moment of an early "miraculous relation" against the Order of the World was the beginning of Schreber's contact with God and the onset of soul murder, to which we turn next.

SOUL MURDER

Soul murder is the second phase in the first stage of the second illness that developed during Schreber's stay at Flechsig's Hospital and became a critical turning point. The hospital went under a number of names, and the question arises: what's in a name? Inaugurated in 1882, it was at first called an *Irrenklinik*, or asylum for the insane, as distinct from an *Irrenanstalt*, a public hospital for the insane. However, as more genteel euphemisms took over, it became *Die Universitäts-Psychiatrische und Nervenklinik*, while the *Irrenanstalt* came to be called *Heilanstalt*, a treatment center, even though the "treatment" was merely custodial, as in Schreber's case at Sonnenstein. As psychiatrist, Flechsig was called a *Nervenarzt*, nerve doctor, and it may have been one of the reasons why Paul Schreber insisted on being called a *Nervenkranke*, a nervous patient. By law, as a *Nervenkranke* with depression in 1884, Schreber was able to resume his career as judge. As *Geisteskranke*, or statutorily insane person in 1894, his judicial career was doomed forever. This explains the fatefulness of his ending up in Sonnenstein (which ironically, Niederland referred to as a 'sanatorium'), as a result of soul murder plotted by Flechsig and others. Here is how it happened.

After over three months at Flechsig's, the agitated, suicidal depression changed drastically: a cosmic and personal catastrophe, soul murder, befell Schreber which he considered fateful for himself and, in his mood of self-absorption, for mankind as a whole. What follows is a general outline of how Schreber depicts the genesis of soul murder as a form of psychiatric abuse:

> "The voices which talk to me have daily stressed ever since the beginning of my contact with God (mid-March 1894) the fact that the crisis that broke out in the realms of God was caused by somebody having *committed soul murder*; at first Flechsig was named the instigator of soul murder" (Schreber, 1903, 23; emphasis Schreber's). ... "It seems very probable that contact with divine nerves was granted to a person who specialized in nervous illnesses, partly because he would be expected to be a highly intellectual person, partly because everything concerning human nerves must be of particular interest to God, starting with His instinctive knowledge that an increase in nervousness among men could endanger his realms. Asylums for the mentally ill were therefore called in the basic language 'God's Nerve-Institutes'" (Ibid., 25).

Note that Schreber portrays Flechsig as the instigator, as a Satan-like seducer who suggests to God that He visit disasters upon Schreber. Under the cover of this fantasy Schreber deploys his mordant irony to mock the God-like behavior of Flechsig who abuses his power as director of his 'nerve-institutes' fatefully to intervene in the life of mortals like Schreber. In the passages below, Schreber depicts his fall and redemption in the fantastic style, to which I have added the bulleted graphic arrangement in order to highlight the various components of soul murder:

Professor Flechsig had found a way of raising himself up to heaven and making himself a leader of rays. ... In this way a plot was laid against me (perhaps March or April 1894), the purpose of which was

- to hand me over to another human being
- after my nervous illness had be recognized as, or assumed to be, incurable,
- in such a way that my soul was handed over to him,
- but my body — transformed into a female body and, misconstruing the above-described fundamental tendency of the Order of the World
- was then left to that human being for sexual misuse
- and simply 'forsaken,' in other words left to rot.
- One does not seem to have been quite clear as what was to happen to such a 'forsaken' human being, or whether this actually meant his death (Schreber, 1903, 56).
- Being buried alive was also repeatedly mentioned as a way of ending my life.
- From the human point of view, ... it was ... very natural for me to see my real enemy only in Professor Flechsig or his soul, and to regard as my natural ally God's omnipotence, which I imagined only Professor Flechsig endangered (Ibid., 59).
- God himself must have known of the plan, if indeed he was not the instigator, to commit soul murder on me and hand over my body in the manner of a female harlot, [i.e.] unmanning me for purposes contrary to the Order of the World (that is to say, for the sexual satisfaction of a human being) and later at destruction of my reason.
- From this apparently unequal battle between one weak human being and God himself, I emerge, albeit not without bitter sufferings and depriva-tions, victorious, because the Order of the World is on my side (Ibid., 61).
- And so I live in the confident faith that the whole confusion was only an episode which will finally lead one way or another to the restoration: the personal misfortunes I had to suffer and the loss of the states of Blessed-ness may even be compensated for, and ... through my case, ... the incalculable gain it would be for mankind if, through my personal fate, particularly as it will be shaped in the future, the foundations of mere materialism and hazy pantheism would once and for all be demolished (Ibid., 62-63).

Let us unpack the above narrative, presented in the style of magical realism, akin to the story of the *Book of Job* and Goethe's *Faust,* in the language of the imaginary, of fantastic daydreams and delusions, transmitted in *Grundsprache* and *Nervensprache,* but *not* in the language of schizophrenia. It is *Wahn* as poetic imagining, as found in Goethe and other creative writers (Freud, 1907; Lothane, in press — a); and it is also a *Verfolgungswahn,* the delusion of persecution, his only one, because Schreber considers Flechsig to be his *only* real enemy.

This account of soul murder is a memory and is created retrospectively to explain how Flechsig caused Schreber's downfall, by disappointing Schreber's expectation, based on the successful outcome of his first depressive episode of 1884, to cure him of his second illness. Adding insult to injury, Flechsig invoked the University Hospital by-laws (Flechsig, 1882), which I found in the Dresden State Archives, limiting a patient's stay to six months and thus giving him the excuse to end the treatment and 'forsake' the patient once his illness was judged to be incurable, to condemn Schreber to be 'buried alive' in a soul-killing, reason-destroying public asylum and 'left to rot' there until he died. This soul murder, a word in 19th century German dictionaries, not a schizophrenic neologism, is primarily defined as spiritual (Lothane, 1992 b, n. 30), and its sexualization (as sexual abuse is secondary). It is noteworthy that Schreber does not state that it was Flechsig who intended to abuse him sexually or otherwise, but that he was handed to "another human being" for such abuse, a role for which Flechsig's cruel attendants qualified in no small measure, and those at Sonnenstein as well. The accusation also mocks Flechsig as 'God' who "*did not really understand the living human being* and had no need to understand him, because ... He only dealt with corpses" (Schreber, 1903, 55; Schreber's emphasis): Flechsig was not interested in Schreber as a human being, only in obtaining his brain at autopsy and adding it to his collection in the brain museum next to his office (Flechsig, 1888).

Like a dream, Schreber's *Wahn* has a grain of truth in it, as presciently stated by Freud in 1907:

"if a patient believes in his delusion so firmly, this is not because his faculty of judgment has been overturned and does not arise from what is false in the delusion. On the contrary, there is a grain of truth concealed in every delusion, there is something in it that really deserves belief ... the true element, however, has long been repressed. If eventually it is able to penetrate into consciousness, this time in a distorted form, the sense of conviction attaching to it as though by way of compensation and is now attached to the distorted substitute of the repressed truth, and protects him from any critical attacks. ... We all attach our conviction to thought-contents in which truth is combined with error, and let it extend from the former over the latter" (Freud, 1907 a, 80-81).

He reaffirmed this idea 30 years later: "there is not only method in madness, as the poet [i.e. Shakespeare in *Hamlet,* Z. L.] has already perceived, but also a fragment of historical truth ... The vain effort would be abandoned of convincing the patient of the error of his delusion and of its contradiction of reality; on the contrary, the recognition of its kernel of truth would afford common ground upon which the therapeutic work could develop" (Freud, 1937 d, 267-268).

Schreber knew this as well, and in fact, he differentiated the two varieties of *Wahn*. During the first week at Flechsig's, following a fight with attendants to which we shall return below, while

> "regarding [himself] totally lost, he made a naturally unsuccessful attempt during the night to hang himself from the bedstead with the sheet. ... [He] knew that this was not permitted in asylums, but [he] labored under the delusion that when all attempts at cure had been exhausted, one would be discharged — solely for the purpose of making an end to one's own life either in one's own home or somewhere else" (Schreber, 1903, 41).

On the other hand, in his ideas about soul murder he was not a paranoiac, as he is still being branded in certain quarters, but a poet, a *Dichter* more than a *Richter* (judge). He earned the title of paranoiac thanks to the pathologizing attitudes of his psychiatrist Weber who could not relate to Schreber as an imaginative creator writing a supernatural narrative about the titanic battle between himself, God, the psychiatrists and his wife. In that battle a mundane *Komplott* (conspiracy) was hatched, and it had more than a grain of reality, as is evident from the documents in the *Personalakte* (personal file) of Paul Schreber, for the discovery of which we owe a great debt of gratitude to Devreese. However, Devreese did not sufficiently appreciate the importance of the political and forensic implications of soul murder. Frau Schreber, Professor Flechsig, and Carl Edmund Werner (Präsident des Königlichen Oberlandesgericht in Dresden), among others, were co-conspirators in that *Komplott,* which evolved in the first two trimesters of 1894, in two stages. First came the replacement of Schreber by another judge, as announced in a Leipzig newspaper, historical information found by our indefatigable Devreese.

Schreber may have seen the following announcement in the *Beilage zum Leipziger Tageblatt und Anzeiger* vom 14 März 1894, Nr. 133:

> "Königreich Sachsen. Leipzig, 14. März. Von anscheinend gut unterrichteter Seite wird uns aus Dresden gemeldet, dass im Justizdepartement vom 1. April ab mehrfache Veränderungen in Kraft treten. Danach rückt Oberlandesgerichtsrat Seyfert zum Senatspräsidenten auf, die Landgerichtsdirectoren Dr. Von Schwarze in Chemnitz, Rudolph in Freiberg und Hallbauer in Leipzig werden Oberlandesgerichtsräte [it has been learned from reliable sources that many changes are taking place in the Department of Justice starting on the first of April. ...]."

Schreber had himself been *Landgerichtsdirector*, or administrative judge, in Freiberg prior to his nomination as Senatspräsident in Dresden, and was now being replaced by others. The changes in the Department of Justice may have been made after an opinion rendered by Flechsig about Schreber's poor prognosis.

Schreber may have alluded to these developments it in the passage that follows:

"I recollect that about the middle of March 1894 when communication with supernatural powers was well underway, a newspaper was put in front of me in which something like my own obituary notice could be read; I took this as a hint that I could not longer count on any possibility of a return to human society. I dare not decide whether what I saw actually happened or whether it was a visual hallucination. I only retained the one impression, that if this and other occurrences really were visions, there was method in them [this allusion to *Hamlet* later confirmed by his quoting "there is something rotten in the state of Denmark," Schreber, 1903, 203, Z. L.], i.e. they were connected in a certain way which enabled me to realize what one had in store for me (Ibid., 81).

Schreber's return to society was blocked by his worsening sickness, by Flechsig's increasing indifference, by the developments at the Ministry of Justice, and by a critical deterioration in his relations with his wife Sabine:

"a further decline in my nervous state and an important chapter in my life commenced about the 15th of February 1894 when my wife, who until then had spent a few hours every day with me and had also taken lunch with me in the Asylum, undertook a four day journey to her father in Berlin, in order to have a holiday herself, of which she was in urgent need. My condition deteriorated so much in these four days that after her return I saw her only once more and then declared that I could not wish my wife to see me again in that low state into which I have fallen. From then on my wife's visits ceased; when after a long time I did see her once again at a window of the room opposite mine, such important changes had meanwhile occurred in my environment and within myself that I no longer considered her a living being but only thought I saw in her a human being produced by miracle in the manner of 'fleeting phantoms [*hingemacht*].' Decisive for my mental collapse was one particular night during which I had a quite unusual number of pollutions (perhaps half a dozen) (Ibid., 44).

The wish for his wife to have a well-deserved vacation is only a thin disguise for the rage at her for abandoning him to discuss the gravity of the situation with her father, the powerful opera director Heinrich Behr, in Berlin. The rage was compounded by the mounting sexual frustration as a result of his wife's coldness, his possible potency problems, or his illness. Moreover, consider the effect the enforced sexual abstinence would have had on this man in his fifties over the long years of incarceration at Sonnestein and on the content of his various sexual imaginings (Lothane, 1993 c; Lothane, in press — b).

By May 1894, the breakdown in the marital relationship culminated in Schreber's refusal to sign receipts against which his wife would collect his monthly salary from the Ministry of Justice. Sabine's attempts to sign the receipts herself were denied by Carl Edmund Werner as illegal, whereupon he advised Frau Schreber to make an application to have Schreber declared mentally incompetent and gain control of the money via a court appointed guardian (Oberjustizrat Clemens Schmidt), as is detailed in Schreber's aforementioned *Personalakte*. These developments would later doubly seal Schreber's fate at Sonnenstein with Superintendent Weber's diagnosis of chronic and incurable paranoia and his reports to the court, whereby the previously imposed temporary incompetency status was made permanent in 1900.

Fighting for his civil rights and his freedom, Schreber rightly insisted throughout the *Memoirs* and in his writ of appeal (1901) that he was not insane in the legal sense of the word, that he was a *Nervenkranke* and not a *Geisteskranke*, that is, he was not somebody deserving to be *entmündigt* (declared legally insane) and *freiheitsberaubt* (deprived of his liberty and civil rights). I have documented extensively in my book, that he saw these motions as a result of the *Komplott* hatched behind his back by the aforementioned co-conspirators. That is why Schreber asked, against Guido Weber, a psychiatrist who was even more hostile to him than Flechsig, "whether it is within the bounds of possibility that my delusional system, as one is pleased to call it, is founded on some truth" (Schreber, 1903, 412), especially since Weber only cared to know "the pathological shell, as I would like to call it, which concealed my true spiritual life" (Ibid., 424).

It would have never occurred to Guido Weber to interpret Schreber's delusions as having anything to do with homosexual desire because Freud's ideas were unknown to him. Weber, the venerable forensic expert and bourgeois *pater familias*, was scandalized by the "content of his writings, ... the abundance of indiscretions relating to himself and others contained in them, the unembarrassed detailing of the most objectionable (*bedenktlichsten*) and esthetically unacceptable (*unmöglichsten*) situations and events, the use of the most offensive vulgar words" and that "a man otherwise tactful and of fine feeling could propose an action [i.e. publishing the *Memoirs*, Z. L) which would compromise him so severely in the eyes of the public" (Weber, 1900, Schreber, 1903, 402). Nor could Weber relate to Schreber's mystical views of hermaphroditic sexuality or his experimentation with gender identity (Lothane, 1998 b, Lothane, in press — b; Lothane, forthcoming): these were heresies and blasphemies against the middle-class Order of the World. Commenting on this very statement by Weber Freud could not hold back his indignation: "Surely one can hardly expect that a case history, which sets out to give a picture of deranged humanity and its struggles to rehabilitate itself should exhibit 'discretion' and 'aesthetic' charm" (1911 c, 37), seemingly endorsing Schreber's proud declaration to the court:

"Besides, my Memoirs are not written for flappers or High School girls;

no understanding person will therefore want to blame me if I have not always hit the form of expression which sensitive school matrons think fit for their charges. A person who wishes to pave a way for new conception of religion must be able if need be to use flaming speech (*Flammenworte*) such as Jesus Christ used towards the Pharisees or Luther towards the Pope and the mighty of the world. (Schreber, 1901, 1903, 444).

Schreber should rather have spoken of spirituality, not religion, for his aim was to uphold the spiritual nature of sexuality. Thus, in his appeal Schreber (1901) considered it advisable to avoid any further discussion concerning his "supposed hallucinations and delusions but rather to convince the judges that he was in full possession of *"the capacity for reasonable action in practical life"* (Ibid., 412; Schreber's italics). There is, of course, a difference between Schreber's profound spiritual insights and his defensive clinging to divine influence to explain his residual symptoms: the continuing attacks of bellowing he called *Brüllwunder*, the snapping of his piano strings, or the involuntary "convulsive twitchings, that is to say cramp-like contractions of the musculature particularly of the face" (Ibid., 418). Not having the concept of unconscious motives of action at his disposal, Schreber ascribes these effects to divine miracles. But it was the discoverer of the dynamic unconscious who said this about Schreber's end-of-the-world fantasy: "He builds up the [destroyed world, Z. L.] by the work of his delusions [*durch die Arbeit seines Wahnes*, on an analogy with dream-work, Z. L.]. *The delusional formation, which we take to be a pathological product, is in reality an attempt at recovery, a process of reconstruction"* (1911 c, 71; Freud's italics). This is a revolutionary insight about love lost and love regained and disorder as a method of self-cure. Freud also realized that Schreber had an intuitive grasp of unconscious processes, as shown in "the distinction [Schreber] draws between the man Flechsig and the 'Flechsig soul.' ... Psychiatrists should at last take a lesson from this patient, when they see him trying, in spite of his delusions, not to confuse the world of the unconscious with the world of reality" (1911 c, 43). That is why Freud wanted to introduce *Grundsprache* as a technical term for primary process, that is why he wrote to Jung that Schreber deserved to be nominated professor of psychiatry. And that is why I consider him in many ways saner than the mad-doctors.

In due course, soul murder, the evil "unmanning" of disease and disorder, was transformed into good unmanning, in consonance with the Order of the World, with a recovery of the states of Blessedness. Here, a healing grace is achieved through cultivation of femininity, aspects which Devreese (1996 a) and myself have discussed elsewhere (Lothane, 1992 b, 1993 c).

THE DOCTOR PATIENT RELATIONSHIP

We now return to the initial phase of Schreber's second illness, prior to the eruption of supernatural themes. Around the 8th or 9th of November 1893, Schreber tells us, as his illness "began to assume a menacing character, I took a week's sick leave, which we were going to use to consult Professor Flechsig, in whom we place all our faith since his successful treatment of my first illness. ... Early the following day ... we [he and wife, Z. L.] travelled to Leipzig ... A long interview followed in which I must say Professor Flechsig developed a remarkable eloquence which affected me deeply. He spoke of the advances made in psychiatry since my first illness, of newly discovered sleeping drugs, etc., and gave me hope of *delivering* me of the whole illness through one prolific sleep. ... my mood thereupon became steadier. ... Unfortunately, ... [d]espite [the drugs] I spent the night almost without sleep, and once [I made] some kind of a suicidal attempt by means of a towel [which] awoke my wife who stopped me. The next morning my nerves were badly shattered ... my mood was gloomy in the extreme and Professor Flechsig ... therefore advised my admission into his Asylum, for which [I] set out immediately by cab accompanied by him. ... I passed days in endless melancholy; my mind was occupied almost exclusively with thoughts of death" (Schreber, 1903, 39-40; emphasis added).

The word 'delivering' does not exist in the original: it was inserted by the English translators of the *Memoirs* and made Lacan (1977, 190-191) laugh because he thought they had procreation in mind and not the idea of being delivered from suffering, i.e. helped by the doctor. The missing verb, however, seems to indicate that the doctor and the patient were not communicating: it was a complete disjunction. Once again, Flechsig was resorting to "*white lies*," just like nine years earlier, when he "wanted to put down my illness solely to poisoning with potassium bromide" (Schreber, 1903, 35). "It seems to me in retrospect," writes Schreber about Flechig's therapy of his second illness, "that Professor Flechsig's plan of curing me consisted in intensifying my nervous depression as far as possible, on order to bring about a cure all at once by a sudden change of mood" (Ibid., 40), accurately alluding to the pharmacological regimen Flechsig applied to patients suffering from epilepsy, with dire results (Lothane, 1992 b). However, the patient yearned for psychotherapy, sympathy and understanding.

Flechsig unpsychological method stood in stark contrast to what was offered to Schreber by Flechig's "Assistant Physician, Dr.Teuscher," misspelt as Täuscher -a word play on hope that ended with a disappointment- who would later become director of his own private hospital, Der Weisse Hirsch.

Here is what happened:

"about the fourth or fifth night ... I was pulled out of bed by two attendants in the middle of the night and take to a cell fitted out for dements (maniacs) to sleep in. ... I was naturally terrified in the extreme by this event ...The way led through a billiard room; I thought he had to resist, a fight started between myself clad only in a shirt, and the two attendants, during which I tried to hold fast to the billiard table, but was eventually overpowered and led to and removed to the above-mentioned cell. ... Regarding myself as totally lost, I made a naturally unsuccessful attempt during the night to hang myself. ... [added in n. 23: during a later conversation Professor Flechsig denied the whole occurrence and all connected with it, and tried to make out that it was only a figment of my imagination — [which] from then on made me somewhat distrustful of Professor Flechsig" (Schreber, 1903, 41).

The next day the good doctor Teuscher "appeared and told me that there was no intention whatsoever of giving up treatment; this coupled with the manner in which he tried to raise my spirits again -I cannot deny him also my appreciation of the excellent way he spoke to me on that occasion- had the effect a very favourable change in my mood ... *the only day on which I was enlivened by a joyful spirit of hope*" (Ibid., 42; Schreber's emphasis). The good mood did not last long, he became sleepless again and was given "*Nekrin*," actually narcein, an opium compound, which Schreber transformed into a word suggesting death rather than hope. As a result, "attendant R, [who the day before] had behaved most tactfully and skillfully in his whole conversation ... in the same way as Dr. Täuscher" appeared to him next day with "totally distorted features" (Ibid., 42): the loss of hope was attended by an accession of rage, projected into the distorted face of the doctor.

But in the following days and weeks, even in spite of occasional visits at home with his mother, he went from bad to worse. Parallel to the aforementioined deterioration of the relationship with his wife there occurred a worsening of his relations with Flechsig, symbolized by the appearance of "the first signs of communication with supernatural powers" (Ibid., 44). Schreber later recalled that "about the beginning of March 1894 ... [occurred] the *very first* vision in which God, if I may express it so revealed Himself to me, ... I do remember that I told Professor Flechsig on the following morning something about the content of this vision and that I had a conversation with him on this topic" (n. 103; Schreber's emphasis). We can only imagine the Professor's horrified expression. From then on Schreber experienced further supernatural impressions, pointing to the widening gulf of mistrust between him and the doctor, "of nerve contact which Professor Flechsig kept up with me in such a way that he spoke to my nerves without being present in person. From then on I also gained the impression that Professor Flechsig had secret designs against me; this seemed confirmed when I once asked him during a personal visit whether he really honestly believed that I could be cured, and he held out certain hopes, *but could no longer* — at least so it seemed to him, *look me straight in the eye*" (Ibid., 45; Schreber's emphasis). It was only after three months of life as a free man that Schreber was able retrospectively to accuse Flechsig of malpractice, still not directly, but in the guise of "delusions", as spoken by departed souls, "because of their innate tendency to express themselves hyperbolically" (Ibid., xi).

From the beginning of soul murder, in March of 1894, Schreber was merely a custodial case in Leipzig: "This was the time when, as previously mentioned, I was kept in bed continuously day and night; whether for weeks and if so how many, I cannot say" (Ibid., 81), in keeping with the old-fashioned idea of bed rest as treatment, or "every night went to bed in [his] padded cell" (Ibid., 98). Note that the bed rest cure, rather than promoting self-healing insights, may have increased Schreber's inclination to voluptuous sexual broodings.

One day in June he was had a false "feeling of liberation," when "early one morning three attendants appeared in my cell with a suitcase in which were packed my few belongings, and told me that I was to get ready to leave the Asylum" which he did "without seeing Professor Flechsig again" (Ibid., 99). In this way he was propelled from "Flechsig's Hell," via "the Devil's Kitchen" (Pierson's asylum) to be warehoused for eight and a half years in "the Devil's Castle," that is, Sonnenstein Fortress. The former fortress had been converted in 1811 into the jewel in the crown of royal Saxon public asylums and flourished under the directorship of Guido Weber who retired in 1910, one year short of its centenary, to die and be buried there in 1914, three years after the death in the Leipzig-Dösen asylum of the most famous patient in psychiatry.

THE INTERPRETATION: ETHICAL BREACHES IN DEALINGS WITH SCHREBER AND HIS STORY

We will now consider the lapses committed by psychiatrists (misdiagnosis and mistreatment) and psychoanalysts (misinterpretation).

The most obvious such breach is that the psychiatrists lied to him or about him. Flechsig rejected as a figment of a sick imagination Schreber's legitimate complaints about the attendants and Weber lied in his report lied about the length of time Schreber spent in seclusion. Flechsig resorted to white lies, Weber fashioned a false (in Schreber's phrase: *Fälschung*) diagnosis. They were in turn deceived by their own biases as organic and forensic psychiatrists and had no personal interest in the patient and did not care about the consequences of their actions toward Schreber. Later psychiatrists, among them Otto Gross (1904), Jung (1907), Bleuler (1911), Kraepelin and Jaspers (1913), did not give the *Memoirs* the close reading they deserve, never consulted Schreber's complete clinical chart still available then at Sonnestein (including the manuscript of the famous expurgated Third Chapter of the *Memoirs*). Thus, owing to the incompleteness of their descriptions and other biases, they continued to view Schreber as the paradigmatic paranoid schizophrenic he never was. This assessment has been reinforced countless times since.

An example of such a biased approach is Spitzer et al. (1981), who lump together early and late events to conclude that "all of these features suggest a diagnosis of schizophrenia ... if the first signs of the illness appear before age 45. In Dr. Schreber's case this seems likely" (Spitzer et al., 1981, 341). But this "if" never happened. They diagnose catatonic stupor and deny the pertinence of "depressive stupor" arguing falsely that "apart from suicidal ideas there is no other reference to characteristic depressive symptomatology," in the face of Schreber's repeated descriptions of symptoms of severe anxiety and melancholia (also neglected by Freud and Weber). With one exception (Koehler, 1981), no psychiatrist has paid attention to chronology and to the change in the clinical picture in March 1894, in the phase of soul murder; with two exceptions (Koehler and Lipton, 1984), none has considered the differential diagnosis of schizophrenia, or that Schreber suffered from a mood disorder (Lothane, 1989 b, 1992 b); with one exception (Szasz, 1976), no psychiatrist has been concerned with the ethical issues in the incompetency ruling, but even Szasz did not consider the effect of Schreber's year-long imprisonment on the content of his symptoms.

Among psychoanalysts, the First Psychoanalyst was the first offender. Like the others, Freud read the *Memoirs* selectively, only to prove the correctness of the formula that paranoia is caused by homosexual desire, a clinical observation which in 1908 he converted into a psychoanalytic dogma, in collaboration with Ferenczi and Jung (Lothane, 1997 b). Two years later, for reasons never explained, Jung gave Freud Schreber's Memoirs to read, and the theory took off like wild fire. Not only was Freud mistaken in applying the formula to Schreber, he also vacillated about Schreber's diagnosis, converting Weber's classical paranoia into dementia paranoides, or paranoid schizophrenia, and remaining blind to the mood disorder. While clinically heuristic, Freud's formula has been found neither universal nor adequate to explain the varieties of paranoia, of schizophrenia, or of homosexuality. Therefore, his epoch-making essay of 1911 is not about Schreber the man (Lothane, 1995 c, d) but an illustration of his formula: it is a sensational Schreber myth, but one that rescued Schreber from oblivion, an indisputable merit.

Sparing himself the effort of traveling to Leipzig and Pirna, let alone of writing to Flechsig and Weber for information, Freud did not even bother to consider Schreber's book in its entirety, or to rely upon Schreber for the facts of the story, quoting at length from Weber's tendentious reports. Freud's first sin is that of misdescription and the second is misidentification and misinterpretation. Thus, Freud rearranges the chronology of events, alters Schreber's text, violating the principle of the sanctity of the text, and theorizes from unproven assumptions rather than from historical facts as presented by Schreber. In sum, while Freud chooses the easier route of applied armchair analysis over hands-on historical research, he has at least the decency to admit:

"Any one who was more daring that I am in making interpretations, or who was in touch with Schreber's family and consequently better acquainted with the society in which he moved and the small events of his life, would find it an easy matter to trace back innumerable details of his delusions to their sources and so discover their meaning, and this in spite of the censorship to which the *Denkwürdigkeiten* have been subjected. But as it is, we must necessarily content ourselves with the shadowy sketch of the infantile material which was used by the paranoic disorder in portraying the current conflict" (Freud, 1911 c, 57).

However, this admission did not stop Freud from inventing a paraphrase of Schreber's nonexistent homosexual scenario to explain the entire second illness, which has gone unchallenged for almost nine decades and still has analysts criticizing me for attacking Freud. In fact, I have in several instances defended Schreber against misrepresentations, and corrected Freud's mistaken opinions about Schreber (Lothane, 1992 b; Lothane, 1995 a — g). On the other hand, I have also defended Freud against his detractors (Lothane, 1996 c, d; 1997 e; 1998 c).

Freud conflates a number of glosses and interpretations, all erroneous because unsupported by historical or textual evidence from Schreber. These are as follows:

1. The unwarranted assumption that Schreber's dream of the return of his previous illness and of what a woman feels in sex are both related to Flechsig and constitute a wish to be castrated and copulated anally by Flechsig:

> "During the incubation period of his illness, ... (that is, between June 1893, when he was appointed to his new post, and the following October, when he took up his duties), he repeatedly dreamt that his old nervous disorder had returned. Once, moreover, when he was half-asleep, he had a feeling that after all it must be nice to be a woman submitting to an act of copulation. The dream and the phantasy are reported by Schreber in immediate succession; and if we also bring together the subject-matter, we shall be able *to infer* that at the same time as his recollection of his illness, a recollection of his doctor was also aroused in his mind, and that the feminine attitude which he assumed in phantasy was from the first directed towards the doctor. ... Perhaps that illness had left behind in him a feeling of affectionate dependence upon his doctor, which had now, for some unknown reason, become intensified *to the pitch of erotic desire*. ... The patient was in fear of sexual abuse at the hands of the doctor himself. The exciting cause of his illness, then, was an outburst of homosexual libido ... and his struggles against the libidinal impulse produced the conflict which gave rise to the symptoms" (Freud, 1911 c, 42-43; emphasis added).

Men are not born with a wish to be anally penetrated by another man but they may acquire such a desire, or habit. Moreover, anal eroticism per se, which Schreber expressed in abundance, is not to be confused with a preference for anal sexual intercourse. Freud had no evidence that Schreber had acquired such a libidinal predilection in his childhood and formed the developmental basis for such a desire in the incubation period, prior to setting eyes on Flechsig again. Nor did Freud know, as we do not, which issues Schreber had repressed which may have returned in the hypnopompic fantasy about a woman in intercourse, and thus had no basis for inferring that during the incubation period, Schreber consciously desired Flechsig, and with such intensity. Last but not least, Freud bases his inference on Schreber's fears of sexual abuse by Flechsig, presumably drawn from the generalization that a fear always implies a wish. But even if it were true, that supposed fear occurred months later after the wish, and its cause, soul murder, as already discussed, was far greater than sexual fear, as was the return of the former disease in and of itself.

Using a strategy known from his other works, Freud disarms our anticipated disbeliefs but he cannot dispel his own doubts:

> "The question why this outburst of homosexual libido overtook the patient precisely at this period (that is, between the dates of his appointment and of his move to Dresden) cannot be answered in the absence of more precise knowledge of the story of his life. ... I can well imagine what a dubious hypothesis it must appear to be to suppose that a man's friendly feeling towards his doctor can suddenly break out in an intensified form after a lapse of eight years and become the occasion of such a severe mental disorder. But I do not think we should be justified in dismissing such a hypothesis merely on account of its inherent improbability ...". (1911 c, 46)

I think we are so justified.

2. To rescue the dubious hypothesis, Freud invokes a generalization, "generally speaking, every human being oscillates all through his life between heterosexual and homosexual feelings" (1911 c, 46) and a formula: "the patient's friendly feeling towards his doctor may very well have been due to a process of 'transference'... to put the matter in a more concrete form: the patient was reminded of his brother or father by the figure of the doctor, he rediscovered them in him ... a longing for a surrogate figure reappeared in him and operated with a violence that is only to be explained in the light of its origin and primary significance" (1911 c, 47). But Freud had no biographical infantile material at his disposal to show that Schreber's tie to his father and brother had been erotic in nature, nor has anyone else since, because such material has not survived, which would furnish evidence for the transference in question, such as knowledge of the real relations that existed between Schreber, his brother and his father.

3. Freud argues self-servingly that it is "not an act of irresponsible levity, an indiscretion and a calumny to charge a man of such high ethical standing as the former Senatspräsident with homosexuality" because the "patient has himself informed the world at large of his phantasy of being transformed into a woman" and "in translating it into the technical terminology of medicine we have not made the slightest addition to its content" (1911 c, 12:43). But such a prima facie assumption is false, in view of known cases of transsexual fantasies without homosexual desire, such as described by Schreber himself and the fact that identification with a person and a desire for that person are not the same. Moreover, translation into the terminology of medicine is a significant alteration of the author's intention and meaning, and such intention cannot be claimed on the author's behalf without having his spontaneous corroborating statements, as would happen in the analytic situation.

4. By using the aforementioned construction as proof that the same wish toward Flechsig is contained in a censored way in Schreber's soul murder, Freud makes use of circular reasoning. Here, Freud dismantles an imagined counter claim: "But it is nowhere expressly stated that the transformation into a woman which he so much dreaded was to be carried out for the benefit of Flechsig," by denying the truth of the very words of Schreber that Freud himself italicizes: "'*I should be handed over to a certain person.*'" This he does via the confident assertion that "It is unnecessary to remark that no other individual is ever named that could be put in Flechsig's place," while in the very next sentence Freud says, apparently without any feeling of self-contradiction, "Towards the end of Schreber's stay in the clinic at Leipzig, a fear occurred to his mind that 'he was thrown to the attendants' for the purpose of sexual abuse (Schreber, 1903, 98)" (Freud, 1911 c, 12:44). But how is Flechsig the same as attendants? After all, it was the attendants who attacked him physically.

5. A further spurious argument in favor of Freud's formula is the equation Flechsig = God, ergo: fucked by God = fucked by Flechsig. But Schreber's God-discourse is a very elaborate treatise, which Freud reduces to its simplest homoerotic denominator. Thus, in the very beginning Schreber warns us not to loose sight of the fact that "The Christian teaching that Jesus Christ was the Son of God can be meant only in the mystical sense which but approximates the human sense of these words, because nobody would maintain that God, as a being endowed with human sexual organs, had intercourse with the woman from whose womb Jesus Christ came forth" (Schreber, 1903, 3). Indeed, in many religious medieval paintings the conception of the Virgin is portrayed as rays emanating from the Heavenly Father into Mary's ear, as a representation of the old hymn: "Gaude Maria, mater Christi, que per aurem concepisti" (hail Mary who has conceived through the ear). Schreber explains his own transformation, by dint of "divine miracles," into a child-bearing woman, not a harlot to be misused sexually:

> "Something like the conception of Jesus Christ by an Immaculate Virgin — i.e., *one who never had intercourse with a man* [emphasis added] — happened in my own body. Twice at different times (while I was in Flechsig's Asylum), I had a female genital organ, although a poorly developed one, an in my body felt the quickening like the first signs of a human embryo: by a divine miracle God's nerves corresponding to a male seed had been thrown into my body; in other words fertilization had occurred." [Ibid., n. 1]

Are we to understand the words 'seed' and 'fertilization' literally and sexually, or metaphorically and therefore mystically? Schreber pays Flechsig back for his arrogance, his 'Professorendünkel' (professorial arrogance) and the hypocritical manner in which he "repeatedly exclaimed, as if astonished: 'is he not unmanned yet?'", just as "God's rays frequently mocked [him] as 'Miss Schreber'" (Ibid., 127). This Schreber did by having visions in which "Professor Flechsig called himself 'God Flechsig' to his wife, so that she was inclined to think he was mad" (Ibid., 82). In his "Open letter" (1903) he asks Flechsig more pointedly: "I beg you therefore, my dear Sir — I might almost say: I *implore* you— to state without reservation: ... (3) Whether during my stay in you Asylum *you yourself also* received visions or vision-like impressions particularly in dreams ... and many other matters mentioned in my 'Memoirs.' I hasten to add that from the numerous communications I received from the voices that talked to me at that time, I have the most weighty indications that you yourself had similar visions" (Ibid., xi-xii). Paranoid projection or true intuition? Flechsig suffered from sleeplessness and two students of his claimed he suffered from a mental disorder (Lothane, 1992 b).

6. Freud's final argument asserts that "the basis of Schreber's illness was the outburst of a homosexual impulse ... harmonizes with a noteworthy detail of the case history, [i.e.] the fresh 'nervous collapse,' which exercised a decisive effect upon the course of his illness, at as time when his wife was taking a short holiday on account of her own health. ... 'What especially determined my mental break-down was a particular night, during which I had quite an extraordinary number of emissions' [Ibid., 44]. ... It is easy to understand that the mere presence of his wife must have acted as a protection against the attractive power of the men about him. ... [Thus] We shall be able to supplement the patient's emissions by assuming that they were accompanied by homosexual fantasies that remained unconscious" (Freud, 1911 c, 45). But there is no warrant for such an assumption, no hint in the entire *Memoirs* of a homosexual wish, and Freud's act of supplementing is tendentious and betrays a penchant for totalizing. Freud should have first pursued remarks about the male climacteric to explore fully Schreber's heterosexual conflicts, his fear of impotence and his wife's frigidity, let alone the sexual frustration of a sexually vigorous man of 51 imprisoned for years without a sexual outlet. Whither Freud's insights about actual-neuroses or defense neuro-psychoses as a reflection of present-day conflicts, not just rigid repetitions of infantile material? Whither the revolutionary revelations in *Die Traumdeutung* (Freud, 1900), which led to the homology, not just analogy, between *Traum-bildung* (dream formation) and *Wahnbildung* (delusion formation), *Traumarbeit* (dream work) and *Wahnarbeit* (delusion work), *Traumdeutung* (dream interpre-tation) and *Wahndeutung* (delusion interpretation)? Toward the end Freud concedes that "the attempt at recovery, which observers mistake for the disease itself, does not, as in paranoia, makes use of projection, but employs a hallucina-tory (hysterical) mechanism" (1911 c, 77). But since the same is true for symptoms, the rigid division between the paranoid and the hysterical mechanisms can no longer be maintained.

So, Freud's theory that Schreber became ill with dementia paranoides because of his negative oedipal transference towards Flechsig as older brother and father, such that soul murder, a metaphorical "rape of mind and soul," was really a wish for rape of his rectum, remains unproven. Schreber never hinted at such a thing. Rather, he said he would first be transformed into a woman and then abused sexually as a female harlot. In addition to a complex transsexual scenario,

Schreber connected the cultivation of femininity with a no less complex theology and a dispute with God shaped by the Book of Job and Goethe's *Faust*.

Moreover, Freud shows a glaring blind spot concerning the role of mother, wife, father-in-law and other family members in the story; of colleagues and superiors at the Oberlandesgericht; of the fact that Flechsig was not prima facie a figure for an older brother transference, being five years younger than Schreber. He fails to discern that the more relevant father-transference person was Weber, five years older than Schreber, let alone the traumatic nature of the hospitalization at Sonnenstein. With one exception (White, 1961), no analyst has taken into account the role of the mother, while Niederland first acknowledged it partially, and only by 1989 began to speak more about this factor (Niederland, personal communication).

7. Freud's fixation on the erotic father-transference led him to another blind spot: the role of aggression in father-son relations and the role of a punitive, anti-sensual and anti-sexual conscience, or superego, so crucial for the understanding of Schreber's character and conflicts about both sexuality and aggression. It will be remembered that in discussing Little Hans, who also wanted to bear children but was not branded as homosexual, Freud rejected Adler's 1908 seminal paper on aggression. This becomes evident in a quotation from the *Prolog im Himmel* of *Faust* I by means of which Freud conflates oedipal rebelliousness of another unnamed patient towards his father and Schreber's erotic desire for the father as expressed in the equation sun=father, with Nietzsche thrown in for good measure. Taking "the sun ... as nothing but another sublimated symbol for the father, ... symbolism [that] overrides grammatical gender — at least as far as German goes, for in most other languages the sun is masculine. Its counterpart in this picture of the two parents is 'Mother Earth'" (1911 c, 54), Freud glosses over the obvious importance of Mother Earth but rather pursues this patricentric reading of the sun's meaning for Schreber via "one of my patients, who had lost his father at a very early age, was always seeking to rediscover him in what was grand and sublime in nature," finds further corroboration in the notion that *Nietzsche's hymn Before Sunrise* is an expression of the same longing," adding in a footnote: "it was only as a child that Nietzsche too knew his father" (Ibid., 54). But Schreber lost his father at age 19 — which Freud knew, as acknowledged in his footnote (Ibid., 51) — experiencing great loss, not oedipal disobedience nor a "father complex [in which the] feminine wishful phantasy is simply one of the typical forms taken by the infantile nuclear complex" (Ibid., 55). Compare this with Freud's undiminished awareness of how "Schreber's God and his relation to Him exhibited the most curious features: how they showed the strangest mixture of blasphemous criticism and mutinous insubordination on the one hand and reverent devotion on the other" (Ibid., 51), rather than merely erotic desire.

The analytical issue is to demonstrate specifically how aggression become erotized, which Freud only dimly hinted at in the famed syllogism: I love him — I hate him — he hates me. Why this sequence, rather than a simple denial and projection: I love him — I do not love him — he loves me?

CONCLUSION

The story of Schreber is a source of many lessons about the ethics of psychiatry. My revision of the interpretive myths about Schreber carries a message for the differentiation between method and theory, between methodology and mythology. The two are dialectically complementary, and to borrow from Kant, to forgo one for the other is to end in a metaphysical illusion, or in totalization, or in reductionism. The other message is about love and ethics. In imitation of Schreber, I define psychoanalysis by means of two oxymorons: as a historical science and as a science of love ethics.

As far as history and psychoanalysis are concerned, we can again borrow Kant's words to say, that psychoanalysis without history is empty, for it must resort to empty clichés and formulas, while history without psychoanalysis is blind, it is a mere chronicling of events, without understanding the inner meaning, or message. I begin where my predecessors end: by fulfilling Freud's wish to know as much history as possible to understand Schreber's meanings and messages.

In his life story, and in its mythical-fantasmatic transformation in the ever-fascinating *Memoirs*, Schreber was concerned with some of the perennial problems of mankind: the nature of love, happiness, sexuality, faith in God or the Devil, good and evil. He was also concerned with the relation between God and the individual and with the question asked by Job and the Psalmist: why does God allow innocent people to suffer? To these questions he presented his own odyssey, his own private little Holocaust. In the historical Holocaust, the Jews also asked: why does God permit such evil? In both cases the answer was renewal of faith. I have made it my goal to understand and to disseminate both the personal and ethical messages of Paul Schreber and his *Memoirs*.

Schreber also discussed the reciprocity of perception and imagination, as did Freud, and debated Kraepelin's theories of hallucinations. In ancient Greek *theoria*, from the root related to theater, spectacle, meant viewing, speculation, contemplation, the contemplative life, the reciprocity of seeing real things and 'seeing' images, that is, being in dreams, hallucinations and delusions. Kant referred to theories as metaphysical dreams. In a letter to Fliess, Freud complains that Breuer treats his theories as fashioned by a man suffering from 'moral insanity' or 'paranoia scientifica' (Freud, 1985 c, 185). The great Ferenczi (1932) viewed "certain of the doctor's theories" as "scientific delusions" (1932, 94). I end with a paraphrase on Freud (1911): it remains for the future to decide whether there is more delusion in my theory than I should like to admit, or whether there is more truth in Freud's (here any other substitution is permitted) delusion than other people are as yet prepared to believe.

'A MAN LYING IN THE MANNER OF A WOMAN': SOUL MURDER, DEMONOLOGY, SODOMY AND THE FATHER IN THE *MEMOIRS* OF D. P. SCHREBER

Daniel Devreese

"Why do you not say it aloud?"
D.P. Schreber, *Memoirs*, 48, n. 26.

In a previous article (Devreese 1996 a), I have analyzed Schreber's *Memoirs* and cast them as a condensation of his family romance. That analysis was guided by the semasiology of 'soul murder', in which I deciphered two meanings; a theological one by Luther against Pope Leo X on the liturgy of the Eucharist (1521) and a criminological one by *Senatspräsident* Feuerbach (1832) concerning the crime against Kaspar Hauser. Accordingly, the delusion could be interpreted in the light of both meanings, as a function of his identification with Christ and with Kaspar Hauser. Furthermore, in three literary dramas (Goethe's *Faust*, Byron's *Manfred*, Weber's *Freischütz*), which he considered examples of soul murder, the figure of the father (Daniel Gottlieb Moritz) could be deciphered. The aim of the present study is to enlarge this hermeneutical approach in order to reconstruct the semantics of the concept and to elucidate the role of the father in the "genesis of soul murder" (Schreber, 1903, 22).

In the Old Testament we find forerunners of warnings against false prophets: "Woe to the women who sew magic bands upon all wrists and make veils for the heads of every stature in the hunt for souls!" (Ez. 13: 18). The witch of Endor asks Saul: "Wherefore then layest thou a snare for my soul, to cause me to die?" (1 Sam. 28: 9). The binding of the wrists refers to a magical ritual (Taylor, 123) and the term 'soul murder' was coined by Gregory the Great in his homily about the parable of John 10, which developed the theme of the sheep murdered by the rapacious wolf into an allegory of the soul murdered by the devil (*Homilia* XIV; Grimm 1835, II 832). The demonological meaning of 'soul murder' is articulated in the second Chapter of the *Memoirs* (22-23) and the title of the Good Shepherd appears in 70.

SAINT PETER DAMIAN'S BOOK OF GOMORRAH

Peter Damian (1007-1072) in his *Liber Gomorrhianus* (1049) extended the demonological meaning of soul murder through association with the crime of sodomy between spiritual fathers and their children. This ascetic eremite, who played a preponderant role in the pre-Gregorian Reform of monastic institutions and of clerical morals under Pope Leo IX (1049-1054) was an adversary of anti-pope Honorius II (Cadalus of Parma: 1061-1064), who appears in the *Memoirs*, in the context of a conclave after the death of the Pope (VII 84; Devreese, 1997 a, 245). This tract against sodomy by clerics included proposals of severe punishments against this 'most offending sin against nature'. Damian offered his book to the Pope, who in his reply not only differed from him but issued a mild rebuke. This most vocal spokesman in the anti-sexual campaign of the eleventh century ranked the sin of sodomy as the most offensive act among four kinds of sexual offense: solitary and mutual masturbation, intrafemoral coitus, and last and worst, complete sodomization, considered "the complete act against nature" (Payer, 29). Even bestiality would be preferable to homosexuality, on the grounds that only one, rather than two souls, are damned (Goodich, 19). Thomas Aquinas formalized this when he held that the 'sin against nature' is contrary to right reason and in conflict with the natural pattern of sexuality as fulfillment of procreative ends. As such, sodomy insults God as Creator of nature, and violates the divine order. It is worse than rape or adultery, because these only affect another human being (Goodich, 62-63). This tract is unique in medieval Christian literature, since it is the only treatment of various forms of homosexuality and the circumstances surrounding clerical offenses. Although his program of sexual repression was at first without much influence, it gained momentum in the next century with the rise of heresy, which seemed to confirm the worst fears of the reformers who were prone to associate, if not to identify, theological heterodoxy with sexual nonconformity (Monter, 1032).

In the *Book of Gomorrah* sodomy is compared with diseases, such as pestilence, leprosy and cancer, the latter being a term regularly used for such common afflictions as sores and ulcers: "Vice against nature creeps in like a cancer and even touches the order of consecrated men. Sometimes it rages like a bloodthirsty beast in the midst of the sheepfold of Christ with such bold freedom, that it would have been much healthier for many to have been oppressed under the yoke of a secular arm, than to be freely delivered over to the iron rule of diabolical tyranny under the cover of religion, particularly when this is accompanied by scandal to others" (*Preface*; Payer, 27). The allusion to John 10 is obvious and returns in Chapter V (Payer, 38, n. 21). In an explicit allusion to the punishment of Sodom and Gomorrah (*Gen.* 19), to the nefarious crime of Onan, and to *Lev.* 20: 13 ("If a man lies with a male as with a woman, both of them have done evil and shall be put to death; their blood will be upon them"), Damian considers the unmentionable vice of sodomy to be a mortal sin, by which the cleric forsakes "all dignity in the Church, which is no less the Kingdom of God" (Payer, 35; *Eph.* 5: 5). Since the sodomitical offender is "wandering in a circle in whirling madness" (Payer, 39), he should be punished in the same way, for "it is just enough that those who commit their flesh to the demons through such filthy intercourse against the law of nature and the order of human reason be allotted the common nook of prayer along with demoniacs" (Ibid., 59). "This is why the holy fathers carefully established, that sodomists pray together with the deranged, since they did not doubt that sodomists were possessed by the same diabolical spirit" (Ibid., 60).

Sodomy, demonology and madness (*insania*) are interrelated, and Dante adopted Peter's view on the punishment of sodomites (Pézard, 297, n. 5), for in the seventh circle of hell, on the plain of sterile burning sands, upon which fire fell in flakes like snow, four clerics or men of letters have to run around perpetually, gazing at the naked oiled bodies before them, against which they had offended (*Inferno* XVI, 21-25). In *Paradiso* Peter Damian still laments over the immorality of the clergy (XXI, 114-135).

The sin of sodomy is condemned in the harshest wording, which brings us to the core of my argument. Against the arbitrariness of the penitentials that prescribed "three years to a lay man, while a cleric is ordered to do penance for half a year, the blessed clerics who fornicate, if judged by the judgment of sodomists in fact mete out to others in the same measure. The greedy author of this error [Burchard, *Decretum* 17.39] is satisfied to win souls for the devil, and while he is zealous to destroy monks, he extends his perverse teaching to the order of the clerics. While the murderer of souls [*animarum homicida*] was not able to satisfy the stomach's gluttony for malice with the death of monks alone, he desired to satiate himself from another order" (Payer, 52). And again: "Truly, this vice is never to be compared with any other vice, because it surpasses the enormity of all vices. Indeed, this vice is the death of bodies, the destruction of souls [*interitus est animarum*]. It pollutes the flesh; it extinguishes the light of the mind [*mentis lumen extinguit*]. It evicts the Holy Spirit from the temple of the human heart; it introduces the devil who incites to lust" (Ibid., 63). Peter Damian condemned Burchard's apocryphal canon about sodomy as the "most pestilential queen of the sodomists" (Ibid., 63). Sodomy is the most offensive crime, not only for the fact "that those fornicate irrationally, who mix with cattle or who are polluted with males", but by the fact that "the one partner could not die in sin without the other dying also" (Ibid., 64). "To die in sin" is the second death, that of the soul: "homicidia spirituale dell'anima", hence: "Seelenmord: *est extinctio, perditio animae*; Grimm, *DWB*, X 24). In other German nineteenth-century dictionaries, 'Seelenmord' is described as: "die gänzliche sittliche Verderbung eines Menschen" (Heinsius, 1822, IV 486), or: "ein arges, seine Existenz ge- fährdendes, oder sie vernichten des Unrecht" (Sanders, 1876, II 331).

In 'A mournful lament for the soul, who is given over to the filth of impurity', Peter apostrophizes the clergy committing sodomy as "*Unmanned man*, speak! Respond, *effeminate man*! What do you seek in a male which you cannot find in yourself? What sexual difference? What different physical lineaments? What tender, carnal attraction? What pleasant, smooth face? Let the vigour of the male appearance terrify you, I beseech you; your mind should abhor virile strength. In fact, it is the rule of natural appetite that each seek beyond himself what he cannot find within the cloister of his own faculty. Therefore if contact with male flesh delights you, turn your hand to yourself" (Payer, 68). Sodomy is a plague, such as "the plague of Gomorrah, that now lives in the dwelling of your body - the pestilence which condemned the house of Joab with revenge for cruel homicide" (Ibid., 69). Sodomy is drawn in parallel with contagious diseases, such as leprosy and pestilence, the first being considered as a disease of the soul and the latter being a metaphor for heresy (Mitre Fernandez, 71, Moore, 3-5). He refers to the Fathers of the Church, Ambrose and Augustine, "who disputed sharply against different sects of heretics" such as the Manichees (Payer, 88). Against those who would "preserve the stricture of silence about those *murderers of another's soul*" (Ibid., 87), he argues: "if blasphemy is the worst, I do not know in what way sodomy is better. Blasphemy makes a man to err; sodomy, to perish. The former divides the soul from God; the latter joins it to the devil. The former blinds the eyes of mind; the latter casts in the turmoil of ruin" (Ibid., 89).

In the Western theological and legal tradition, sodomy as a crime against nature was considered for the first time as a *crimen majestatis* or high treason against God, in the decree *Vergentis in senium* (1199) of Innocent III, which was important in the institutionalization of the Inquisition (Chiffoleau, 294). The criminological meaning of soul murder in early German penal codes was an offense against religion (*Religionsdelikt*) (Küper, 112) and depended upon its theological meaning. Schreber considered soul murder to be the cause of the "crisis in the realms of God" (Schreber, 1903, 22). The association in canon law of soul murder with sodomy as the most offensive act in the hierarchy of sins, had an apparent effect, being the judicial basis for the pursuit of heresy as the perversion of the Christian religion. For this meaning of soul murder, explicitly related to sodomy, played a fundamental role in the Inquisition. In 1208 Innocent III ordered Dominicus Gutzman, the founder of the Dominican Order, to organize the Inquisition against the Albigensian Neo-Manichean heresy, modeling this new procedure on *Gen.* 18: 21, where God says of Sodom and Gomorrah: "I will go down and see whether they have done according to the cry that is come unto me" (Kelly, 995). In 1252 Innocent IV in his bull *Ad extirpanda* introduced torture and capital punishment into the inquisitorial procedure, stigmatizing heretics as "robbers, killers of souls and thieves of the sacraments of God" (Shannon, 80). In 1307 King Philip IV of France opened the trial of the Order of the Temple with a charge of sodomy: "A bitter thing, a lamentable thing, a thing which is horrible to contemplate, terrible to hear of, a detestable crime, an execrable evil, an abominable work, a detestable disgrace and a thing almost inhuman, indeed set apart from all humanity" (Barber, 45). After being tortured, they were sentenced to the stake and in 1312 Pope Clement V suppressed the Order.

The identification of sodomy with heresy by sixteenth century German illiterate peasants was not an instance of "conceptual confusion" (Sabean, 237), for both concepts had long been irrevocably linked by ecclesiastic authority that was prone to interpret Neo-Manichean ascetic aversion to heterosexuality as proof of perversion by heretics (Monter, 1024). Schreber feared soul murder, homosexual attacks and castration by Flechsig (Schreber, 61; Baumeyer, 1955, 516) and he identified with two famous victims of the Inquisition: the Bohemian reformer John Huss (Ibid., 410), who was sentenced by the Council of Constance in 1415, and Joan of Arc (Ibid., 77), who was burned at Rouen in 1431.

SOUL MURDER: SODOMY AND HERESY IN THE MEMOIRS

In the *Memoirs*, we find two passages that hint at sodomy and heresy. First, the apocalyptic delusion began with catastrophes, such as those of Sodom and Gomorrah (Ibid., 60), or with the reappearance of such "devastating epidemics as leprosy and plague hardly yet known in Europe and signs of which were visible on my own body" (Ibid., 91). He also had "to recite certain strange-sounding incantations, such as 'I am the first leper corpse and I lead a leper corpse' - incantations which, as far as I could understand, were connected with the fact that lepers had to consider themselves doomed to certain death" (Ibid., 92). In the *Book of Gomorrah* leprosy and pestilence are metaphors for sodomy, while "Flechsig should have destroyed the basis of religion (Ibid., 91). The delusion is framed by Manichean theology which is characterized by the antagonism between Ariman and Ormuzd, impure and pure rays, darkness and light, deceit and truth. Flechsig is identified with Ariman, the God of evil in Manichean gnosis, who sent the plague of homosexuality (Hoheisel, 298), while the father *Gottlieb*, whose third Christian name *Moritz* represents a loose anagram of Ormuzd, is identified with the God of truth and light (Devreese, 1998 a, 151).

Other important clues for the offense which Schreber attributed to Flechsig are written down in paratextual passages: in footnotes, or in addenda. Footnote 62 about the 'System des Darstellens' is evidence of the fact that he thought of soul murder as heresy and sodomy. For he gives two specific examples in the same context about the threat of unmanning and trans-sexualization as 'Miß Schreber', adding that the hallucinatory voices were threatening him ignominiously by the words: "Sie sollen nämlich dargestellt werden als *Gottesleugner*, als einer, der *Seelenmorde* getrieben". Footnote 62 refers to the sentence in Chapter IX p. 128, where the voices repeat *ad nauseam*: "Sie sollen nämlich als *wollüstigen Ausschweifungen* ergeben *dargestellt werden*". Both accusations that reappear as examples of the *Denkzwang* (Schreber, 1903, 218) are the matter itself, for "given to voluptuous excesses" and "denier of the existence of God" hint at the crime of sodomy, viz. at heresy. Hence, he refers to II 23, which deals with the accusation of soul murder and its inversion, the "System des *Darstellens*": "at first Flechsig was named as the instigator of soul murder, but of recent times, in an intended attempt to reverse the facts, I myself have been accused [*dargestellt*] as the one who committed soul murder" (Ibid., 23). The "System des Darstellens" levels an accusation, which oscillates between the defense and the plaintiff. It is followed by a version of the selling of one's soul to the devil by a written pact and "the torturing of the soul which in the end gave the devil special pleasure" (Ibid., 23). In his *Volksbuch vom Doctor Johann Faust* (1587), the Lutheran publisher Johann Spiess warned against the "Leibs und Seelen Mord" by the devil (Petsch, 4). In Chapter IX his being accused of soul murder hints at sodomy, for in that chapter and at that stage of transsexual delusion, he was forced by the voices to take a 'female posture' which *Lev.* 20: 13 condemned as that of a passive sodomite.

The concept 'Darstellen', which Macalpine renders as 'to represent', pertains to the *Grundsprache* and means 'to accuse': "zeugen darstellen: testes ad judicium producere" (Grimm, *DWB* II, 791). From the same entry, the Biblical context is evident: "dasz sie die Zeichen ihrer Hurerei von ihrem Angesichte weg tue und die Zeichen ihrer Ehebrecherei zwischen ihren Brüsten, auf daß ich sie zur Strafe nicht nacket ausziehe und darstelle wie sie war, wenn sie geboren ward" (Hosea 2: 5). The juridical and heresiological meaning is apparent from other quotations: "wir werden alle vor dem Richtstuhl Christi dargestellt werden *Röm.* 14, 10" and: "die so der Ketzer Irrthum beschirmen und durch ihre Gewalt aufhalten, das Sie in des Richters Gewalt Sie zu verhören nicht dargestellt werden, *Luther* 1. 18".

In 1816, Byron had to leave England as a social outcast, after the scandal about three crimes (murder, sodomy and incest with his half-sister Augusta Leigh), which he confessed to his wife Annabella Milbanke: "I'm a villain - I could convince you in three words" (Crompton, 214). Sir Ralph Noel "treated his son-in-law of public proceedings, calling on facts capable of the clearest proof and asserting that his own action would bear the test of the most rigid public investigation" (Knight, 59). "Taking with her that statement made by her son-in-law, Lady Noel sought legal advice from an ecclesiastical lawyer, Dr. Stephen Lushington, who ruled that Lady Byron should never return to her husband" (Ibid., 75). In his *Byron and Greek Love*, Crompton (164) quotes an anonymous pamphlet about *The Trying and Pilloring of the Vere Street Club*, which in 1810 attracted an enormous crowd in London. In Regency England sodomy was punished by pillorying and hanging. In *Manfred*, written in the first year of exile, Byron's capacity to hint at the hidden, unspeakable crime of his *alter ego* Manfred against Astarte, is paired with a denial of the sale of his soul to the devil: "my past power/ Was purchased by no compact with thy crew" (III 4, 113-114).

For Freud, this was evidence of the fact that the "essence and secret of the whole work lies in - an incestuous relation between a brother and a sister" (1911 c, 44), this being the kernel of soul murder. "A terrible crime, a frightful transgression lies in the background and the past of these figures; but what it was we are never told, or at best are given only hints of. Those hints suggest a violation and destruction of another personality or at least an attempt at it. It is not simple murder that appears to haunt these men, but the murder of a soul" (Peckham, 103). The pact was supposed to be ratified by sexual intercourse with the devil, and since he is a father figure, the pact represents an implicitly incestuous sexuality (Jones, 199). "Manfred's explicit incestuous love represents an implicit diabolic pact", while his self-reproaches "bear an uncanny resemblance to melancholia" (MacDonald, 30, 32).

In light of the semasiology of soul murder verses like: "loved each other as we should not love" (II 1, 27), "some half-maddening sin" (II 1, 31), and above all: "the deadliest sin to love as we have loved" (II 4, 123), must be related not merely to incest, but to marital sodomy (Crompton, 353, n. 14), which Lady Byron, "apparently under the seal of uttermost secrecy" (Knight, 75) avowed to her ecclesiastical lawyer. Astarte, then, is less a person than the expression of Byron's love-life as a whole and the condensation of at least two women, his wife Annabella Milbanke and his half-sister Augusta Leigh, reflecting the crimes of sodomy and incest. In Manfred's prayer to the Sun and repudiation of the Abbot of St. *Maurice*, which is an equivalent for *Moritz*, Schreber portrays a heretical stance for the drama that ends with verses (III 1, 4748; 54-55), which are negations of two sayings of Christ (Mt. 5: 17; 1 Tim. 2: 5) (Looper, 237). Manfred died unrepentant, in a state of mortal sin, his soul succumbing to the second death. The Manichean inspiration is obvious and the 'Globe of Fire' on which Arimanes is enthroned "surrounded by the Spirits" (*Manfred* II 4), hints at the 'Feuerkugel', the house in Leipzig in which Schreber's mother was born and which Goethe as a law student inhabited and praised in *Dichtung und Wahrheit* (Devreese, 1996 a, 920).

The dialectic of mutual accusation and of crime and punishment is the principle of the transformations that Schreber, his wife and Flechsig underwent. This chain of crime and punishment is borrowed from juridical, Biblical or mythological sources. The first sanction is expressed by the term 'flüchtig hinmachen' (fleeting-improvised-men; Schreber, 1903, 44). His wife was the first victim of that sanction, which represents a condensation of a medieval sanction for people who could not pay their debts and were driven out of the city (*flüchtig machen; profugus*: His, 450) with *hinmachen*, the colloquial verb for to murder (Grimm, *DWB* IV 1455). This sanction was first extended to her relatives and to some jurists (Schreber, 1903, 4, n. 1)! By this negative hallucination, that was the onset of the apocalyptic delusion, he declared her, and subsequently the whole world, dead. This interpretation is confirmed by a vision that is inspired by the destruction of Sodom: "I walked as though across a large cemetery where, coming upon the place where Leipzig's inhabitants lay buried, I crossed my own wife's grave" (Ibid., 74).

Years ago, in researching the third chapter of the *Memoirs*, I discovered the real cause for Schreber's aggression towards his spouse in the *Personalakte* (personal file) at the Ministry of Justice (Dresden). It contains a letter dated the 15th of June 1894 by Dr. Clemens Werner, the President of the Court of Appeal in Dresden, to the Department of Justice. He stated that Schreber's wife complained about his opposition to signing the monthly pay slips. He included also a letter by Flechsig stating her complaint. The Department ordered that in the future she should cash the cheques, provided that he sign them as well (Devreese, 1986, 208 - 210). In the Leipzig idiom, this procedure was called a 'Seelenverschreiber' (Grimm, *DWB*, X 37). The conflict over the cheques was the onset of the plot Schreber feared between his wife, Flechsig and the 'Gottesreiche' (the Department of Justice), being the core of Flechsig's *Seelenpolitik*, i.e. the transfer of his patient to the asylum of Coswig on the previous day (14 June) and to Sonnenstein, "amongst the fossils" (Schreber, 1903, 118, n. 58) at the end of the same month (Devreese, 1986, 164-166). About his intermediary stay at the 'Devil's Kitchen' in Coswig, Schreber wrote that his "fellow lodger [in Dresden] von W. [= Johann Georg Freiherr von Welck; *Staatshandbuch 1894*, 505] had given false evidence about me in some State inquiry, either on purpose or through carelessness and particularly to have *accused me of masturbation*; as *punishment* for this he had now to be my servant in the form of a fleeting-improvised-man"

(Schreber, 1903, 108). The motive for this accusation by "the soul of von W., that hung on the opposite wall of my bedroom, *when I was lying in bed*" (Ibid., 194), appears much later: "the abdominal putrefaction of von W. who probably had the most impure nerves and therefore exhibited the most abominable intent towards me, expressing himself with unabashed impudence, for example 'permit me to dislodge him from his position'" (Ibid., 194; my own translation). Freiherr von Welck was the *Kreishauptmann* of Zwickau, a town in South Saxony, where Flechsig was born in 1847. In this function von Welck was subordinated to Rudolph Schurig, the Minister of the Interior, who was also Prime Minister and Minister of Justice.

The second stage, fear of violation by Flechsig, is expressed by "*liegen gelassen werden*, wie eine weibliche Dirne" (Ibid., 56). The expression is borrowed from Ez. 16: 38-39), where Yahweh punishes His brides Ohola and Oholiba (a metaphor for Sodom and Samaria) for their fornication with Israel's enemies and their idolatry of false gods. In the *Memoirs*, idolatry is present in the accusation of his spouse, who after his recovery from the first illness in 1885 "worshipped Professor Flechsig, as the man who had restored her husband to her; for this reason, she kept his picture on her desk for many years" (Ibid., 36). If his fear of violation by 'God Flechsig' is inspired by the Book of Ezekiel, his transsexual ritual, "standing in front of the mirror with female adornments (ribbons, trumpery necklaces and suchlike) with the upper half of my body exposed" (Ibid., 429) is likewise borrowed from Ez. 16: 1-7, which precedes the damnation of the Lord's Bride. He also feared "being buried alive" (Ibid., 59); in German medieval law, this was a punishment for virgins who had illicit intercourse and were buried alive under the gallows (Grimm, 1828, 691). Flechsig himself wrote that Schreber feared the "homosexual love [*Urningsliebe*] of certain persons" (Baumeyer, 516). The term was coined in the 1860's by Karl Ulrichs, a German jurist and poet who was also the author of *Incubus* (1869) (Leibbrand, II 574, n. 4).

The third stage consists of his 'vision' about Flechsig, who should have committed suicide in the police prison of Leipzig and then been buried in an ignominious way, outside the city, at the Thonberg (Schreber, 1903, 82). The vision appeared around the middle of March 1894, after "a newspaper was put in front of me, in which *something like* my own obituary notice could be read" (Ibid., 81). The *Leipziger Tageblatt* of 14 March 1894 does not contain his obituary (Lacan, 1959, 208), nor that of his father or his brother (Niederland, 83-84), but the announcement of the promotion on the first of April of Ernst Hugo Seyfert to the Superior Court in Dresden (Devreese, 1997 a, 254). He interpreted that promotion as his own replacement, as his death and hence, as a plot "in March or April 1894" (Schreber, 1903, 56) of Flechsig with the Department of Justice. As a reaction, "he wanted to become a Roman Catholic in order to escape from persecution [*Nachstellungen*]" (Baumeyer, 1955, 516). Hence, his revenge on Flechsig who was punished as a "fleeting-improvised *charwoman*" (Schreber, 1903, 108, n. 56). In note 8, he wrote that he was reading Greek authors in the original text. The metamorphosis of men into women is borrowed from Plato's

Timaeus, being the punishment for cowards and unrighteous men (*Tim.* 90 e), who after death and metempsychosis (Schreber, 1903, 85) become women or, in the worst case, birds. It is also the philosophical source of the delusion about the enchanted birds. Ezekiel and Plato's cosmology (*Tim.* 91 a; Schreber, 1903, 150) are sources for his transsexual delusion, which is entirely based on the concept of metamorphosis [*Verwandlung*] (Devreese, 1996 b). The punishment is a mirroring penance (*spiegelnde Strafe*), based on the *jus talionis* practiced in German medieval law (Schild, 197). For it implies the previous soul murder by Flechsig, i.e. the sexual abuse of his patient as a harlot, who is 'liegengelassen', by her enemies (Schreber, 1903, 56, 59). Buried in a footnote he imposed another ignominious penance on Flechsig, "having to perform drayman's work [*Kärrner-dienste*]" (Schreber, 1903, 13, n. 7). He described this punishment as rather moderate [*glimpflich*] (n. 56), in contrast with the words the Judges at the Royal Court used in 1902, about "the defamation [*Verunglimpfungen*] which Professor Flechsig suffers in the *Memoirs*, as he is accused of soul murder and worse [*Seelenmord und noch viel Schlimmeres*]" (Ibid., 514).

For those eminent Judges who read the uncensored manuscript of the *Memoirs*, the accusation was twofold: "soul murder and worse". Yet, the latter offense, a homosexual assault, is unmentionable, after the introduction in 1891 of the Lex Heinze (Röhl, 127) and the Judges add: "the danger of being sued by Flechsig for libel is not very great, particularly as certain alterations are to be made in the manuscript before it is printed" (Ibid., 514). After censoring the third Chapter and many footnotes, Schreber reintroduced the accusation of homosexual assault by means of hypnosis (Ibid., xi) in the *Open Letter to Professor Flechsig* (March 1903), which is a substitute for the third Chapter (Devreese, 1997 b).

SOUL MURDER: KASPAR HAUSER AND THE JESUITS

As can be inferred from their Christian names (David, Salomo, Daniel, Johann, Gottfried, Gotthilf, Gottlieb), the Schreber family was deeply rooted in the German pietistic tradition. Barbara Schreber, a daughter of Hans Schreber (? - 1547), married Valentin Braun (1498-1601), Luther's amanuensis (Lothane, 1992, 110). Johann David Schreber (1669-1731) was a theologian before becoming Rector at the famous *Fürstenschule* in Pforta (1716 -1731), where Klopstock, Lessing, von Ranke and Nietzsche would study. In 1688, Johann David wrote a theological dissertation *De libris obscoenis* at the University of Leipzig in which he inveighed against the Latin erotic authors Ovid, Catullus, Juvenal, Horace and Martial, but also against *De matrimonio* by the Spanish Jesuit Thomas Sanchez about the casuistics of confession (Tabouret-Keller, 290). He called on Christians to reject and to burn such books (Lothane, 1992, 110). According to L. Marcuse (20; 24), the German puritanical tradition originated with that booklet. D.G.M. Schreber was a chip off the old block, for his pedagogic maxims are inspired by August Hermann Francke, the founder of the *Waisenhaus* in Halle, where Johann

Christian Daniel von Schreber, the entomologist and pupil of Linné, published in 1759 his first booklet *Novae Species Insectorum*, which reverberate as newly created insects in Chapter XVIII of the *Memoirs*. That ennobled great-uncle of Daniel Paul was the instigator of a feud in the family by taking over the legacy of his half-brother Daniel Gotthilf (Devreese, 1996 a, 730). In the view of his family tradition and of the *Jesutengesetz* in 1872, that in Saxony, the cradle of Lutheranism, had force of law until 1918, torture is attributed to the Jesuits. Martin Delrio attacked in his *Disquisitionem Magicarum Libri Sex* (Louvain, 1599) Johann Weier's revolutionary views on the witches as the product of a rabid dog, while at the same time he underpinned with scholarly erudition the *Hexenhammer* (1487) of Sprenger and Institoris (Baschwitz, 129-130).

Schreber considered the Jesuits to be instigators of the Inquisition. In an anonymous German drama about their alleged role in the Portuguese regicide (1758), they were branded as *Seelenmörder* (Lübeck, 1759; *GV* 133 p. 53). In 1773, the Society of Jesus was suppressed by Clement XIV, but was reestablished in 1814. Schiller's *Geisterseher* (1786; VI 77) was also inspired by the fear in Protestant Württemberg of the political intrigue of the Jesuits, who tried to convert Protestant princes to Catholicism (Hoppe, 242). In his family romance, D.P. Schreber *is* a Prince of Baden (1812-1833). One day before the last Margrave Ludwig of Zähringen died on 30 March 1830, Feuerbach wrote to Hegel's brother-in-law and Hauser's legal guardian, *Gottlieb* von Tucher, that his pupil had been barred from the throne by a plot in which "stupidity and religious fanaticism elevated to insanity and to diabolic, calculating evil play the leading role and which in due course will give an idea about the machinations of the Jesuit Congregation in our days" (Mayer & Tradowsky, 402)[1]. Anti-Jesuit pamphlets used four complexes of imaginary figures, which are tributary to heresiology: metaphors of light against darkness, of ambush and trapping, of animality (scorpions, hungry wolves concealed under sheepskins) and of disease (leprosy and plague) (Cubitt, 182-185). In German *Kulturkampf* the same metaphors were used (Schuselka, 162-171; Kißling, I, 330). Like Satan, they would annihilate the human soul in confession and seek to conquer the world by seducing widows and kidnapping their children. Béranger's popular song *Les Révérends Pères* (1819) suggests that they have a predilection for corporal punishment in education: "Hommes noirs, d'où sortez-vous?/ Nous sortons de dessous la terre;/ Moitié renards, moitié loups,/ Notre règle est un mystère./ Nous sommes fils de Loyola;/ Vous savez pourquoi l'on nous exila./ Nous rentrons; songez à vous taire!/ Et que vos enfants suivent nos leçons./ C'est nous qui fessons/ Et qui refessons/ Les jolis petits, les jolis garçons" (Béranger, 181)[2]. According to the Jules Michelet, who published the Templar trials in 1841, and in 1843 wrote a tract against the alleged machinations of the Jesuits, the human soul could not survive their suspicious policy, nor their mechanical methods in education: "La mort ne tue que le corps; mais l'âme tuée, que restet-il?" (Michelet, 42). In Eugène Sue's *Le Juif errant* (1844), a roman-feuilleton which dwelt upon the mythology of Jesuit devilry, conspiracy and murder, which spawned five different German translations in the following years (*GV* 142, 218), the Jesuits are portrayed as the murderers of the seven Protestant heirs of M. Rennepont, who knew the secret about the murder of Henry IV (1610) by 'the Jesuit Ravaillac'.

In Schreber's political-religious delusion, it was his "basic idea" as "a champion for the German people", that the Pope who bears "a scorching ray" (Schreber, 1903, 49), was conspiring with the Jesuits (Ibid., 49), the Jews and the Slavs against the German people (Ibid., 84), which "in modern times (perhaps since the Reformation), is God's chosen people, whose language He preferred to speak" (Ibid., 14). In this way, the Jewish people was displaced by the German, a paranoid delusion which coincides with the rise of political anti-semitism in Germany (Devreese, 1997 a, 273). Anti-semitism is also evident in the delusional idea that "a Viennese nerve specialist and baptised Jew produced in place of my healthy natural stomach a very inferior 'Jewish stomach'" (Ibid., 151), and in the Jewish stigma on the delusional genealogy, which he attributed to Flechsig (Ibid., 24) (Devreese, 1998 a).

Insofar as Jesuits are *Seelenmörder,* the obscure final fragment of the apocalyptic delusion can be elucidated: "I could tell of wandering clocks, that is to say souls of departed heretics said to have been preserved for centuries under glass [*Glasglocken*] in medieval cloisters (here too there is an undercurrent of something like *soul murder*), who announced their survival by a vibration connected with an infinitely monotonous and doleful humming noise" (Ibid., 96). But what about the glass bells under which those heretics are preserved? The fragment can be traced back to the custom of installing the mummified corpses of Jesuits under glass bells in the crypt of the church of St. Ignace at Klattau (Ibid., 85) in Bohemia (Gorys, 224). In the Hussite revolt the Dominican cloister of Klattau was destroyed and under the Black Tower, adjacent to the Jesuit Church, there is a torture room (Gorys 225). After the death of John Huss and the persecution of his followers, Taborite chiliasm urged "that all those desiring to be saved from the wrath of the Almighty God, which was about to be visited on the whole globe, should leave their cities, as Lot left Sodom, and should go to one of the five cities of refuge", including Klattau, where in 1424 a Taborite Synod was held (Kaminsky, 311-312; 500). The voices proposed him to become after his death a Jesuit Novice in Ossegg, the town he mentioned just before Klattau (Schreber, 1903, 85). Accordingly, he described an attempt at conversion by "*Catholic scorpions*, tiny *crab- or spider-like* creatures, which were put on my head", in order "to carry out some work of destruction". "Departed souls of former Jesuits tried to put in my head a different determinant nerve [*Bestimmungsnerv*], which was to change my awareness of my own identity; the inner table of my skull was lined with a different brain membrane, in order to extinguish my memory of my own ego [*Identitätsbewußtsein*]" (Ibid., 95). This attempt at conversion *is* the extinction of his soul. It harkens back to beliefs about the Jesuits' ability to annihilate the individual personality (Cubitt, 53) and to their machinations aimed at the conversion of Protestant princes. Yet, as can be inferred from the medical terminology, another instigator lurks behind it: his father as a Jesuit and hence, as soul murderer, extinguishing his identity of Kaspar Hauser, who according to Feuerbach had been eliminated from the throne of Baden by a Jesuit plot in the era of Restoration.

CHAPTER XI AND SOUL MURDER: SODOMY AND THE FATHER

On a hermeneutical basis, I have reconstructed the delusional positions between Schreber, his wife and Flechsig, which Freud (1911 c, 62-65) in his theory about the clinical forms of paranoia (persecution; erotomania; jealousy and megalomania) deduced from a single unconscious proposition: "I (a man) love him (a man)". The logical problems inherent in such a grammatical deduction, in order to present the switch of the relation to the other by all the different ways of denying a basic proposition expressive of homosexual love, remain unquestioned (Lacan, 1959, 188), even after the study of Bruss (1976). J. Forrester (1980, 155) has argued that in Freud's theory intended to contribute to a general theory of paranoia, the level of the primal sentence and that of the text, or clinical detail, never meet. As demonstrated, two forms of paranoia (jealousy towards his wife and persecution by Flechsig), are ubiquitous. Yet, it was Freud's aim to demonstrate that Schreber's anxiety about sexual abuse by Flechsig was primarily a homosexual *wish* for him (1911 c, 72). In our view, his "delusional homosexuality" (Lacan, 1959, 219) was primarily *anxiety* about sexual abuse by Flechsig, but also by another physician: his father. Although F. Baumeyer in 1955 published his medical chart with the entry by Flechsig that "he feared the homosexual love of certain persons" (516) - an entry Freud never read! - Macalpine (1955, 377) and Lothane criticized the role of homosexuality in general. Lothane even "argued for the non-sexual and interpersonal interpretation of soul murder as a rape of the mind, the sexual fantasy being a metaphor for political reality, sexual abuse standing for moral abuse" (1993, 132). By this hermeneutics of locutions that enact Schreber's transformations as well as those of his antagonists, we can conceive the chain in which the erotic aggressions experienced by the subject were formed (Lacan, 1959, 219). The permutation from a delusion of jealousy towards a delusion of persecution ends in the position of the object of an "érotomanie mortifiante" (Lacan, 1969, 76) towards God, viz. the father. Moreover, framed by soul murder as sodomy and demonology, the "essential genetic relation" which Freud (1911 c, 34) postulated between the transformation into a woman and the favored relation to God can be reconstructed from the *Memoirs*. Freud's theory about paranoid psychosis as the return of a repressed homosexual fantasy about the father, can be endorsed within this matrix, which is homologous with that of demonology, the Inquisition and the orthopaedic instruments of his father.

Although Chapter XI about torturing and miracles is the somatic argument for Chapter II about soul murder, it is impossible to trace the whole catalogue of wonders and of all kinds of machines back to the orthopaedic instruments of his father, as Niederland (1974) and Schatzman (1975) had proposed. They never analyzed the concept of soul murder, but inversely defined it as the cluster of more or less stringent parallels between the delusion of the son and the medical instruments, or the pedagogic rules of his father. The catalogue of tortures in Chapter XI is heterogeneous and, *as a whole*, cannot be traced back to his instruments, for one miracle, the 'putrefaction of the abdomen' [*Unterleibsfäule*

= peritonitis] (Schreber, 1903, 153) was his lethal symptom. 'Putrefaction' is displaced onto von W., who accused him of masturbation; "but putrefaction could be removed again by God's rays, which pushed their way into my intestines like a wedge" (Ibid., 154). Three 'miracles' hint at his childhood fantasy of being sexually abused by the father, thus combining soul murder and sodomy in accordance with the literary version about the father (Daniel) as a devil: Samiel, the Black Hunter in the *Freischütz* (Devreese, 1996 a, 918), or as a Black Man: a Jesuit. Weber's opera set after the Thirty Years' War, was inspired by Bohemian witch-trials. The *Freischütz* was the oldest stratum of his family romance, for in nineteenth-century German bourgeois ritual, it was the first opera children attended (Mayer, 69). Moreover, two of the *dramatis personae* are Kaspar (an equivalent of Kaspar Hauser), who out of jealousy for Agathe barters his soul to the devil, and Anna, a "young relative" hints at his sister Anna. Wilhelmine Schröder-Devrient, an acquaintance of Schreber's mother, performed the role of Agathe in the Vienna première of 1822 (Devreese, 1996 a, 920). Within this matrix a cluster of miracles can be described which hints at three torture machines of the Inquisition, and at the same time, at three orthopaedic instruments of the father. The latter are isomorphic to the former and imply his role as the devil, which in the *Memoirs* is hinted at through contiguity or condensation with the Jesuits (Schreber, 1903, 95; 116), parallel to the double identity of the son: D.P. Schreber / Kaspar Hauser.

The first homology exists between the torture of the 'Kopfzusammen-schnü-rungsmaschine' (Ibid., 159) and the inquisitorial "head crusher, in which the victim's chin is placed on the lower bar and the cap forced down by the screw" (Held, 62, fig. 23). Our author describes torture with the head-compressing machine as follows: "The *little devils* stood on both sides of this cleft [*Spalte*] and compressed my head as though in a vice by turning a kind of screw, causing my head temporarily to assume an elongated almost pear-like form" (Schreber, 1903, 159). The cleft corresponds with the torture of the "inner table of my skull that was lined with a different brain membrane, in order to extinguish my memory of my ego" (Ibid., 95), which was first ascribed to the Jesuits. The form of the machine is isomorphic with the famous *Kopfhalter* of his father, which binds the head of the child in leather belts and is fixed by a bar to the back (Schreber, 1858 a, 220, Niederland, 54, fig. 5), in order to secure the symmetrical growth of the skeleton. Moreover, the accusation of his father as a sadistic devil and soul murderer corresponds with that of Faust about his father as a "freche Mörder" (*Faust*, v. 1055), who was also a physician and used instruments: "Du alt Geräte, das ich nicht gebraucht/ Du stehst nur hier, weil dich mein Vater brauchte./ Was Du erberbt von deinen Vatern hast,/ erwirb es, um es zu besitzen" (*Faust*, v. 676-677; 682-683).

The second, the compression of the chest-miracle [*Engbrüstigkeitswunder*] (Schreber, 1903, 150), was a predominant symptom in the demonological night-mare [*Alpdruck, Nachtmännlein*], implying the posture of the succubus, "weil es den Patienten vorkommt, als lege man ihnen eine grosse Last auf der Brust" (Zedler, I, C. 1327). The "little devils, who walked around on my head" (Schreber,

1903, 158), do not originate from his father's *Pangymnastikon* (Niederland, 95) but from the punishment for sodomites in Canto XVI of *Inferno*. The devil sitting on the breast of a sleeping woman is well-known in art since *The Nightmare* (1782) by Henry Fuseli. In the context of torture the miracle corresponds with the "crushing under hundreds of pounds of deadweight, a punishment called the turtle" (Held, 69, fig. 55). Significantly, the prodromal stage of his psychosis was characterized by the dream, "that it must be beautiful to be a woman succumbing to intercourse" and also by insomnia, by nightmares and palpitations (IV 37).

The third miracle is the "coccyx miracle [*Steißwunder*], an extremely painful caries-like state of the lowest vertebrae. Its purpose was to make sitting and *even lying down impossible*" (Schreber, 1903, 160). It is a delusional return of the 'Judas cradle', "by which the victim is hoisted up and lowered unto the point of the pyramid, in such a way that his weight rests on the point positioned in the anus, in the vagina, under the scrotum or under the coccyx" (Held, 50, fig. 37; 138, fig. 118), being a torture frequently inflicted on witches. The meaning of phallic penetration is obvious and this instrument designed by Girolamo Menghini, a Sienese judge and author of *Flagellum daemonum* (Venice, 1587), was also called the *Veglia* (the nightwatch), because the torture took place at night (Helbing, 196). The most famous victim of the Veglia was Beatrice Cenci who "after long and vain attempts to escape from a perpetual contamination both of body and mind by her father, at length plotted with her mother-in-law and brother, to murder their common tyrant" (Shelley, 272). Count Cenci was accused in 1594 of having sodomized his youngest son but escaped prosecution by buying papal indulgences. In Shelley's drama *The Cenci* the father suffering from venereal disease curses Beatrice: "Earth, in the name of God, let her food be/ Poison until she be encrusted round/ With leprous stains!" (IV 1, 128-130). Before Cenci was murdered, his wife Lucretia said to him: "She [Beatrice] bids thee curse;/ And if thy curses, as they cannot do,/ Could *kill her soul...*" (IV 2, 168-169). After the torture and death of all conspirators by the Roman Inquisition in 1599, the famous aristocratic family was extinguished.

The 'coccyx miracle' is linked to the "female posture in bed during intercourse" (Schreber, 1903, 166) and the concept of 'Darstellen' also appears in the description of the torture of lying in bed which in turn implies the sin of sodomy: "one did not want to admit that what had happened was not my fault, but one always tended to reverse the blame [*Schuldverhältnis*] by way of 'representing' [*Darstellen*]" (Ibid., 160). Symptomatically, he refers to his father's *Medical Indoor Gymnastics* (1856), in order to assure himself about the female posture: "Souls knew very well that a man lies on his side in bed, a woman on her back (as the 'succumbing part' [*unterliegender Teil*], considered from the point of view of sexual intercourse)" (Schreber, 1903, 166). Yet, after reading p. 102 of that book, he had to conclude "that even physicians do not seem to be informed about it". For on page 102 he could only find instructions against morbid and weakening *pollutions in boys*, which his father would suppress by 16 gymnastic exercises, by sitz baths in cold water, anal water clysters - and by the *exceptional* prescription of the sideways position in bed, instead of the 'normal' dorsal one. Yet, he referred to the wrong book! Only in the *Schädlichen Körperhaltungen* (1853) could he find an instruction *for girls in puberty*, that they never should sleep on their side, but always on their back. As a remedy, his father proposed a bed with belts, which is isomorphic with the torture of the rack, with "strait belts, applied to the victim's waist. His or her wrists are locked into the rings at the flanks, and he is thus subjected to torture. The devices were all-purpose bond, present in every prison and in insane asylums the world over" (Held, 120 fig. 50). Could the binding of the wrists, which in Ezekiel 13: 18 is a magical practice of witches, hint at his mother? In that book (Schreber, 1853, 11, 36-37, Niederland, 1974, 52, fig. 1 & 2), the father-devil towards his son in the pose of a *succubus*, is apparent. "Succubus" literally means: "unterlieger, succubus [*in coeundo*], der beim Alpdruck *quasi loco feminae* liegende Alp" (Höfler, 372).

'Liegen' is a nodal signifier which occurs in all dreams, fantasies and symptoms about sexual abuse, viz. metamorphosis. In reference to 'soul murder' as a demonological possession, this can be interpreted as an anal-masochistic phantasm, which some authors consider the "prerequisite of paranoid development" (Bak, 299, Green, 206). Parallel to soul murder, a chain of psycho-sexual positions was developed from his childhood-identification with Kaspar Hauser, towards the incubation period of psychosis and the dream "that it really must be rather beautiful [*recht schön*] to be a woman succumbing [*unterliegt*] to intercourse" (Schreber, 1903, 36). At a literal level, "unterliegen" is the expression of a 'female erotic position', while metaphorically it implies a male aggressor.

After his wife's two miscarriages in 1890 and in 1892 (Lothane, 1992, 39) all hope of progeniture was illusionary (Schreber, 1903, 36). The dream is the expression of a wish to have a son by himself (Freud, 1911 c, 58): as a feminine *succubus* to the devil. The dream appeared in June 1893, after "I was informed by the Minister of Justice Dr. Schurig in person of my impending appointment as *Senatspräsident* in Dresden" (Schreber, 1903, 36). "Wollust pflegen" is his term for voluptuousness towards God and "an obsolete expression used in *Genesis* 18: 12, when Sarah, old and barren, is promised a son by the Lord, but says to Him: *Nun ich alt bin soll ich noch Wollust pflegen?*" (Macalpine, 401). After His promise of a future progeny to Abraham and Sarah, He revealed the destruction of Sodom (*Gen.* 18: 20). About the end of the world that was the effect of soul murder, i.e. of the "rent [*Riß*; II 22] in the natural bond [*Band*] that holds God and mankind together" (Schreber, 1903, 60), he considered himself as Lot the righteous (*Gen.* 18: 23). In the frame of the "*genesis* of soul murder" (Ibid., 22) and a son lying bound by his father, the first instigator of soul murder "*Abraham* Fürchtegott Flechsig" (Ibid., 24) refers to the *Akeda* episode in Genesis (Rosolato, 71), where God orders Abraham to take "thine only son Isaac, whom thou lovest" to Mount Moriah (*Gen.* 22: 2). Before Abraham took his knife to slay him, he "bound Isaac and laid him on the altar upon the wood" (*Gen.* 22: 9). Schreber identified with the son and victim (Isaac/ Christ) and later on with their mothers (Sarah/ Mary), but his ubiquitous passivity is a symptom of the traumatic binding by his father, who prescribed that posture for girls during puberty: the "flappers and High School girls", for whom the *Memoirs* were *not* written

(Schreber, 1903, 443). The feminine fantasy originated about 1853, but forty years later, on the occasion of the memorial of his father's death, it was projected onto Flechsig as a defense against his "much too persuasive suggestive invigoration, in which he indulged on the subject of the promises of a sleep cure" (Lacan, 222 n. 10). The female position during that thaumaturgic cure prescribed by the wizard Flechsig (Schreber, 1903, 91) at his Nerve Clinic in Leipzig, near the Orthopaedic Clinic of his father, repeats the infantile complex about the father as a sodomist.

The demonological version of soul murder refers to one book by his father. But in his youth, the leading psychiatric theory about madness refers to an implicit demonological pact. Heinroth, the first professor of psychiatry in Leipzig (1811-1843) is generally considered as the most important exponent of that romantic-theologic doctrine in German psychiatry (Dörner, 255). As a friend of the family of Pauline Haase, and as a mentor of D.G.M. Schreber, in 1839 he became godfather of their first-born son Daniel Gustav (Busse, 108). After his death in 1843, the first chair of psychiatry in Europe remained vacant for an entire generation, until it was occupied in 1882 by Flechsig, who in his inaugural speech at the University Church ridiculed the obsolete moral theory of his predecessor (Flechsig, 1927, 25). In his *Lehrbuch der Störungen des Seelenlebens* of 1818, Heinroth considered mental illness to be caused by vice and sin, offering a transposition of old demonology into a moral theory about the copulation of the feminine soul with masculine evil, generating the child of mental illness (Dörner, 259). "The origin of mental illness is not only to be compared with conception but identified with it. Who are the parents of this family? Obviously, the mother is the soul itself. It is also easy to identify the procreator: it is always evil which copulates with the soul in many forms. For the soul is joined with evil, as the sexes are always joined: by love. The love of the soul for evil is called with a very expressive word, the proclivity to evil, for the soul can only join with evil through abasement and falling low [*Hinabneigen und Sinken*]" (Heinroth, I, 194)[3]. Flechsig's materialistic "Hirnmythologie" (Jaspers, 16) is diametrically opposed to Heinroth's moral aetiology of mental illness, but also to Schreber's demonological delusion.

That Schreber perceived Flechsig as a devil (*Zauberer*; n. 46) can be inferred from another symptom, where he had "Flechsig's soul and most probably his whole soul temporarily in my body. It was a fairly bulky ball or bundle, which I can perhaps best compare with a corresponding volume of wadding or cobweb which had been thrown into my belly by way of miracle, presumably to perish there" (Schreber, 1903, 82). Psychoanalytically, this represents the introjection of the bad object Flechsig which was later vomited (Ibid., 83); but in a demonological cast of thought, Johann Weier considered "one of the best-known symptoms of bewitchment: the vomitting of bones, nails, needles, *balls of wool*, bunches of hair, and other things" (Graham, 101-102).

After the expulsion of Flechsig's soul and about the "new human beings out of Schreber's spirit", he writes that he "had the God or Apostle as a soul in my body, more specifically in my belly" (Ibid., 115). This is his fertilization by

Gottlieb, who was a *Gesundheitsapostel* (Niederland, 61). The solution was achieved by splitting of the instance of the father and by the permutation from demonology towards orthodox religion. The father is the pivot in the permutation from the negative instance of the devil (Samiel = Daniel) to that of Moritz/ Ormuzd, or Gottlieb (= Theophilus). The delusion of being the Virgin Mary was the theological apex of the solution to the problem of soul murder, which was first formulated in a heresiological idiom. In the seminal legend about Theophilus of Adana, the Holy Virgin is the rescuer of the bond with the devil (Roskoff, I 285). The word "unversehrt" (Schreber, 1903, 93, n. 48) belongs to the *Grundsprache* and hints at bodily integrity (Ibid., 148), but also to the Catholic dogma of the Immaculate Conception (Grimm, *DWB*, XI 2092), which was proclaimed in 1854 by Jesuit propaganda (Perry, 116). It is also the central model of trans-sexualization: "Something like the conception of Jesus Christ by an Immaculate Virgin happened in my own body" (Schreber, 1903, 4, n. 1). The posture of a *Luder* (= lewd: Ibid., 136), he had to take up in catatonic stupor towards the *lower* Gott Ariman, was accompanied by the attempt of "tested souls to falsify my own frame of mind of a frivolous human being given only to the pleasures of the moment (to represent [*darstellen*] me as such, (*compare n. 62*)" (Ibid., 144). It is followed by a self-reference of Mephistopheles, the "Lord of the Flies" (= Ariman) in *Faust* (v. 1337): "Ein Teil von jener Kraft,/ Die stets das Böse will und doch das Gute schafft" (Ibid., 145). Those verses that precede the pact (*Faust*, v. 1413) mark the beginning of sexual transformation "in accordance with the Order of the World". For by a "great triumph of my dialectical dexterity" (n. 63) the evil is integrated in "the Order of the World, that carries its own remedies for healing the wounds inflicted upon it" (Ibid., 31).

All delusional sexual positions are borrowed from religious, mythical or juridical contexts, which specify punishments for whores or unfaithful women, or for 'a man lying in the manner of a woman', i.e. the sodomitical offense he feared from Flechsig, but which harkens back to the posture in bed his father prescribed for girls in puberty. Schreber's "elegant solution" (Lacan, 212) is dialectical, consisting in the permutation of a humiliating feminine posture, into a positive religious imago of the Virgin, who gives birth to the Divine Child, being the inversion of his initial identification with the dying Christ. That birth-fantasy occurred at Christmas 1900 with a couvade-symptom (*Hexenschuß*: lumbago: Schreber, 1903, 321) and this very fact refutes the theory about an "endless postponement of the realization of its aim" (Lacan, 1959, 211). This demonological symptom (Höfler, 1899, 598) or coccyx miracle (*Steißwunder*) is inversed into a positive symptom, with God/ *Gottlieb* as father of the "new human beings out of Schreber's spirit" (Schreber, 1903, 115), which was the climax of the reconstruction of the world. As Freud (1911 c, 78) pointed out, the acceptance of a feminine role was the condition for his asymptotic recovery, which was reached at Christmas 1900 in parallel with the writing of the *Memoirs*, which was the only product of delusion and which represents his spiritual child [*Geisteskind*] (Devreese, 1990, 210).

The turning point was reached in November 1895 (Schreber, 1903, 181) when

147

all previous relations with the *lower* God Ariman and with the *upper* God Ormuzd
were inverted. Nocive miracles were reduced to mere boyish pranks [*harmlosen
Schabernack*] and verbal hallucinations to neutral nonsense, such as "David and
Solomon" (Ibid., 181), the names of two Pietistic ancestors. In the end, "all
nonsense cancels itself" (Ibid., 182) and verbal hallucinations which initially
caused "mental torture" (Ibid., 132), were reduced to "the sound of sand trickling
from an hour glass" (Ibid., 311, 462). The "particularly dangerous 'scourge of
von W.' that used to move a little scourge about in my skull, and with it caused
serious destruction and often fairly severe pain" (Ibid., 194), was transformed
into the miracle of "golden drops [*Goldtropfen*] usually practised only by God's
omnipotence in which some fluid like balsam was placed on damaged parts of
my head and elsewhere, so that all at once an immediate curative effect was
achieved" (Ibid., 195). 'Goldtropfen' is a pietistic metaphor for the blood of
Christ (Langen, 74). Schreber's characterization of his progeny as "flesh from
my flesh and blood of my blood" (Schreber, 1903, 116) is the hybrid product of
the Old and the New Testament, being a combination of Adam's words after the
creation *in a deep sleep* of Eve, out of his rib ("this is now bone of my bones and
flesh of my flesh", Gen. 2: 23), with the words of Christ, the second Adam, at
Last Supper ("this is my flesh and my blood", John 6: 54). Transsubstantiation
becomes a theological version of metamorphosis. Yet in 1893, far from parodying
"the situation of a couple of ultimate survivors, following some human catastrophe" (Lacan, 1959, 211), he imitates the creation of the first couple (Schreber,
1903, 256), while transcending the identification with the agonized Christ. The
"*new* human beings" out of Daniel Paul Schreber's belly are borrowed from the
Pauline theologemenon about the new man in the flesh and blood of Christ (Gal.
6: 15; Eph. 2: 15; 4: 24).

The analysis of all delusional images demonstrates that from the beginning
to its end, he took a female posture, which was his way of answering the question:
"how can I a man, be in the process of having or actually have children? To live
through the various possibilities was his psychosis" (Macalpine, 386). Nevertheless, Freud's theory that paranoid psychosis consists in the break-through of a
repressed feminine fantasy, is correct. The reconciliation [*Versöhnung*; Freud
1911 c (GW VIII). 272, 284] with a homosexual attitude towards the father was
the solution of the problem and the end of the delusion. In that light, the problem
of the inversion about November 1895 (Schreber, 1903, 176) can be solved. The
evolution of his psychosis was determined by two 'anniversary reactions' (Pol-
lock). His psychosis broke out in November 1893 after the day of remembrance
of the death of his father (10 November 1861). In 1895, the son who was born in
1842, reached the same age as his father (1808-1861), i.e. 53 years. It is as if only
after reaching the same age and by enacting the lethal symptom (*Unterleibsfäule*;
Ibid., 153) of his father on his own body, could he repeat under a positive sign
the infantile feminine position towards the dead father "which in religion is the
symbolic Father insofar as he signifies the Law" (Lacan, 1959, 199). The
permutation towards femininity is a "deferred obedience" that Freud also described in the Haizmann case (1923, 88). The demonological-perverse *Seelen-*

mord is transformed into a state of spiritual and ennobled *Seelenwollust* (Schreber, 1903, 190), which as a prerequisite for falling asleep (Ibid., 178), never exceeds religious and moral limitations (Ibid., 282).

DEMONOLOGY AND THE THIRD ILLNESS

Schreber's paranoid illness was brought by his profound unconscious insight into a unique form of self-therapy which remained stable until November 1907, when his wife suffered from an apoplectic stroke resulting in aphasia, after which he was admitted to the psychiatric asylum of Dösen, near Leipzig. In 1908, five entries on his medical chart hint at demonology and trans-sexuality. In February, he "addressed the doctor angrily on his morning visit 'apage Satanas'" (Bau-meyer, 66). In March, he "asks the doctor entirely unexpectedly: 'When did Gustav Adolf reign? 1611 to 1632, wasn't it? (1611 - 1632 +). Has attempted to jump through the window" (Baumeyer, 66). That symptom has never been interpreted, but as can be inferred from his own words, he repeated the defenestration of the Catholics Martinitz and Slawata in Prague on 23 May 1618 by the Protestant Bohemian nobility (Rößler, 163). As if by a miracle, both lived through this attack, which was the immediate cause of the Thirty Years' War between German Protestantism and the Counter-Reformation. Gustav Adolf of Sweden, the liberator of Lutheran Germany, fell on 15 November 1632, in the battle of Lützen near Leipzig. The allusion to the suicide of Gustav by gunshot and to the salvation of the 'Feuerkugel', his mother's birthplace, in the devastating siege of Leipzig on 21 October 1642 (Müller, 48), is obvious. In 1905, on the occasion of her 90th birthday, he wrote a poem about that house with a charade on its name (Israëls, 58; 82). In that poem of 434 verses, "ein Stück Erinnerung aus alter Zeit" (v. 410) and the final poetical elaboration of his family romance, the word 'father' never occurs.

In May 1908, a transsexual symptom originates: "*lies down* on the lawn, with his waistcoat and shirt open over his chest" (Baumeyer, 66). The dorsal pose on the lawn, with his chest exposed to the sun, is borrowed from his father's *Buch der Gesundheit*, which prescribed sunbaths as a means to regenerate the nerve ends of the body by lying naked on a mattress in the garden (Schreber, 1839, 84). On the title page of that book he cited a poem by Fr. Rückert: "Bedenke, daß ein Gott in Deinem Leibe wohnt,/ Und vor Entweihung sei der Tempel stets verschont".

In June Schreber asked his doctor: "Why do the other Satans not come too? Why only you alone?" (Baumeyer, 66). Like his father, Flechsig and Dr. C.G. Ackermann of Sonnenstein (*Algemeine Zeitschrift für Psychiatrie*, 1906, Vol. 63, 922), who was called by the talking birds in the same breath with the lower God, "Ariman/ Ackermann" (Schreber, 1903, 210), the doctors at Dösen are devils too. Dr. Weber, who invited Schreber to his family table, never became a devil, nor can he be included in the delusional genealogy attributed to Flechsig (Lothane, 295).

In August we read: "Dresses and undresses several times a day. Lies down on his bed, then stands up again, to sit rigidly in the armchair for hours on end in his shirt" (Baumeyer, 66). His father in his last years wrote, that sun rays could be a powerful remedy against infantile illnesses, such as cretinism (Schreber, 1858 b, 169). One of Schreber's last scribbles before dying was: "auch nicht wollüstigen Ausschweifungen" (Israëls, 117), the central accusation in the second illness. The delusion began as an *Imitatio Christi* after the *Lutherfeiertag* (10 November 1893), which was instituted by the Gustav Adolfs-Verein, but he died on Good Friday 14 April 1911. In this way the infernal circle was closed.

The kernel of Schreber's *fantasy* about his father as homosexual violator, can be grasped in one medical document of 1853. Our theory does not imply a real anal violation by the father (de Mause, 1987) which Lothane (1992, 185) rightly criticized as an absurdity. Rather, his treatment against pollutions with anal water clysters is isomorphic with the wedge and with the Judas Cradle. After the accident with a ladder in 1851, he suffered from severe headaches and "Zwangs-vorstellungen mit Mordtrieb" (Lothane, 1992, 117), which may have been auxiliary to his role as sadistic devil. In 1852 he drew up the final version of his genealogy including his five children. In the same year Feuerbach's secret *Mémoire* about the real identity of Kaspar Hauser was posthumously published, Schreber constructed his family romance about the identification with that foundling who lived many years in a dungeon before being brought into the Vestner Gate Tower at Nuremberg in 1828 (Mayer & Tradowsky, 25), which had a torture room. In Bavaria in 1806, *Senatspräsident* Feuerbach abolished torture and inquisition on his own accord (Radbruch, 74-75). In Saxony, it had been abolished in 1770. But in Baden it existed as late as 1831 (Williams, 78). Schreber's identification with Kaspar Hauser and the construction of his exalted family romance around 1853 implies the forclusion of the 'Name of the Father' (Lacan, 1959, 220). The motive for his studying law and not medicine is obvious. Hauser's real noble title was the model for the delusional title Margraves of Tuscany and Tasmania, which is the reflection of his ambi-sexual conflict: man or woman? life or death? (Devreese, 1996 a, 729).

EPILOGUE: SCHREBER & HAIZMANN

At the dawn of psychoanalysis, when Freud discovered themes of witchcraft in the hysterical symptoms of Emma Eckstein and in paranoid patients, who complained about being sexually abused at night, he wrote to W. Fließ on 24 January 1897, that he had just ordered a copy of the *Hexenhammer* (1487) by the Dominican inquisitors Sprenger and Institoris, which he planned to study dili-gently (Freud, 1985 c, 239). On 21 September of that year, he transformed his theory of traumatic seduction into a theory of infantile sexual fantasy, under the influence of Johann Weier (1515-1588), the Dutch physician and author of *De Praestigiis Daemonum* (1563), who defended witches by arguing that their admissions were shaped by the coercive suggestions of the inquisitors (Swales, 331-333). Freud could have read about Weier in a work of Binz (Bonn, 1885), that was reissued in Berlin in 1896. In the meantime, on Easter 17 April 1897

Freud and Fließ visited Nüremberg and probably also the torture chamber (Swales, 339; 351, n. 8), with the famous Iron Maiden (Held, 25, fig. 1). Although he declared in the Haizmann case that the "demonological theory of those dark times has won in the end against the somatic views of the period of 'exact' science" (1923, 72) and that "the father is the individual prototype of both God and the Devil" (1923, 86), in his interpretation of the Schreber case he did not incorporate the demonological theme, which is the clue to the solution. In his opinion, "the fact that in our analyses we so seldom succeed in finding the Devil as a father-substitute may be an indication that for those who come to us for analysis this figure from medieval mythology has long since played out its part" (Freud, 1923 d, 87, n. 1). Nevertheless, he considered the Schreber case as lateral support for his theory about Haizmann's illness, which also expressed a feminine attitude towards the devil as father-substitute (Ibid., 91-92). The reason for not incorporating demonology in the Schreber case is obvious, since he did not consider 'soul murder' to be a demonological pact, but an expression of an incestuous wish. Accordingly, he regarded the father, a physician, as exclusively good (1911 c, 52; 1923 d, 91), although in a letter to Jung he wrote that "the delightful characterization of God, that he knows how to deal only with corpses and has no idea of living people, is a bitter satire on his father's medical art" (Freud, 1974, 369). As a pupil of Charcot, he considered demonology as belonging exclusively to "those early times" (1923 d, 72), being of no relevance to the case of his contemporary who was born in the heydays of Romanticism. Schreber's delusion is influenced by Heinroth's theory and by the scurrilous medical works of his father, "who legislated as an omniscient God" (Lacan, 1959, 220), but who in his medical practice must have been perceived as a sadistic, devilish Jesuit: 'perinde ac cadaver'.

NOTES

1. "Über die ganze Sache in welcher Dummheit und bis zum Wahnsinn gesteigerter Religionsfanatismus mit teuflisch rechnender Bosheit die Hauptrolle spielen, und welche seiner Zeit einigen Aufschluß über das Treiben des Jesuiten Kongregationen unserer Tage geben wird".

2. "Black men, where do you come from?/ We come from under the earth/ Half foxes, half wolves,/ Our rule is a mystery./ We are the sons of Loyola;/ You know the reason for our exile/ But we shall come back again/ Take care and shut your mouth!/ And see that your children follow our lessons/ For we spank and spank again, the jolly little, little boys".

3. "Einer Zeugung also wurde die Entstehung der Seelenstörungen nicht bloß verglichen sondern auch gleichgesetzt. Welches sind nun die Eltern dieser Familie? Die Mutter ist offenbar die Seele selbst. Auch der Erzeuger ist nicht schwer auszumitteln; er ist allezeit das Böse, mit dem sich die Seele begattet, in dem sich dasselbe ihr in mannigfacher Gestalt naht. Die Seele und das Böse werden vereinigt, wie überall die Geschlechter vereinigt werden: durch die Liebe. Die Liebe der Seele zum Bösen heißt der Hang zum Bösen, mit einem sehr ausdrucksvollen Worte, weil sich die Seele mit dem Bösen nur durch Hinabneigen und Sinken vereinigen kann".

REFERENCES

Abély, P. (1930). Le signe du miroir dans les psychoses et plus spécialement dans la démence précoce. *Annales medico-psychologiques, 88,* 28-36.

Adler, A. (1908). Der Aggressionstrieb im Leben u. in der Neurose. *Fortschritte der Medizin, 19,* 577-584.

Alzheimer, A. (1907). Über eine eigenartige Erkrankung der Hirnrinde. *Allgemeine Zeitschrift für Psychiatrie, 64,* 146-148.

Andreoli, A. (1976). Corps et psychose a travers les traitements de relaxation. *L'Evolution Psychiatrique, 41 (3),* 933-962.

Andreoli, A. (1981a). A la découverte d'une clinique du corps à travers la relaxation. In W. Pasini & A. Andreoli (Eds.), *Eros et changement. Le corps en psychothérapie* (pp. 73-127). Paris: Payot.

Andreoli, A. (1981b). Pour une théorie psychosomatique de la psychothérapie. In W. Pasini & A. Andreoli (Eds.), *Eros et changement. Le corps en psychothérapie* (pp. 251-300). Paris: Payot.

Andreoli, A. (1984). Le schizophrène et son corps: Remarques sur l'économie psychosomatique des psychoses dissociatives. *Archives Suisses de Neurologie, Neurochirurgie et de Psychiatrie, 135* (1), 87-99.

Aulagnier, P., Castoriadis. (1968). Remarques sur la structure psychotique. *La Psychanalyse, 8,* 47-67.

Aulagnier, P., Castoriadis. (1975). *La violence de l'interpretation.* Paris: Presses Universitaires de France.

Aulagnier, P. (1984). *L'apprenti-historien et le maître-sorcier.* Paris: Presses Universitaires de France.

Aulagnier, P. (1986). Naissance d'un corps, origine d'une histoire. In J. Mc Dougall, F. Gachelin, P. Aulagnier e.a. (Eds.), *Corps et Histoire* (pp. 99-141). Paris: Société d'édition "Les Belles Lettres".

Aulagnier, P. (1992). Voies d'entrée dans la psychose. *Topique: revue freudienne, 22* (49), 7-30.

Bak, R. C. (1946). Masochism in Paranoia. *The Psychoanalytic Quarterly, 15,* 285-301.

Barber, M. (1978). *The Trial of the Templars.* Cambridge: Cambridge University Press, 1995.

Baschwitz, K. (1963). *Hexen und Hexenprozesse.* München: dtv, 1983.

Baumeyer, F. (1956). The Schreber Case. *International Journal of Psycho-Analysis, 37,* 61-74; Der Fall Schreber. *Psyche, 9,* 1955, 513-536.

Beck, A. T. (1976). *Cognitive Therapy and the Emotional Disorders.* New York: International Universities Press.

Bentall, R. P., & Kaney, S. (1989). Content specific processing and persecutory delusions: An investigation using the Emotional Stroop Test. *British Journal of Medical Psychology, 62,* 355-364.

Bentall, R. P., Kaney, S., & Dewey, M. E. (1991). Paranoia and social reasoning:

An attribution theory analysis. *British Journal of Clinical Psychology, 30,* 13-23.

Beranger, P. J. de (1850). *Oeuvres complètes.* Bruxelles: Librairie Encyclopédique de Périchon.

Bleuler, E. (1911). *Dementia Pracox or the Group of Schizophrenias.* Zinkin, J. Trans. New York: International Universities Press, 1950.

Bolton, D., & Hill, J. (1996). *Mind, meaning and mental disorder. The nature of causal explanation in psychology and psychiatry.* Oxford: Oxford University Press.

Brett-Jones, J., Garety, P., & Hemsley, D. (1987). Measuring delusional experiences: A method and its applications. *British Journal of Clinical Psychology, 26,* 257-265.

Bruss, N. H. (1976). The Transformation in Freud. *Semiotics, 17,* 69-94.

Busse, G. (1990). *Schreber, Freud und die Suche nach dem Vater.* Frankfurt: Peter Lang.

Busse, G. (1991). *Schreber, Freud und die Suche nach dem Vater.* Frankfurt: Lang.

Chiffoleau, J. (1996). Contra Naturam. Pour une approche casuistique et procédurale de la nature médiévale. *Micrologus, 4,* 265-312.

Corveleyn, J. (1984). Het gepassioneerde betoog. Alphonse De Waelhens over le duc de Saint-Simon. *Tijdschrift voor filosofie, 46* (1), 57-82.

Corveleyn, J. (1984). De hysterische psychose in het oeuvre van Gisela Pankow. *Psychoanalyse, 2,* 47-56.

Crompton, L. (1985). *Byron and Greek Love. Homophobia in 19th-Century England.* London: Faber and Faber.

Cubitt, G. (1993). *The Jesuit Myth. Conspiracy Theory and Politics in Nineteenth-Century France.* Oxford: Clarendon Press.

Cutting, J. (1997). *Principles of psychopathology: Two worlds - two minds - two hemispheres.* Oxford: Oxford University Press.

deMause, L. (1987). Schreber and the history of childhood. *Journal of Psychohistory, 15,* 423-430.

Devreese, D. (1981). De "Personalakte" van Daniel Paul Schreber bij het "Königliche Justizministerium" te Dresden. In: *Psychoanalytische Perspektieven,* Rijksuniversiteit, Gent.

Devreese, D. (1986). Eléments nouveaux sur Daniel Paul Schreber: sa carrière de magistrat et l'histoire de sa maladie à la lumière de son dossier personnel. In D. Devreese & H. Israels, *Schreber inédit* (pp. 147-255). Paris: Seuil.

Devreese, D. (1989). *De Waan Lezen.* Doctoral dissertation, K.U.Leuven.

Devreese, D. (1990). Imago's en metamorfosen. De transsexuele dynamiek in Schrebers waan. *Psychoanalyse, 6,* 201-211.

Devreese, D. (1996 a). Anatomy of Soul Murder. Family Romance and Structure of Delusion in Schreber's Memoirs. *Psychoanalytic Review, 83/5,* 709-734: 83/6, 913-927. Also : Anatomie du meurtre d'âme. In: Prado de Oliveira, L. E. ed. *Schreber et la paranoïa.* Paris: l'Harmattan.

Devreese, D. (1996 b). Metamorphosis sexualis paranoica. In E.L. Prado de

Oliveira, *Schreber et la paranoa. Le meurtre d'âme* (pp. 237-258). Paris: Editions de l'Harmattan.

Devreese, D. (1997 a). "Ein Kämpfe für das deutsche Volk". Wereldondergangswaan, biografie en geschiedenis in de Denkwürdigkeiten van D.P. Schreber. *Belgisch Tijdschrift voor Nieuwste Geschiedenis, 27,* 243-288.

Devreese, D. (1997 b). Waan, theorie en autobiografie. Freud, Schreber en de hypnose rond 1893. *Psychoanalyse, 11,* 111-134.

Devreese, D. (1998). Genèse et structure des royaumes divins. In D. Devreese, Z. Lothane, & J. Schotte. *Schreber revisité. Actes du colloque de Cerisy* (pp. 133-163). Louvain: University Press.

Devreese, D. (1999). *L'acte manqué paranoïaque. Le délire de Schreber entre les quatre discours universitaires et dans l'histoire allemande de Luther à Bismarck.* Paris: L'Harmattan.

De Waelhens, A. (1961). *La philosophie et les expériences naturelles.* La Haye, Martinus Nijhoff, Phaenomenologica.

De Waelhens, A. (1970). *Une philosophie de l'ambiguïté. L'existentialisme de Maurice Merleau-Ponty.* Louvain/Paris: Nauwelaerts.

De Waelhens, A. (1972). *La Psychose. Essai d'interprétation analytique et existentiale,* Louvain-Paris, Nauwelaerts, 1971; *Schizophrenia. A Philosophical Reflection On Lacan's Structuralist Interpretation.* W. Ver Eecke (tr.). Pittsburgh: Duquesne University Press, 1978.

De Waelhens, A. (1981). *Le duc de Saint-Simon. Immuable comme Dieu et d'une suite enragée.* Bruxelles: Éd. Fac. Univ. St. Louis.

Dolto, F. (1984). *L'image inconsciente du corps.* Paris: Seuil.

Dörner, K. (1984). *Bürger und Irre. Zur Sozialgeschichte und Wissenschaftssoziologie der Psychiatrie.* Frankfurt: Europäische Verlagsantsalt.

Ferenczi, S. (1932). *The Clinical Diary of Sándor Ferenczi.* J. Dupont, ed. Cambridge: Harvard University Press, 1995.

Fine, A. (1992). Quelques aperçus de l'importance du corps dans l'oeuvre de Piera Aulagnier. *Topique: revue freudienne, 22* (49), 129-142.

Flechsig, P. (1882). *Auszug aus dem Statut für die Irrenklinik der Universität Leipzig; Bestimmungen über die Aufnahme, Verpflegung und Entlassung der Kranken enthaltend (1882).* Leipzig: Druck von Frankenstein und Wagner (Source: Flechsig, Personalakte, Staatsarchiv Dresden).

Flechsig, P. (1888). *Die Irrenklinik der Universität Leipzig und ihre Wirksamkeit in den Jahren 1882-1886.* Leipzig: Veit & Co.

Flechsig, P. (1927). *Meine myelogenetische Hirnlehre nebst biographischer Einleitung.* Berlin: Springer.

Forrester, J. (1980). *Language and the Origins of Psychoanalysis.* London: Macmillan Press.

Freeman, T. (1988). *The psychoanalyst in psychiatry.* New Haven: Yale University Press.

Freud, S. (1900 a). *The Interpretation of Dreams. Standard Edition,* 4-5.

Freud, S. (1907 a) *Delusions and Dreams in Jensen's Gradiva. Standard Edition,* 9.

Freud, S. (1911c). Psycho-analytic notes upon an autobiographic account of cases of paranoia (dementia paranoides). (Schreber). In *Standard Edition*, Vol. XII, pp. 1-82.

Freud, S. (1914 c). Zur Einführung des Narziszmus. *Gesammelte Werke X*. Also *On Narcissism*, in *Standard Edition*, 14.

Freud, S. (1915 c). Triebe und Triebschicksale. *Gesammelte Werke X*. Also *Instincts and their vicissitudes*, in *Standard Edition*, 14.

Freud, S. (1917). *Introductory Lectures on Psychoanalysis*. *Standard Edition*, 16.

Freud, S. (1920 g). Jenseits des Lustprinzips. *Gesammelte Werke XIII*. Also *Beyond the pleasure principle*, in *Standard Edition*, 18.

Freud, S. (1923 d). A seventeenth-century demonological neurosis. *Standard Edition*, 19.

Freud, S. (1931). Preface to Bourke's Scatologic Rites of All Nations, *Standard Edition*, 12.

Freud, S. (1937 d). Constructions in analysis. *Standard Edition*, 23.

Freud, S. (1985). *Briefe an Wilhelm Fliess 1887-1904*. Hg. von J.M. Masson. Deutsche Fassung von M. Schröter. Frankfurt: Fischer Verlag.

Freud, S. - Jung, C. G. (1974). *The Freud/Jung Letters*. Edited by W. McGuire, Princeton: Princeton University Press.

Gesamtverzeichnis des deutschsprachigen Schrifttums (GV) 1700-1910, Münich - New York: K.G. Sauer.

Gilmour-Bryson, A. (1996). Sodomy and the Knights Templar. *Journal of the History of Sexuality*, 7, 151-183.

Goethe, J. W. (1812). *Faust. Eine Tragödie*. München: Goldmann.

Goldberg, T. E., Weinberger, D. R., Berman, K. F. et al. (1987). Further evidence for dementia of the prefrontal type in schizophrenia. *Arch. Gen. Psychiatry*, *44*, 1008-1014.

Goldberg, T. E., & Weinberger, D. R. (1988). Neuropsychological studies of schizophrenia. *Schizophr. Bull.*, *14*, 179-184.

Goleman, D. (1995). *Emotional Intelligence*. New York, Bantam.

Goodich, M. (1979). *The Unmentionable Vice. Homosexuality in the Later Medieval Period*. Santa Barbara California-Oxford; England: ABC-Clio, Inc.

Gorys, E. (1994). *Kultur, Landschaft und Geschichte in Böhmen und Mähren*. Cologne: Du Mont.

Graham, Th. F. (1967). *Medieval Minds. Mental Health in the Middle Ages*. London: George Allen & Unwin Ltd.

Green, A. (1986). Réponses à des questions inconcevables. *Topique: revue freudienne*, *16* (17), 11-30.

Green, A. (1972). Aggression, feminity, paranoia and reality. *International Journal of Psycho-Analysis*, *53*, 205-211.

Green, A. (1992). L'originaire et la pensée des origines. *Topique: revue freudienne*, *22* (49), 49-65.

Gregory The Great, Homilia XIV. In J.P. MIGNE, *Patrologiae cursus completus. Series latina*, Paris 1849, vol. 76, col. 1483-1488.

Grimm, J. (1828). *Deutsche Rechtsalterthümer*. Göttingen.

Grimm, J. (1835). *Deutsche Mythologie.* Frankfurt-Berlin-Wien: Ullstein, 1981, vol. II.

Grimm, J. (1854-1954). *Deutsches Wörterbuch.* Leipzig: Hirsel.

Haekens, A. (1998). *Beslissingsbekwaamheid in de gerontopsychiatrische context (Decisional Capacity in a Gerontopsychiatrical Context).* Doctoral Dissertation. Katholieke Universiteit Leuven.

Heinroth, J. C. A. (1818). *Lehrbuch der Störungen des Seelenlebens, oder die Seelenstörungen und ihrer Behandlung. Vom rationellen Standpunkt aus entworfen,* Leipzig: Vogel, 2 vols.

Heinsius, Th. (1822). *Volsthümliches Wörterbuch der Deutschen Sprache,* Hamburg: Hansche Hofbuchhandlung, vol. IV.

Helbing, F., & Bauer, M. (1926). *Die Tortur. Geschichte der Folter im Kriminalverfahren aller Zeiten und Völker.* Berlin: P. Langenscheidt.

Held, R. (1985). *Inquisition/ Inquisicion.* A bilingual guide to the exhibition of torture instruments from the Middle Ages to the Industrial Era. Florence: Qua d'Arno Publishers.

Herner, T. (1965). Significance of the Body Image in Schizophrenic Thinking. *American Journal of Psychotherapy, 19,* 455-466.

His, R. (1920). *Das Strafrecht des deutschen Mittelalters.* Leipzig: Theodor Weicher, vol I.

Hofler, M. (1899). *Deutsches Krankheitsnamen-Buch.* München: Verlag Piloty & Loehle.

Hoheisel, K. (1994). Homosexualität, in: *Realencyklopädie für Antike und Christentum,* Stuttgart, vol. XVI, col. 289-364.

Hoppe, M. (1976). Erläuterungen. In F. Schiller, *Der Geisterseher und andere Erzählungen* (pp. 237-246). Frankfurt: Insel.

Israels, H. (1986). Gedicht zum neunzigsten Geburtstag seiner Mutter. In D. Devreese & H. Israels, *Schreber inédit* (pp. 58-82). Paris: Editions du Seuil.

Israels, H. (1989). *Schreber Father and Son.* New York: International Universities Press.

Jaspers, K. (1913). *Allgemeine Psychopathologie.* Berlin-Heidelberg: Springer Verlag, 1973.

Jaspers, K. (1919). *Allgemeine Psychopathologie.* Berlin: Springer, 1948.

Jones, E. (1912). *On the Nightmare.* New York: Liveright, 1951.

Jung, C. G. (1907). *Psychologie der Dementia praecox.* Halle: Marhold.

Kagan, J. (1996). The Return of the Ancients: On temperament and development. In S. Matthysse, D. L. Levy, J. Kagan, & F. M. Benes (Eds.), *Psychopathology. The Evolving Science of Mental Disorder* (pp. 285-297). New York: Cambridge University Press.

Kaminsky, H. (1967). *A History of the Hussite Revolution.* Berkeley and Los Angeles: University of California Press.

Kaney, S., & Bentall, R. P. (1989). Persecutory delusions and attributional style. *British Journal of Medical Psychology, 62,* 191-198.

Kapsambelis (1994). *Les médicaments du narcissisme. Metapsychologie des neuroleptique.* Synthélabo.

Kelly, H. Ansgar (1993). The Right to Remain Silent: Before and After Joan of Arc. *Speculum, 68,* 992-1026.

Kelly, J. N. D. (1988). *The Oxford Dictionary of Popes.* Oxford New York: Oxford University Press.

Kißling, J. B. (1911). *Geschichte des Kulturkampfes im Deutschen Reiche.* Freiburg im Breisgau: Herder, 3 vols.

Knight, G. W. (1957). *Lord Byron's Marriage. The Evidence of Asterisks.* London: Routledge and Kegan Paul.

Koehler, G. K. (1981). The Schreber case and affective illness: a research diagnostic assessment. *Psycho. Medicine, 11,* 689-696.

Kolle, K. (1931 a). Paraphrenia und Paranoia. *Fortschritte der Neurologie und Psychiatrie, 3,* 319-334.

Kolle, K. (1931 b). *Die primäre Verrücktheit.* Leipzig: Thieme.

Kraepelin, E. (1910). *Psychiatrie, Vol 2: Klinische Psychiatrie, 8th Edition.* Leipzig: Barth.

Kraepelin, E. (1913). *Psychiatrie: ein Lehrbuch für Studierende und Aertze.* Vollständig umgearbeitete Auflage. Bd. III. Leipzig: J.A. Barth.

Kraepelin, E. (1919). Dementia praecox and paraphrenia. In R. M. Barclay (translator), *The 8th German Edition of the Textbook of Psychiatry,* Vol 3, part 2: *Endogenous Dementias.* Edinburgh: Livingstone.

Kraepelin, E. (1923). *Psychiatrie, Vol 3, 9th Edition.* Leipzig: Barth.

Kretschmer, E. (1927). *Der Sensitive Beziehungswahn.* Berlin: Springer.

Küper, W. (1991). *Das Verbrechen am Seelenleben. Feuerbach und der Fall Kaspar Hauser in strafrechtlicher Betrachtung.* Heidelberg: Manutius Verlag.

Lacan, J. (1932). *De la psychose paranoïaque dans ses rapports avec la personnalité.* Paris.

Lacan, J. (1948). Le stade du miroir comme formateur de la fonction du Je, telle qu'elle nous est révélée dans l'expérience psychanalytique. *Revue Française de Psychanalyse, 13* (4), 449-455.

Lacan, J. (1959). On a question preliminary to any possible treatment of psychosis. *Ecrits. A Selection,* New York - London: Norton, 1977, 179-225.

Lacan, J. (1969). Présentation des Mémoires d'un névropathe. *Cahiers pour l'Analyse, 5,* 73-76.

Lacan, J. (1977). *Ecrits. A Selection,* A. Sheridan (tr.). London: Tavistock.

Langen, A. (1968). *Der Wortschatz des deutschen Pietismus.* Tübingen: Max Niemeyer.

Laure, J. C. (1971). Lieux du corps, recension du corps. *Nouvelle Revue de Psychanalyse, 3,* 23-24.

Leibbrand, A., & W. (1972). *Formen des Eros. Kultur- und Geistesgeschichte der Liebe.* Freiburg: Karl Alber, 2 vols.

Lipper, S. & Werman, D. S. (1977). Schizophrenia and Intercurrent Physical Illness: A Critical Review of the Literature. *Comprehensive Psychiatry, 18* (1), 11-22.

Lipton, A. A. (1984). Was the "nervous illness" of Schreber a case of affective disorder? *Amer. J. Psychiatry, 141,* 1236-1239.

Looper, T. (1978). *Byron and the Bible. A compendium of biblical usage in the poetry of Lord Byron,* Metuchen NJ & London: The Scarecrow Press.

Lothane, Z. (1982 a). The psychopathology of hallucinations — a methodological analysis. *Brit. J. Med. Psychol., 55,* 335-348.

Lothane, Z. (1982 b). Dialogues are for dyads. *Issues Ego Psychol., 5,* 19-24.

Lothane, Z. (1983). Reality dream, and trauma. *Contemp. Psychoanal., 19,* 423-443.

Lothane, Z. (1987 a). Love and destructiveness. *Academy Forum* (American Academy of Psychoanalysis), *31* (4), 8-9.

Lothane, Z. (1987 b). The primacy of love: love ethics versus hermeneutics. *Academy Forum, 31* (1), 3-4.

Lothane, Z. (1987 c). Love, seduction and trauma. *Psychoanal. Rev., 74,* 83-105.

Lothane, Z (1989 a). The nature of love. *Academy Forum, 33* (1,2), 2-11.

Lothane, Z. (1989 b). Schreber, Freud, Flechsig and Weber revisited: an inquiry into methods of interpretation. *Psychoanal. Rev., 79,* 203-262.

Lothane, Z. (1989 c). Vindicating Schreber's father: neither sadist nor child abuser. *Journal of Psychohistory, 16,* 263-285.

Lothane, Z. (1992). *In Defense of Schreber. Soul Murder and Psychiatry.* Hillsdale NJ-London: The Analytic Press.

Lothane, Z. (1992 a). The human dilemma: heterosexual, homosexual, bisexual, "holosexual." *Issues Ego Psychol., 15,* 18-32.

Lothane, Z. (1992 b). *In Defense of Schreber: Soul Murder and Psychiatry.* Hillsdale, NJ: The Analytic Press.

Lothane, Z. (1992 c). The missing link — Schreber and his doctors. *History of Psychiatry, 3,* 339-350.

Lothane, Z. (1993). Schreber's feminine identification: paranoid illness or pro-found insight? *International Forum of Psychoanalysis, 2,* 131-138.

Lothane, Z. (1993 a). Schreber's soul murder: a case of psychiatric persecution. In L. De Goei & J. Vijselaar (Eds.), *Proceedings 1st European Congress on the History of Psychiatry and Mental Health Care* (pp. 96-103). Rotterdam: Erasmus.

Lothane, Z. (1993 b). L'assasinio dell'anima di Schreber: un caso di persecuzione psichiatrica. *Giornale storico di psicologia dinamica, 34,* 61-75.

Lothane, Z. (1993 c). Schreber's feminine identification: paranoid illness or profound insight? *Internat. Forum Psychoanal., 2,* 131-138.

Lothane, Z. (1994). The revival of ethics. *Academy Forum, 38* (1,?), 4 6.

Lothane, Z. (1995 a). El caso Schreber: una revision. *Revista Española de Neuropsiquiatríu, 15,* 255-273.

Lothane, Z. (1995 b). Rejoinder to David B. Allison and Mark S. Roberts, *Review of Existential Psychology and Psychiatry, 22,* 49-55.

Lothane, Z. (1995 c). Der Mann Schreber: Ein Leben Neue Sicht und Einsicht. *Psychoanalyse im Widerspruch, 14,* 5-15.

Lothane, Z. (1995 d). Die Wahrheit über Schreber: ein Leben, Neue Sicht und Einsicht. Deutsche Psychoanalytische Vereinigung, Wiesbaden:

Herbsttagung 1995, 95-101.

Lothane, Z. (1995 e). Review of Sander Gilman, Hysteria Beyond Freud, The Case of Sigmund Freud, Freud, Race, and Gender. *Psychoanalytic Books, 6,* 74-87.

Lothane, Z. (1995 f). Review of L. Sass, *Paradoxes of Delusion, Psychoanalytic Books, 6,* 251-257.

Lothane, Z. (1995 g). Freudsche Fehlleistung. *Die Zeit, 18,* April 28, p. 44.

Lothane, Z. (1996 a). Le meurtre d'âme de Schreber un cas de perséciton psychiatrique. In L. E. Prado de Oliveira (Ed.), *Schreber et la paranoïa.* Paris: l'Harmattan.

Lothane, Z. (1996 b). Die Verknüpfung von Sohn und Vater Schreber mit Hitler: ein Fall von historischem Rufmord. *Werkblatt, 36,*108-127.

Lothane, Z. (1996 c). Psychoanalytic method and the mischief of Freud bashers, *Psychiatric Times,* vol. XIII, no. 12, pp. 49-50.

Lothane, Z. (1996 d). Open Letter to Professor Crews. *Bulletin of the American Society of Psychoanalytic Physicians,* LXXXIV, issue 2, 69-71.

Lothane, Z. (1997 a). Omnipotence, or the delusional aspect of ideology in relation to love and power. *Amer. J. Psychoanal., 57,* 21-46. Also in C. S. Ellman & J. Reppen (Eds.), *Omnipotent Fantasies and the Vulnerable Self.* Northvale, NJ, Aronson, 1997.

Lothane, Z. (1997 b). The schism between Freud and Jung over Schreber: its implications for method and doctrine. *Internat. Forum Psychoanal., 6* (2), 103-115.

Lothane, Z. (1997 c). Schreber ermeneutica e storia. Una risposta a Sergio Benvenuto. *Giornale Storico di Psicol Dinamica, 21,* 97-98.

Lothane, Z. (1997 d). Freud and the interpersonal. *Internat. Forum Psychoanal., 6,* 175-184.

Lothane, Z. (1997 e). Review of J. Farrell's *Freud's Paranoid Quest, Journal of the American Psychoanalytic Association, 45* (4), 1319-1323.

Lothane, Z. (1998 a). Morals, ethics, and psychiatry. *Dynamische Psychiatrie,* vol. 168/169.

Lothane, Z. (1998 b). Pour la défense de Schreber: meurtre d'âme et psychiatrie. In D. Devreese, Z. Lothane, & J. Schotte, *Schreber Revisité* (series "Figures of the Unconscious: hors série). Leuven: Leuven University Press, 11-19.

Lothane, Z. (1998 c). The perennial Freud: method vs. Myth and the mischief of Freud bashers (in Spanish). *Revista Española de Neuropsiquiatría, 18,* 269-292.

Lothane, Z. (In press, a). Goethe, Schreber, Freud: Themes in metamorphosis. Read at International Congress of Applied Psychoanalysis, Bolzano, Italy, 29 November 1997 (Il Divano, l'Immaginaorio e la cura); proceedings of the congress in press.

Lothane, Z. (In press, b). Paul Schreber's sexual desires and imaginings: cause or consequence of his psychosis? In C. Socarides, A. Friedman, K. Gould, & S. Kramer (Eds.), *The Sexual Deviations: Theory and Therapy.* Madison, CT: International Universities Press.

Lothane, Z. (Forthcoming), Paul Schreber's ecstasies.

Macalpine, I., & Hunter, R. (1955). *Daniel Paul Schreber. Memoirs of my nervous illness. Translated, edited, with an introduction, notes and discussion.* London: Dawson.

MacDonald, D. L. (1992). Incest, Narcissism and Demonality in Byron's Manfred. *Mosaic, 25,* 25-38.

Mac Dougall, J. (1991). De l'indicible à l'interprétation. *Topique: revue freudienne, 21* (47), 33-56.

Marcuse, L. (1964). *Obszön. Geschichte einer Entrüstung.* Munich: Paul Liszt Verlag.

Matthysse, S., Levy, D. L., Kagan, J., & Benes, F. M. (1996). *Psychopathology. The evolving science of mental disorder.* New York: Cambridge University Press.

Mayer, H. (1969). *Das Geschehen und das Schweigen. Aspekte der Literatur* (pp. 69-100). Frankfurt: Suhrkamp.

Mayer, J., & Tradowsky, P. (1984). *Kaspar Hauser. Das Kind von Europa.* Stuttgart: Urahhaus.

Messy, J. (1992). *La personne âgée n'existe pas. Une approche psychanalytique.* Paris: Éditions Rivages.

Michelet, J., & Quinet, M. (1843). *Des Jésuites.* Paris: J.J. Pauvert, 1966. (German translation: *Die Jesuiten,* Basel 1843).

Mitglieder des Deutschen Vereins für Psychiatrie. In *Allgemeine Zeitschrift für Psychiatrie* (= AZP), 63, 1906, p. 922.

Mitre Fernandez, E. (1995). Muerte, veneno y enfermedad, metaforas medievales de la herejia. *Heresis, 25,* 63-84.

Monter, E. W. (1974). La sodomie à l'époque moderne en Suisse romande. *Annales ESC, 29,* 1023-1033.

Moore, R. I. (1976). Heresy as Disease. In W. Louraux & D. Verhelst (Eds.), *The Concept of Heresy in the Middle Ages (11th-13th C.)* (pp.1-11). Louvain-The Hague.

Moyaert, P. (1982 a). Taal, lichamelijkheid en affect in de schizofrenie. *Tijdschrift voor Psychiatrie, 24* (1), 49-69.

Moyaert, P. (1982 b). Taal, lichamelijkheid en affect in de schizofrenie (II). Enkele psychotherapeutische perspectieven. *Tijdschrift voor Psychiatrie, 24* (2), 696-707.

Moyaert, P. (1988). Schizofrenie en paranoia. In A. Vergote & P. Moyaert e.a. (Eds.). *Psycho-analyse. De mens en zijn lotgevallen.* Kapellen: Pelckmans/De Nederlandsche Boekhandel.

Müller, E. (1931). *Die Häusernamen von Alt-Leipzig vom 15.-20. Jahrhundert mit Quellenbelegen und geschichtlichen Erläuterungen.* Leipzig 1992.

Niederland, W. G. (1974). *The Schreber Case Psychoanalytic Profile of a Paranoid Personality.* New York: Quadrangle.

Niederland, W. G. (1974). *The Schreber Case. Psychoanalytic profile of a paranoid personality.* New York: Basic Books.

Pankow, G. (1956). Structuration dynamique dans la schizophrénie. Contribution à une psychothérapie analytique de l'expérience psychotique du monde. *Beiheft zur Schweizerischen Zeitschrift für Psychologie und ihre Anwendungen, 27,* Bern-Stuttgart: Hans Huber Verlag.

Pankow, G. (1960). Zum Problem des Spiegelbilderlebnisses in der Neurose und in der Psychose. *Confinia Psychiatrica, 3,* 36-56.

Pankow, G. (1968). Du corps perdu au corps retrouvé. Une introduction à une psychothérapie analytique des psychoses. *Tijdschrift voor Filosofie, 2,* 223-247.

Pankow, G. (1969). *L'homme et sa psychose.* Paris: Aubier/Montaigne.

Pankow, G. (1976). Sexe et image du corps dans la psychose. *L'Evolution psychiatrique, 41* (2), 919-931.

Pankow, G. (1977). *Structure familiale et psychose.* Paris: Aubier-Montaigne.

Pankow, G. (1978). Rejet et identité. *Revue française de psychanalyse, 40* (2), 289-299.

Pankow (1981). *L'être-là du schizophrène.* Contribution à la méthode de structuration dynamique dans les psychoses. Paris: Aubier/Montaigne.

Pankow, G. (1982). Körperbild, Übergangsobject und Narzissmus. Ein Beitrag zu vor-konfliktuellen Strukturen. *Jahrbuch der Psychoanalyse, 14,* 84-109.

Payer, P. J. (1982). *Book of Gomorrah. An Eleventh-Century Treatise against Clerical Homosexual Practices.* Translated with an introduction and notes. Waterloo (Ontario): Wilfrid Laurier University Press.

Peckham, M. (1962). *Beyond the Tragic Vision. The Quest for Identity in the Nineteenth Century.* New York: G. Brasiler.

Perry, N., & Echevveria, E. (1988). Under the Heel of Mary. London & New York: Routledge.

Peter Damian (1049). Liber Gomorrhianus. In J. P. Migne, *Patrologiae Latina cursus completus* (pp. 159-190). Paris 1853, *145.*

Petsch, R. (1911). *Das Volksbuch vom Doctor Faust (Nach der ersten Ausgabe, 1587).* Halle: Max Niemeyer.

Pezard, A. (1950). *Dante sous la pluie de feu (Enfer, chant XV).* Etudes de philosophie médiévale XL, Paris: Vrin.

Plato, Timaios. In *Sämtliche Werke,* 5, (trans. Schleiermacher), Hamburg: Rowohlt, 1959, 141-213.

Prado de Oliveira, L. E. (1997). *Freud et Schreber les source écrites du délire, entre psychose et culture.* Ramonville Saint-Agne: Editions érès.

Radbruch, G. (1934). *Paul Johann Anselm Feuerbach. Ein Juristenleben.* Göttingen: Vandenhoeck & Ruprecht, 1969.

Roberts, G. (1991). Delusional belief systems and meaning in life: A preferred reality? *British Journal of Psychiatry, 159* (Suppl. 14), 19-28.

Röhl, J. C. G. (1995). *Kaiser, Hof und Staat. Wilhelm II. und die deutsche Politik.* München: C.H. Beck.

Roosens, E. (1979). *Mental Patients in Town Life. Geel Europe's First Therapeutic Community.* Beverly Hills-London: Sage Publications.

Rößler, H. (1955). *Größe und Tragik des christlichen Europa.* Frankfurt: Verlag Moritz Diesterweg.

Roskoff, G. (1869). *Geschichte des Teufels*. Vienna, 2 vols.

Rosolato, G. (1967). Trois générations d'homme dans le mythe religieux et la généalogie. In *Essais sur le symbolique* (pp. 59-96). Paris: Gallimard 1969.

Rümke, H. C. (1971). *Psychiatrie, deel III. De psychosen*. Amsterdam: Scheltema & Holkema.

Sabean, D. W. (1990). *Das Zweischneidige Schwert. Herrschaft und Widerspruch im Württemberg der frühen Neuzeit*. Frankfurt: Suhrkamp 1990 (= Power in the Blood, Cambridge 1984).

Sanders, D. (1876). *Wörterbuch der deutschen Sprache*, Leipzig: Otto Weigand, vol. II.

Satlow, M. L. (1994). 'They Abused Him Like a Woman': Homoeroticism, Gender Blurring, and the Rabbis in Late Antiquity. *Journal of the History of Sexuality, 5*, 1-25.

Schatzman, M. (1973). *Soul murder. Persecution in the family*. Harmondsworth: Penguin Books.

Schild, W. (1980). *Alte Gerichtbarkeit. Vom Gottesurteil zum Beginn der modernen Rechtsprechung*. München: Callwey.

Schreber, D. P. (1901). Berufungsbegründung. In: Schreber, 1903, original pages 404-451.

Schreber, D. P. (1903). *Denkwürdigkeiten eines Nervenkranken nebst Nachträgen und einem Anhang über die Frage: "Unter welchen Voraussetzungen darf eine für geisteskrank erachtete Person gegen ihren erklärten Willen in einer Heilanstalt festgehalten werden?"*. Leipzig: Oswald Mutze. Trans. eds. Macalpine, I. & Hunter, R. A. *Memoirs of My Nervous Illness*, Cambridge: Harvard University Press, 1988.

Schreber, D. G. M. (1839). *Das Buch der Gesundheit. Eine Orthobiothik nach den Gesetzen der Natur und dem Baue des menschlichen Organismus*. Leipzig: Volckmar.

Schreber, D. G. M. (1853). *Die schädlichen Körperhaltungen und Gewöhnheiten der Kinder, nebst Angabe der Mittel dagegen: Für Ältern und Erziehern*. Leipzig: Fr. Fleischer.

Schreber, D. G. M. (1856). *Ärtzliche Zimmergymnastik*. Leipzig: Fr. Fleischer.

Schreber, D. G. M. (1858 a). *Kallipädie oder Erziehung zur Schönheit durch naturgetraue und gleichmässige Förderung normaler Körperbildung*. Leipzig: Fr. Fleischer.

Schreber, D. G. M. (1858 b). Über Anwendung von Sonnenbäder zu Heilzwecke, insbesondere gegen gewisse chronische Krankheiten des kinderlichen Alters. In *Jahrbuch für Kinderheilkunde und physische Erziehung*, vol. I, (pp. 169-171).

Schuselka, F. (1845). *Der Jesuitenkrieg gegen Oesterreich und Deutschland*. Leipzig: Weidmann'sche Buchhandlung.

Seelenmoerder, oder die Jesuiten bei dem portugesischen Königsmorde. Trauerspiel von einem Preußen. Lübeck 1759, (= GV 133, 1985, 53).

Seidel, P. (1989). Probleme des Zugangs bei Schizophrenen; zum Verständnis des Beitrags von Gisela Pankow. *Jahrbuch der Psychoanalyse, 24* (15),

256-280.

Shannon, A. C. (1949). *The Popes and Heresy in the Thirteenth Century.* Villanova, Pennsylvania: Augustinian Press.

Shelley, P. B. (1819). The Cenci, In *The Complete Works of Percy Bysshe Shelley.* Edited by Thomas Hutchinson, London: Oxford University Press, 1929, 271-334.

Soenen, S., & Corveleyn, J. (1998). De verstoring van de lichaamsbeleving en het lichaamsbeeld in de schizofrenie: waan of werkelijkheid? *Diagnostiek-wijzer: Tijdschrift voor de geestelijke gezondheidszorg, 4,* 166-180.

Spitzer, R. L., Skodol, A. E., Gibbon, M., & Williams, J. B. W. (1981). Dr. Schreber in: *DSM-III Case Book.* Washington: American Psychiatric Association.

Staatshandbuch für das Königreich Sachsen 1894, Dresden 1894.

Stern, D.N. (1985). *The interpersonal world of the infant.* New York: Basic Books.

Swales, P. (1982). Freud, Johann Weier, and the Status of Seduction: The role of the witch in the conception of fantasy. In L. Spurling (Ed.), *Sigmund Freud: Critical assessments*; vol. I, *The origins of psychoanalysis* (pp. 331-358). London: Routledge, 1989.

Szasz. T. S. (1976). *Schizophrenia: The Sacred Symbol of Psychiatry.* New York: Basic Books.

Tabouret-Keller, A. (1973). Une étude: La remarquable famille Schreber. *Scilicet, 4,* 287-321.

Taylor, J. R. (1985). *Ezekiel. An Introduction and Commentary.* Leicester-Downer's Grove, Illinois: Inter-Varsity Press.

Thiel, W. (1971). Über das Wesen der Leibgefühlsstörungen bei den Schizophrenien. *Fortschritt der Neurologie, Psychiatrie und ihrer Grenzgebiete, 39,* 279-287.

Tustin, F. (1986). *Autistic barriers in neurotic patients.* London: Karnac.

Vergote, A. (1982). Pulsion de mort et destins mortifères de la pulsion. *Psychanalyse à l'université, 28* (7), 579-580.

Vergote, A. (1989). De splitsing taal-lichaam in de schizofrenie. In G. Kongs, H. De Cuyper, L. De Vooght & K. Pyck (Eds.), *Psychiatrie tussen mode en model* (pp. 193-210). Leuven: Peeters.

Vergote, A. (1996). *In Search of a Philosophical Antropology : A compilation of Essays by Antoine Vergote.* Amsterdam/Atlanta, GA-Leuven: Rodopi – Leuven University Press.

Wallon, H. (1931). Comment se développe chez l'enfant la notion du corps propre. *Journal de Psychologie,* 705-748.

Weinberger, D. R., Berman, K. F., & Daniel, D. G. (1991). Prefrontal cortex dysfunction in schizophrenia. In H. S. Levin, H. M. Eisenberg, & A. L. Benton (Eds.), *Frontal lobe function and dysfunction* (pp. 275-287). Oxford: Oxford University Press.

White, R. B. (1961). The mother-conflict in Schreber's psychosis. *Internat. J. Psycho-Anal., 42,* 55-73.

Wilden, A. (1968). *The language of the self. The function of language in psychoanalysis by Jacques Lacan.* New York: Dell Publishing Co., Inc.

Williams, J. (1911). Torture. In *Encyclopaedia Britannica*, vol. XXVII, 72-78.

Zedler (1732), Alp. In *Grosses volständiges Universal-Lexikon*, Reprint Graz 1961, vol. I, c. 1327.

FIGURES OF THE UNCONSCIOUS

(Hors série)

- D. DEVREESE, Z. LOTHANE , J. SCHOTTE (éds.), *Schreber revisité*
  1998, 243 p., ISBN 90 6186 908 0, € 30,98

1. PH. VAN HAUTE, J. CORVELEYN (eds.), *Seduction, Suggestion,*
   Psychoanalysis
   2001, 128 p., ISBN 90 5867 127 5, € 21,07
2. A. DE WAELHENS, W. VER EECKE, *Phenomenology and Lacan on*
   Schizophrenia, after the Decade of the Brain
   2001, 338 p., ISBN 90 5867 160 7, € 30,98
3. J. CORVELEYN, P. MOYAERT (eds.), *Psychosis: Phenomenological and*
   Psychoanalytical approaches
   2003, 165 p., ISBN 90 5867 279 4

www.ingramcontent.com/pod-product-compliance
Lightning Source LLC
Chambersburg PA
CBHW062036270326
41929CB00014B/2443